THE DOCTRINE OF MAN IN THE WRITINGS
OF MARTIN CHEMNITZ AND JOHANN GERHARD

THE
DOCTRINE OF MAN
IN THE WRITINGS
OF MARTIN CHEMNITZ
AND JOHANN GERHARD

Edited by Herman A. Preus
and Edmund Smits

Translated by Mario Colacci, Lowell Satre,
J. A. O. Preus Jr., Otto Stahlke, and Bert H. Narveson

CONCORDIA PUBLISHING HOUSE · SAINT LOUIS

This edition published 2005 by Concordia Publishing House
3558 S. Jefferson Ave., St. Louis, MO 63118-3968
1-800-325-3040 • www.cph.org

Cover design by Andrea Otto.

Manufactured in the United States of America

ISBN 0-7586-1002-5

1 2 3 4 5 6 7 8 9 10   14 13 12 11 10 09 08 07 06 05

Preface

One of the strangest phenomena in Protestantism, and particularly in Lutheranism, is the fact that the theology of an entire century has been left buried in dust and mold and a dead language. A half-dozen of the greatest theologians in the history of the Christian church are unknown to English-speaking theologians of today, because their works have never been translated into English. The Roman Catholic Church said shortly after the death of Luther, "If Chemnitz had not arisen, Luther would have fallen." Yet how many American Lutheran theologians today concern themselves seriously with the theology of Martin Chemnitz? Johann Gerhard, who was called to the theological faculties of twenty-four universities, wrote what is generally regarded as the greatest dogmatics since Aquinas' *Summa Theologica*. But how many American theological students are shown the treasures that lie hidden in this basic theology of the Lutheran Church?

The period of Orthodoxy, so-called, runs roughly from Martin Chemnitz (1522-1586) to David Hollaz (1648-1713). Its theology is a closed book to American Protestantism, being commonly brushed off as "dead orthodoxy." The fact that out of that century came some of our greatest Christian devotional literature, like Johann Arndt's *True Christianity* and the immortal hymns of Paul Gerhard,

serves notice that there were deep streams of spiritual life flowing
through the church in that period.

From time to time there have been noble efforts to bring this theology to light and make it available to English-speaking Protestantism. English translations of Gerhard's *Meditationes Sacrae* have
been made but are long since out of print. The most notable contribution to the cause is the English translation of Heinrich Schmid's
Die Dogmatik der evangelisch-lutherischen Kirche by Charles A.
Hay and Henry E. Jacobs, which was published in 1875 and went
through several editions. It has recently been reprinted by Augsburg Publishing House, Minneapolis.

A revival of interest in the Orthodox theologians is apparent in
English-speaking Protestantism. Works of Chemnitz and Gerhard
are being translated into English to make them available to a wider
readership.

In the present volume Martin Chemnitz and Johann Gerhard are
given the principal attention. These two men seem to tower above
the whole galaxy of theologians who have appeared in Lutheranism
since the Reformation. Futhermore, their proximity to Luther and
the Reformation gives them a unique authority in Lutheran theology.
Chemnitz's life overlapped that of Luther and Melanchthon, whose
friend and pupil he was. When the very existence of Lutheranism
was threatened by synergism and by the erosion of sacramental
thinking following the death of Luther, Chemnitz stepped into the
breach and with a few of his colleagues reestablished the theology
of the *Augsburg Confession* in the last Lutheran Confession, the
Formula of Concord.

Johann Gerhard followed on the heels of Chemnitz and has gained
the title of Lutheranism's greatest dogmatician. It was Jacques
Bossuet, the court theologian of Louis XIV, who called Johann
Gerhard "the third man of the Reformation, after Luther and Chemnitz." Throughout his great *Loci Theologici* he evinces his unswerv-
ing loyalty to the inspired Scripture and to the theology of Luther
and the Lutheran Confessions. His theological insight and scholarship have hardly been surpassed since the Reformation.

For this volume on *The Doctrine of Man* we have drawn prin-
cipally on the *Loci Theologici* of Chemnitz, where the doctrine is

treated exhaustively. However, the "image of God" gets a more thorough treatment in Gerhard's *Loci Theologici,* which is therefore used in the first chapter.

The editors are grateful for the painstaking work of the translators, for the careful checking of references to the Fathers by Paul Hasvold, James Preus and Donald Berg, and for the generous help of Pastor Robert Anderson and Carlyle Haaland in the final preparation of the manuscript.

Attention is called to the fact that a few sections or paragraphs of the original text have been omitted in order to avoid repetition and lengthy quotations of unimportant theologians. With great difficulty all but a very few of the quotations from the Fathers have been found and checked in Migne. The footnotes are added for the orientation of the average pastor and to help the scholar doing research in this field. Historical difficulties were encountered in this connection because of the neglect of the entire period in the subsequent history of church and dogma.

In the present dialogue between churches it is vital that the representatives are thoroughly conversant with the historic theology of their respective church bodies. It is our hope that this volume will contribute to the cause of unity in the faith. The Roman Catholic Church has rediscovered her Aquinas and her Scotus. It is time that Lutherans rediscover their counterpart in the Church of the Reformation, Martin Chemnitz and Johann Gerhard.

HERMAN A. PREUS

What Is Lutheran Orthodoxy?

Among all the living creatures on earth man has the unique privilege to be moved not only by biological needs and instincts, but also by ideas and doctrines. Doctrines are able to rally men and nations to unite in a cause, as well as to divide them into armed camps.

At present one hears many voices depreciating the importance of doctrine for the life of the church. How hollow these sound if one brings to mind the experience of Christian believers of the past! The men of the early Christian church "devoted themselves to the apostles' teaching" (Acts 2:42).[1]

Far from being willing to allow the teaching of right doctrine to assume a secondary role, Martin Luther as the leader of the Reformation emphasized its importance in the strongest possible terms. "Doctrine is heaven, life is earth," he writes. "One little point of doctrine is of more value than heaven and earth; and therefore we cannot allow the least jot of it to be corrupted. But we can very well

---

[1] They persevered in it, "they strongly adhered to it," as the Greek word expresses it.

disregard offenses and lapses of life."[2] For Luther every human life, even that of a believer, inevitably includes some confusion, error, and sin. Where then can we find the true light which is able to guide our way to heaven? Only in the pure doctrine, answers Luther.

The term "orthodoxy" is applied by the Greek Church Fathers to signify that which is the true faith and right teaching. Orthodoxy arises out of the passionate zeal of the church to find the true insights and to express them in scrupulously correct statements; the sacred treasures of the church must be safeguarded with loving care and preserved inviolate.

But this zeal of the church is not motivated by a purely theoretical concern. Firm adherence to right doctrine has an intimate relationship to the proper conduct of a man's life, as Luther indicates in another passage: "When we are speaking about godliness and ungodliness we are not speaking about manners, but about convictions which are the fountainheads of the moral life. The man who is orthodox concerning God cannot help but do good works and be good in his life. Even if he falls seven times a day, he rises again just as many times. But the ungodly fall to the ground and do not rise again."[3]

The first centuries of the Christian church marked an agonizing effort to establish the true doctrine and to fight against the insidious invasion of error.

The Protestant Reformers of the sixteenth century felt called to renew the struggle to retain the original doctrine. Thus Martin Chemnitz, prince of the Lutheran Orthodox theologians, could write: "Our Lord, being merciful to his church, sent Dr. Martin Luther,

---

[2] WA 40/2, p. 52. WA is the abbreviation for Dr. Martin Luther's *Werke Kritische Gesamtausgabe,* Hermann Boehlaus, Nachfolger (not yet finished). *Weimar* (1883-1960).

[3] WA 5, p. 28. What is important here is that orthodoxy is not merely a correct intellectual construction but the very foundation of a Christian's life. Consequently, heresy is not simply an intellectual misconception, but a pattern of thinking and living which is no longer Christian.

"Consider those who are of a different opinion about the grace of Jesus Christ which has come to us, how opposed they are to the will of God," writes Ignatius of Antioch in his *Epistle to the Smyrnaeans* (6:12). "They have no regard for love; no care for the widow or the orphan or the oppressed, for the bond or the free, for the hungry or the thirsty."

who started to purify the doctrine of the church. He directed her path to the living source of Scripture and to the rule of the prophetic and apostolic faith. However, his work was not finished. In the first place, there was the purely technical difficulty that the insights of Martin Luther and his explanations were scattered about in many different volumes, so that it was indeed very difficult to develop from them an integrated body of doctrine. Moreover, as it turned out, the statements of Martin Luther were interpreted in various ways."[4]

Perhaps one might represent the case this way, that Martin Luther opened new horizons of the ancient church which had become obscured through the ages. However, to give aid to the lesser guide of the solitary traveler, the single shepherd of a local flock, there was needed a road map and a compass. At one point Luther compared himself to a pioneer and woodcutter chopping down the trees of the forest and clearing the way. After him subtler scholars would be needed, highly skilled agriculturists or gardeners, who would cultivate the soil and raise the growth with loving care.[5]

The first and most outstanding man to meet this need was Phillip Melanchthon (1497-1560). Luther was strongly appreciative of Melanchthon's *Loci Communes* of 1521, which he rated the finest manual to instruct the evangelical bishop and theologian and make him powerful in the preaching of Christian doctrine. In later editions of the *Loci*, however, Melanchthon adopted some peculiar positions which aroused sharp controversy among the Lutheran scholars, most of whom had been his own pupils. Nevertheless, on the strength of his historical position and his influential part in the making of Orthodox methodology, Melanchthon may well in this respect be called the "father of Lutheran Orthodoxy."

Following Melanchthon in the sixteenth century we meet Lutheran Orthodoxy in the strict sense, that is, the body of doctrine which has been accepted within the greater part of the Lutheran Church as the theology of the Lutheran Confessions. Chief among the lead-

---

[4] Loci Theologici DN Martini Chemnitii, editi opera et Studio Polycarpi Leyseri D., Francofurti et Wittebergae, sumptibus Chr. H. Schumacheri, 1653, pars I, p. 11.

[5] e.g. WA 30/2, p. 68.

ers of the movement was Martin Chemnitz (1522-1586),[6] who, together with Jacob Andreae (1528-90) and Nicolaus Sellnecker (1530-92), composed the *Formula of Concord.* Other teachers of the same century who delineated the Lutheran doctrine over against the Reformed teaching were Egidius Hunnius (1550-1603), Leonhard Hutter (1563-1616), and Balthasar Mentzer (1565-1627).

The Lutheran theologians of the seventeenth century found their principal spokesman in Johann Gerhard (1582-1637),[7] and after his death this place was accorded to Johannes Hülseman (1602-61). Distinguished positions among the theologians of the time were held also by Solomon Glassius (1593-1656) within philology and hermeneutics, by Balthasar Meisner (1585-1626), a lover of philosophy, and by Caspar Erasmus (Jasper Rasmussen) Brochmand (1585-1652), who was called by his contemporaries "the father of Danish theology."

To us in the twentieth century the era of Gerhard and Hülseman appears full of contrasts between the sharp polemical attacks and outbursts of enthusiastic praise, between zeal and skill and a deep-seated piety. Among the great theologians is Johann Konrad Dannhauer (1603-66), highly esteemed in the eighteenth century for his devout spirit; as well as Abraham Calov (1612-86), an erudite and very polemical Lutheran, yet showing at the same time a profound mysticism in his doctrine of the Sacraments. Johannes Musaeus (1613-81) and Johannes Meisner (1615-84) stood for a more conciliatory attitude in their polemical writings, but give evidence of a rationalistic outlook. The aspiration of the men of this time to achieve a highly integrated dogmatic system is prominently represented in Johann Friedrich König (1647-95), Wilhelm Baier (1647-95), and especially in Johannes Andreas Quenstedt (1617-84).

The last of the great masters of Lutheran Orthodoxy was David Hollaz (1615-84). He formulated the theory of verbal inspiration of the Scriptures in a very strict form. In spite of his critical attitude

---

[6] Main works of Chemnitz (Chemnitius): 1) *Loci Theologici* (1543), editions of 1653 and 1690; 2) *Examen Concilii Tridentini* (1565-1573), edition of 1641, Jacob Stoer, Geneva.

[7] Main work of Johann Gerhard: *Loci Communes Theologici,* Exegesis and 9 Volumes, written 1610-1622.
Quoted edition: 1657, Zachariae Hertelii, Francoforti et Hamburgi.

toward pietism, certain latent pietistic tendencies can be detected in his work, as for example in his treatment of the *via salutis*.

In order to characterize some of the salient features of the Lutheran Orthodox way of thinking, four topics will be discussed: (1) *Inspiration of the Scriptures;* (2) *Faith and Reason;* (3) *Traditions of the Church;* and (4) *Theology for the Practical Life.*

I

Inspiration of the Scriptures

If anything is fundamental for Lutheran Orthodoxy, it is the authority of the Scriptures. The seventeenth century did not invent the teaching of verbal inspiration. This view of the Scriptures has taken many forms during the history of the church and is to be found among the earliest Fathers of the church. When the first Apostolic Fathers called the Scriptures *"Logia,"* they meant "divinely inspired sayings."[8]

Centuries later, at a time when the Bible appeared to be virtually crowded out by the voluminous systems of scholastic theology, Martin Luther restored the reverence for this Book of Books as the one divine source of truth. For him here was the greatest miracle, that God himself came down and humbled himself so deeply as to "immerse himself in the letters."[9] "The Holy Scriptures are God's guarantee. If you embrace them, you are blessed."

Some divergence of interpretation concerning Scriptural inspiration may be observed between the Orthodox theologians of the Lutheran and those of the Reformed Confessions. Although the latter stressed that Scripture was verbally inspired, they differed from the Lutheran writers in ascribing to it a merely instrumental func-

---

[8] One finds this, for example, in I Clement 53:1, 13:3-4, 57:3-4 and in 19:1: "The generations before us who received his Oracles (Logia) in fear and truth," and again in 45:2, "You have contemplated the truthful Scriptures, which are given by the Holy Spirit." Other examples which might be cited include Ignatius of Antioch (*Philadelphians*, 5:1-2, 8:2, 9:2), Justin Martyr (*Dialogue*, 52 and 65), Theophilus (*To Autolycus*, 2:10), and Pseudo-Justin (*To the Greeks*, 12). In Irenaeus a similar view is expressed: "Scripture is perfect, that is, it is spoken by God's Word and his Spirit" (*Contra Haereses*, 2:28: 2), and "All Scripture is given us by God" (2:28:3).

[9] WA 34/2, p. 487.

tion. They stoutly maintained that Holy Scriptures has no power in itself; instead, it resembles some inanimate tool, a saw or a hammer, which becomes effective only when the master-workman especially deigns to take it into his hands and operate with it. Thus the Holy Writings cannot work except through some special decision and operation of the Holy Spirit, who in this case "exalts" the instrument and works with it upon the listener or reader.

Lutheran Orthodox theologians did not countenance such a restriction upon the efficacy of the Holy Scriptures. In their polemical writings they emphasized the organic character of the content, designating it as a "thing which is alive" *(res animata).* They preferred to compare the Scriptures to the "living incorruptible seed" (1 Peter 1:23), a seed that grows by itself (Mark 4:26-29), penetrating fire (Jeremiah 23:29), oil and wine (Luke 10:34), bread and food, rain that refreshes the earth, shining light, and healing medicine. Here the intrinsic value of Scripture was strongly manifested. The understanding was that the divine revelation and its expression in the Scriptures are so completely united that to divorce them would create a serious distortion. This view inspires greater confidence in the holy will of our Father in heaven than a view which leaves the inspiration of Scripture in suspense. Even the Gentiles can receive God's light through the reading of the Holy Scriptures. No peculiar decision of the inscrutable will of God is any longer needed. God has already decided to regenerate you and has sent you his grace; the gates of revelation are not closed. Then take and read his Word, fearing only lest you should resist its power.

The emphasis by the Lutheran Orthodox theologians upon the perspicuity of Biblical teachings should not be misinterpreted. In fact, these men are on the whole more cautious here than Martin Luther himself in his dynamic work, *On the Bondage of the Will.* Clarity is to be achieved only gradually; the Scriptures open piece by piece to zealous students, and just that much light is given to the individual believer as is needed for his life situation. The Bible is the perfect guide for believers, but it is a very profound book. The majesty of its content is so great that there is some necessary darkness; no human mind can exhaust divine mystery.

Even the church, the only proper and competent interpreter of the Bible, must humble itself before the majesty of the divine writings, and is not authorized to add anything to the Biblical message. In a characteristic phrase Martin Chemnitz writes that "the church is only the philologist" (ecclesia tantum debet esse grammatica),[10] whose assignment is to investigate the proper use of the words and to uncover their deeper meaning. The church should not fabricate new ideas and dogmas, but proclaim those which have been imparted by the Holy Spirit.

II
Faith and Reason

"All the properties of God ought to be as rational as they are natural. I require reason in his goodness, because nothing else can properly be accounted good than that which is rationally good." These words, although spoken somewhat over-emphatically by Tertullian,[11] might strike a sympathetic chord in the Orthodox theologians. As much as they base their insights on revelation and faith, they nevertheless try to give full satisfaction to the demands of reason for clarity and consistency in argument. Orthodoxy has an inherent aversion to irrationality.

Martin Luther sometimes speaks about the sacrificing or even the "killing" of reason by the godly for the sake of "entering with Abraham into the darkness of faith."[12] Nevertheless, it would be a serious mistake to call Luther an irrationalist. In the same work, the *Commentary on Galatians*, he writes: "Now Christ is apprehended not by the law, not by works, but by reason or understanding (ratione seu intellectu) enlightened by faith."[13] On other occasions as well Luther praises reason highly, calling it, for example, a "numen," or spiritual guiding power.[14]

Between the content of faith and the requirements of reason in theology Luther insists upon a "dialectical" union. Here he uses the

---

[10] Loci 2, p. 202.
[11] Against Marcion 1:23, PL. 2, p. 272.
[12] WA 40/1, p. 362.
[13] *Ibid.*, p. 444.
[14] *Ibid.*, 39/1, p. 175.

term "dialectical" in a special sense to mean a union of unequal opposites. Certainly there can be only one way of co-existence and cooperation between them; reason must subordinate itself to and serve faith. Such a synthesis can take place in the regenerated mind of the believer, but remains impossible for the unregenerated reason fighting against the insights of the faith. Through the union of faith and reason in the mind of the believer a new "speculative life" arises which is neither empty theorizing nor an amorphous emotionalism; it is the "theological, faithful beholding of the serpent on the pole; that is, of Christ hanging on the cross for my sins."[15]

Similarly, Lutheran Orthodoxy builds upon the presupposition of a very extensive cooperation between faith and reason. Faith is the undisputed leader, but reason follows. Even though a theologian may be forced on occasion to admit that he is unable to reconcile certain theological statements,[16] he does not renounce his striving for logical consistency and harmony.

The patristic and scholastic ages shared a conviction that there can be no real contradiction between the statements of revelation and those of reason when working in a truly responsible way, except that reason is inherently inadequate for grasping the eternal truth without the aid of faith. And even in this case we are looking in a mirror darkly and seeing enigmatic forms (1 Cor. 13:12).

In this respect Lutheran Orthodoxy agrees firmly with the patristic and scholastic traditions. It is persuaded that there is an ultimate harmony between faith and right reasoning. In spite of the heresies which these theologians see to have arisen out of the philosophical schools, they show a broad appreciation of philosophy both as a method of systematic thinking and as the ceaseless quest of an inquiring mind.

Yet, the members of the Orthodox tradition do not claim that even the best possible human theology will attain to the formal perfection of a "closed system." Our theology at its best is not "archetypal," that is, the wisdom of God himself; it can only be "ectypal," a reflection of God's revelation within the limited human mind. What

---

[15] *Ibid.*, 40/2, p. 447.
[16] As for example *Formula of Concord* XI, Sol. Decl. 53.

we possess is the *theologia viatorum,* the theology of travelers, who are not yet at their heavenly home and lack the comprehensive knowledge given to the blessed after the resurrection.

III
Traditions of the Church

The Protestant Reformation, which possessed throughout an acute awareness of the frailty of human reason and its liability to error, dealt a crushing blow to the over-heavy medieval reliance upon an accumulation of traditions. However, the Reformers were very far from rejecting the value of tradition altogether. Instead, they summoned Christians everywhere to re-examine and screen the received traditions for the purpose of re-establishing the authentic testimony of the primitive Christian community.

Existing as it did in the shadow of the Roman Council of Trent, the Lutheran Orthodox movement was impelled to re-define further the Reformation position.[17]

---

[17] Accordingly, Martin Chemnitz in his *Examination of the Council of Trent* distinguishes eight varieties of tradition.

First and underivatively authoritative are the traditions which Christ and the Apostles delivered by living voice and which were later set down by Apostles and Evangelists in the *Scriptures* themselves. A second kind of tradition is the *transmission of the Holy Scriptures* by the church, joining the writings in a proper order in the canon and preserving them faithfully for posterity. Following these is the class of immediate summaries of Scriptural thought and expression in the *credal statements,* most prominently represented in the Apostles' Creed.

The fourth form of traditional testimony concerns the proper *exposition of the Scriptures.* For this purpose one should begin by choosing passages which are truly clear and unambiguous, and proceed from there to other texts where the discovery and formulation of the proper sense is more difficult. Since the Apostles' Creed is based on scriptural teaching, and more indirectly on the Nicene and Athanasian Creeds as well, their articles are able to provide a key for further interpretation.

To the fifth kind of tradition belong those dogmas which are not explicitly expressed in the words of Scripture, but which are deduced by cogent *inference from the scriptural witness.* Within this group are some ancient teachings which are implicit in the Biblical text, such as, for example, the dogma that the Son is of the same essence (homoousios) with the Father.

The testimonies of the Church Fathers, which constitute the sixth set of traditions, receive from the Orthodox theologians profound respect whenever they

In their own theological work the Orthodox theologians exhibit considerable flexibility, and avoid attempting to develop their theology from a single deductive principle or the teaching of a single man (like Luther).[18] Important as the teaching of justification by faith is, it is not the only basis for the deduction of Orthodox doctrine. Rather, these men hold as the "regulative principle" that one ought to take Scripture in its wholeness.

Again, if the Orthodox Lutheran theologians follow in the footsteps of Martin Luther, this is not because they accord Luther special authority as a prophet, but simply because in their judgment he understood how to extract the genuine sense of the Biblical text. Direct quotations from Luther are very sparingly employed. In following him the Orthodox teachers are not primarily concerned with Luther's statements themselves, but with the light which they cast upon the Biblical truth.

The same attitude is shown toward the *Book of Concord*. No doubt this book is their norm, but it is not called an absolute or infallible norm. Instead, it is treated as normative in a relative sense *(respective)*. By holding to this norm we demonstrate the unity of the

---

are consonant with the Scriptures themselves. "We diligently inquire into the consensus of scholarly and ancient authorities," writes Chemnitz. "We love and exalt that witness of the Fathers which agrees with the Scriptures. Our standpoint is that in religious controversies the judge is God's Word itself, which is later joined by the confession of the true church" (Examen p. 71).

Seventh in Chemnitz's listing come the *liturgical traditions*, which have not been delivered in writing, and which are not dogma in the proper sense of the term. Although these solicit respect as ancient and beneficent usages of the church, they are not binding upon us: "The apostolic rites are to be tempered with Christian liberty" (*Ibid.*, p. 75).

The eighth class of traditions includes all those which not only lack any basis in Scripture, but in fact run contrary to it. The *contra-scriptural traditions* are merely the expression of human subjectivity; they arise often out of the "lapses of good men or the tricks of evil men." Unfortunately, a great number of such groundless traditions are enjoined by the Roman Catholic Church, as a result of the time when the Council of Trent ordered that church to honor them with the same reverence (*pari pietatis affectu*) as the Scriptures themselves. To fight against this kind of tradition and to establish positively the true Biblical doctrine were two of the main tasks of Martin Chemnitz's *Examen*.

[18] H. E. W. Turner writes of the orthodoxy in the patristic era that it is not a single melody or motif, but a whole symphony consisting of a great diversity and complexity of motifs (*The Patterns of Christian Truth*, p. 9). The same could be said about Lutheran Orthodoxy.

church. Sacred Scripture contains everything to be believed and done, whereas symbolical books reflect only limited aspects of the Biblical teaching.

IV

Theology for the Practical Life

For Thomas and the majority of medieval thinkers theology was primarily a speculative science rather than a practical one. The Lutheran Orthodox movement, on the other hand, strongly resisted this tendency to make of theological study predominantly an intellectual inquiry and described it instead as a *habitus animi practicus,* a total attitude or disposition of the mind, heart, and will. Theology is the practical wisdom for man, the sinner, which will teach him all things necessary for the true faith in Christ and the sanctification of his life and for guidance toward eternal beatitude.

In emphasizing the practical nature of theology, the Orthodox teachers followed closely on the work of Luther. On several occasions Luther warned others against speculating about God's majesty instead of concentrating theology around man, the lost sinner, and his Savior. "For the proper subject of theology is man guilty of sin and lost, and God who justifies him and who is the Savior of man the sinner. Whatever else theology is looking for and discussing is error and poison."[19] As Johann Gerhard indicates, the centering of theology in man, the sinner, does not contradict its centering in Christ, but these two topics necessarily involve each other.[20]

Who then can be a theologian? If theology is a matter of heart and will, and not of the reason alone, then there is properly speaking only the *theologia regenitorum,* the theology of believers who as sinners are regenerated through grace. [21]

---

[19] WA 40/2, p. 328.

[20] Loci Exegesis Prooemium 27, p. 7.

[21] Quenstedt of later Orthodoxy says that divine enlightenment (*informatio*) by which men become theologians is an operation of the Holy Spirit. He aids men in the search for truth but leaves to the theologian who is rooted in Scripture the choice of the proper expression. To a certain extent such assistance can be given also to the unregenerated and the ungodly. For those who are theologians in name and in reality, however, who are not only instructed in

Within Biblical exegesis the Orthodox teachers manifested their practical concern with a "spiritual interpretation" of Scripture. By this they do not advocate farfetched allegorizing or intellectual gymnastics to find the most bizarre analogies. On the contrary, "the spiritual understanding is this one, where the literal sense of difficult things is transferred by the Holy Spirit into practical use and generates pious movements of the heart."[22] That is to say, the Word of God is interpreted "spiritually" when it is refracted through the Christian's experience and his decisions, and when it involves his whole personality.

The theology of Lutheran Orthodoxy, then, is "totally orientated toward the practical life."[23]

In the case of some Orthodox teachers the connection with church practice is evident at first sight. The writings of Brochmand, for example, treat hardly a question which does not have visible roots in situations of preaching, pastoral care, and parish administration. When theological discussion is carried on by other men at a more abstract level, a close scrutiny will reveal the same practical motivation. Even in his article on the divine attributes, Johann Gerhard is concerned to indicate two applications of such knowledge, namely, consolation and guidance.[24]

---

theological methods, but reborn, theology is not only from the Holy Spirit, but with the Holy Spirit; that is, it is associated with the gracious indwelling of the Holy Spirit (Johann Andrea Quenstedt, *Theologia Didactico Polemica sive Systema Theologicum*, Lipsiae, Fritsch 1715, pars I p. 23).

In its primary sense the term "theology" refers to the revealed wisdom of God himself, which is the formative power which molds men's hearts and souls and which calls and inspires the church. Although the word is used in another sense as well, to describe the "human superstructure built upon the Scriptures and entirely dependent upon them," this man-made edifice is possible only because God speaks to us through his Word. "Theology is primarily an inner Godward-orientated disposition, and only in a secondary, derivative sense is it a doctrine, a speech, a book, or a system" (*Ibid.*, p. 16).

[22] Vide Hollaz, *Examen Theologicum Acroamaticum*, ed. R. Teller, Holmiae et Lipsiae, 1750. p. 15.

[23] Gerhard, 12; compare Hollaz, p. 10.

[24] (a) *Consolation.* The divine attributes are not some changeable peculiarities (accidens mutabile) in God, but his very essence. (Gerhard, *Loci* I, p. 265; cf. Quenstedt, p. 432). Accordingly, we may be sure that his love is more ardent than we could ever imagine. Whenever we meditate upon the divine attributes we may be reassured concerning our future hope: As God is unchangeable, so is his mercy, so are his promises.

A pastoral counselor knows that the comforting word must be a strong word—delivered unambiguously, without doubt, and with firm persuasion—or it will not be effective. If the teacher refuses to speak about the attributes of God, does it not hint that he is in some doubt about them? He must be rash indeed if he does not fear that his doubts may be communicated to his students and undercut the consolation and stability they could have derived from the doctrine.

For the modern clinically-trained chaplain it should be of special interest to learn that in the Orthodox age theology is called a "spiritual medicine."[25] The inward goal of theology, according to Balthasar Meisner, is to cure *(medicari theologicum)*, that is, "to work on behalf of the man who is to be saved." A theologian who is faithful in his duty does not omit anything in his power to heal and to restore men.[26]

A chaplain or a pastoral counselor may be excused if he becomes frustrated at some skillfully woven spider web, which tickles his intellect but gives him no practical help. A theology neatly separated from faith, kerygma, and edification might well strike him as being pebbles instead of grapes *(sic)*, and he might yearn to pull some present-day theologian a bit closer to everyday life.

This is exactly where the Orthodox theologians could make a surprising contribution. The pastor must meet his parishioners in their need and not leave them stumbling along like sheep without a shepherd. A mature Christian personality must have sharply defined goals, clear criteria, and stable moral principles, says Luther.[27]

Every teacher of theology has had some gifted students with a keen interest in religious problems, yet at the same time a pronounced distaste for anything "dogmatic" or "orthodox." What hap-

---

(b) "Our changeable nature ought to regard the immutable divine goodness as the ideal for its aspirations, so that by his immutability the fickleness and instability of our goodness may be absorbed" (Gerhard, I, p. 268). Here we must learn to desire the perfect goodness to which we shall be carried in the life eternal.

[25] *Ibid.*, p. 7.

[26] Balthasar Meisner, *Philosophia Sobria*, III, p. 112. Vide Joh. G Baieri *Compendium Theologiae Positivae*, ed. C. F. G. Walther, 1879. Prol. c. I § 16, ant. b) vol. 1, p. 37.

[27] WA 18, p. 656.

pens when one of these students becomes a pastor responsible for his flock? It is easy to predict: Little by little he falls out of love with his own doubts and finds the sweetness of rebellion fading away. Instead of delighting himself and dazzling others with his dialectical skill, he discovers that he must search for a simple and direct means of presenting the true doctrine of the Apostles. In other words, our young friend is drifting toward a form of orthodoxy, whether or not he wishes to admit the fact to himself. In the case of a Lutheran this orthodoxy to which he inclines might very likely be the same seventeenth century orthodoxy which he once rejected, but in an oversimplified and slightly twisted form. He would eventually recognize that what Martin Luther affirmed is true: The Holy Spirit is not a skeptic; he does not come with vague conjecture, but writes in our hearts assertions which are stronger than any experience, yea, than life itself.[28]

EDMUND SMITS

---

[28] *Ibid.*, p. 605.

Contents

Preface v

Introduction: What Is Lutheran Orthodoxy? ix

PART ONE: THE IMAGE OF GOD
Johann Gerhard, *Loci Theologici* IV, Locus 9

    Introduction 27
    I. The Nature of the Image of God in Man 32
    II. The Image of God Not a Supernatural Gift 41
    III. The Image of God Not the Substance of Man 43
    IV. Immortality as a Part of the Image of God 46
    V. The Image of God in Man's Body 49
    VI. The Image of God in the Woman 52
    VII. The Dwelling of the First Man 54
    VIII. The Propagation of the Soul 58
    IX. The Loss of the Divine Image Through the Fall 61
    X. Definition and Application of the Doctrine 65

PART TWO: FREE WILL
Martin Chemnitz, *Loci Theologici*, Locus 6

    Introduction 69
    I. The Freedom of the Will in External Conduct 81
    II. The Bondage of the Will 88
    III. Concerning Spiritual Powers in Man 95
    IV. Augustine's Distinctions in the Doctrine of Grace 102
    V. Is the Will Purely Passive in Conversion? 119

PART THREE: SIN

Martin Chemnitz, *Loci Theologici*, Locus 7

Introduction 131
I. A Comparison of the Doctrines 136
II. The Classification of Sin 139

ORIGINAL SIN

III. Regarding Testimonies or Proof Passages 142
IV. Regarding Questions of Method 149
V. The Chief Perversions of the Doctrine 154
VI. The Arguments of the Pelagians 164
VII. The Remnants of Original Sin After Baptism 177

ACTUAL SIN

VIII. The Gravity of Actual Sin 198
IX. Actual Sin in Relation to Original Sin 204

Appendix: Biographies of Johann Gerhard and Martin Chemnitz 219

Index 231

PART ONE

The
Image
of
God

by
Johann Gerhard

Introduction

1^1 (1) God's deliberation in the creation of man.

God created man according to the counsel of his will[2] which he made before the foundation of the world. In the beginning, in six distinct days, the divine architect created with his omnipotent Word the heaven, the earth, the sea, and all the things therein. Finally, not without previous deliberation,[3] he came to the creation of man.

God "deliberated" about the creation of man in a new and thus far unusual way. The reason for this is to be found, not in the weakness of the Creator, but rather in the excellence of the work itself. As Tertullian rightly remarks: "Man was made by God not with a word of command, as the other animals, but with a friendly hand, pre-

---

[1] The numbers in the margin are the paragraph numbers in Cotta's 1787 edition of Johann Gerhard's works, the edition used here.

[2] See Eph. 1:4, 5: ". . . . he hath chosen us in him before the foundation of the world . . . having predestinated us unto the adoption of children by Jesus Christ to himself . . ." Lutheran Orthodoxy recognizes only single predestination based on God's grace and mercy "with the purpose to give man eternal life" (Gerhard IV:237).

[3] Gerhard is not to be indicted here for having an anthropomorphic conception of God. He has in mind the succession of time depicted in the Creation account of Genesis 1. The timing in this account is meaningful in that it places a special value upon man.

ceded by that gracious utterance: 'Let us make man in our own image and likeness.' "[4] And Gregory the Great says: "This was done in order that he who was to be made in the image of his Maker should exist, not through the voice of a command, but through the dignity of an act."[5]

4   (2)   Let us make man

Whom does God address by saying "Let us make"? Not himself indeed, because he does not say, "Let me make" but "Let us make"; not the angels, because the angels are servants of God, and the servants cannot share the work proper of the Master, as the works cannot participate in the operation of their Maker: but he speaks to his Son,"[6] through whom, and to the Holy Spirit, in whom, all things were made. . . .[7]

When he says, "Let us make," one operation of three Persons is expressed. On the other hand, when he says, "In our own image and likeness," the one and equal essence of the three Persons is indicated. Thus, in the creation of the first Adam, the mystery of the most holy Trinity is set forth, though in a rather obscure and indistinct way. This mystery was later clearly revealed for the sake of our regeneration in the baptism of the Second Adam, i.e., Christ.

7   (3)   The counsel of God concerning man

In that council of infinite wisdom of the three divine Persons, i.e., the Father, the Son, and the Holy Spirit, a great counsel indeed was set forth on behalf of us sinners. Actually, it was the outcome of a divine soliloquy rather than of a senatorial deliberation.[8] Do you think that any of the things which had to be done for us were missed? There, in the midst of that divine council, the whole cause concerning us was set down. There our coming perdition and death were foreseen,[9] and the whole matter concerning man was planned in such a

---

[4] *Adversus Marcionem* 2:4; P.L. 2:288C, 289A.

[5] *Expositio in librum b. Job* 9:49.75; P.L. 75:900B, C.

[6] Ambrose, *Hexaemeron* 6:7; P.L. 14:257B.

[7] It is interesting to note Gerhard's emphasis on the presence of the Holy Spirit in creation. The whole universe is created "in him," thereby being made alive and holy by the Spirit himself.

[8] I.e., not God deliberating with an assembly but God deliberating with himself.

[9] The meaning is certainly "foreseen" (perspecta) and not "predestined" (praedestinata).

way that each divine Person would contribute to it. There it was decided that what the Father would create, the Son afterwards, in the fulness of time, would redeem from perdition, and the Holy Spirit would bring about the remission of sins and the resurrection of the flesh. Hence, with a counsel of all the three Persons the things lost since the beginning of the ages would be restored in man and the foundations of generation and regeneration established. Therefore, "praise be to the wisdom of the Creator; honor to the grace of the Liberator; thanksgiving to the power of the Illuminator; adoration to the one and indivisible Trinity by whom all things were created, were redeemed, and are governed."[10]

8 (4) All things on behalf of man

Man was created after the work of heaven and earth was completed. He was created after all other creatures. For man is the epitome of all other creatures. All the things which in the other creatures are found separately, are found in man jointly. In fact, man partakes of both spiritual and physical nature. In the words of Augustine, "In man is found almost every creature; man is the center of creation and nature."[11]

All things were created on behalf of man. For, as man was made for God in order that he might serve him, so the world was made for man in order that it might serve man. Man, therefore, was set in the middle in order that he might be served and, in turn, that he himself might serve. Thus, that man is obeyed and that he himself obeys are both for his own benefit. For God intended that he should be served by man in such a way that not God, but rather man, might be benefited. Everything, then, was intended for the good of man; both that which was made on his behalf, and the purpose for which he himself was made.

Since man was created to be the most quiet dwelling-place of the holy Trinity, God rested from his work after creating man. Therefore let man seek in God the true rest of his heart, for there he will find it. Let him make use of the creatures, and yet not abuse them.

---

[10] Rupertus, *De Trinitate et Operibus eius* 2:42, P.L. 167:248A. Rupertus or Rhodbert (d. 718) was a member of the Merovingian family; he became Bishop of Worms and was active in spreading Christianity in southern Germany.

[11] *De Civitate Dei* 10:12. The quotation is not in the place indicated by Gerhard, but the thought itself is Augustinian.

Let him make use of the creatures not as the ultimate end of his desire, but as means to render homage and service to the Creator. Let the brooks lead to the source, and the road to its destination.

12   (5)   Whence the soul of man

Man was made out of the dust in order that such an origin should be a safeguard and reminder of man's low estate, and, moreover, that it should bear witness that man before God is like clay in the hands of the potter. For we are all dust and ashes (Gen. 18:27). However, the one who was able to make the body of man out of the clay will be able also to raise it out of the dust. His might and power are not diminished by years.

While the body of man was made out of the dust of the earth, the soul, which is the essential breath of life, came to him inside his body, through the breathing of God. Lactantius remarks: "After the body of man was made, God breathed into it the soul out of the vital source of his eternal Spirit in order that man might bear the image of the world itself which is constituted of opposite elements.[12]

As without hands God had fashioned the body of man, in like manner without lungs he breathed into it a created spirit.[13] God's breathing in the face of man actually means putting a living soul into his body.[14] For God did not breathe the soul of man out of the inner source of his divine essence in the same way as the Father with the Son from eternity breathes the Holy Spirit within the divine essence; but, in time, he breathed in man a created soul outside of his divine essence. The breath of life, which is man's soul, was made by God, not out of God.

13   Man was made in the image and likeness of God, and hence he received supreme dignity and preeminence above all physical creatures. Oh that the image of God in man would be as clear to us for the right knowledge of him as it was once so excellent as to render

---

[12] *Divinae Institutiones* 2:12; P.L. 6:519C. An African by birth and a pupil of Arnobius, Lactantius was a Christian apologist of the early 4th century.

[13] By "without hands" and "without lungs," Gerhard means that both the created body and the inbreathed spirit of man are above the crude physical level.

[14] *Anima rationalis*, lit. rational soul, has here essentially the same content as *nephesh hayah* and *psychē zōsa*, i.e., living soul.

man worthy of the supreme divine grace! However, because of sin, all the divine things by which we were made in God's image were so lost that scarcely any little remnants of them are left. Yea, scarcely a shadow of a great name remains. No wonder, then, that our intellect cannot grasp the full knowledge of him, for that knowledge is lost. In such darkness we shall follow the torch of the Holy Scriptures.

The Nature of the Image of God in Man

15 (1)   The meaning of the divine utterance
"And God said, Let us make man in our image, after our likeness" (Gen. 1:26).[1] According to Pererius, "This divine utterance can be understood in two different ways, i.e., either of the image which is in God, so that the essential nature of God would be like an original pattern after whose likeness man was made, or of the created image which is in man. According to the former interpretation, the meaning of the divine utterance would be: 'Let us make man such as we ourselves are,' whereas according to the latter the meaning would be: 'Let us make man so similar to us that he himself might be an image and a likeness reflecting our own nature, power, wisdom, etc.' "[2] Actually, both interpretations go back to the same meaning. In fact, since goodness, wisdom, and righteousness constitute the very essence of God, man who was made in the image

---

[1] The *Authorized Version* is followed predominantly except where another version is indicated or where the author has his own unique translation.

[2] *Commentariorum et Disputationum in Genesim* 4:472. Benedict Pererius (Pereira, Pereyra, Perera) was a Jesuit philosopher, theologian, and exegete of the late 16th and early 17th centuries.

of God was created in goodness, wisdom, and righteousness. On the other hand, since in man shines the image of divine goodness, wisdom, and righteousness, it is rightly said and believéd that he was made in the image of God.

16 (2) Image and likeness

Do these two words indicate something different, or rather the same thing? According to many of the old scholars, man was made "in the image of God" with regard to the essential faculties of the soul, i.e., mind, will, and memory; whereas, on the other hand, he was made "in the likeness of God" with regard to the *qualities* of the soul, in the sense that the mind or intellect is illuminated by faith, the memory confirmed by hope, and the will by love.

This distinction of old is followed by Bellarmine; and hence he attributes a note of heresy to all those who hold that through sin the image of God, as far as spiritual things are concerned, was lost and erased.[3]

17 It would indeed be a great error and heresy to refer the image of God in man to the very essence of the soul and, consequently, to say that such an image was lost. If this were the case, man by his fall would have lost the very essence of his soul, and hence it would follow that after the fall a new souɪ subject to sin was created. However, such a new soul could not be attributed to the devil because it was a created soul;[4] on the other hand, it could not be attributed to God because of its being subject to sin.

18 As far as our understanding is concerned, we do not distinguish between image and likeness as referring the former to the essence of man's soul, the latter to holiness, righteousness, knowledge of God, and so on. We hold that both words indicate the same thing. In this we follow Pererius who argues as follows:[5]

(a) As in Gen. 1:26 man is said to have been made in the image and likeness of God, so later in Gen. 5:6 it is stated that Adam begot his son Seth in his own image and likeness. Now, in the latter the

---

[3] *De Notis Ecclesiae* 4:9. Robert Bellarmine (1542-1621) was a learned and eloquent Roman Catholic theologian. A bitter opponent of Protestantism, he sought to overcome it by means of rational argument.

[4] The devil is unable to create. Cf. below, §97.

[5] *Ibid.*, p. 474.

distinction claimed above cannot be applied. Therefore, the two words do not mean two different things.

(b) The Apostle Paul often uses the word image in the sense of likeness, which image or likeness is said by Paul to consist in freely given and supernatural gifts. Thus in 1 Cor. 15:49: "As we have borne the image of the earthly, we shall also bear the image of the heavenly"; and in Col. 3:10: ". . . the new man, which is renewed in knowledge after the image of him that created him."

(c) The Scriptures in this respect speak in various ways. Sometimes they put both words, image and likeness, in the same case, as in Gen. 1:26: "Let us make man in our image, after our likeness"; sometimes in different cases, as in Wisdom 2:23: "God created man in the image of his likeness"; sometimes they omit the word likeness and use only the word image, as in Gen. 9:6: "In the image of God made he man."

19   To these arguments of Pererius we shall add the following remarks, also from the Scriptures.

According to Gen. 1:26, God says: "Let us make man in our image, after our likeness"; to which Moses adds: "And God created man in his own image, in the image of God created he him" (Gen. 1:27). Here the word likeness is omitted, and hence we gather that what was indicated before by the two words image and likeness is now expressed by one word, i.e., image, and, therefore, only for the sake of clarification was it said before that the image was going to be in the likeness of the original type.

20   Since not every image is like the original type and, on the other hand, since the essential nature of the image of God in man could be understood differently, as the different opinions of the Fathers testify, God himself indicated how to find its true meaning. By adding the word likeness he taught that man was originally made so that in him the image of the Creator should appear in every respect like the Creator. As Pererius rightly remarks: "The Hebrew word *selem* [image] properly means a shadow or a shady likeness, that is, an imperfect image, a representation, whereas the Hebrew word *demuth* [likeness] indicates a perfect likeness."[6]

21   Hence Luther writes: "After careful observation I discovered that

---

[6] *Ibid.,* p. 472.

they called *selem* the image or figure, as when Scripture says: 'Destroy the altars of your images.' There the word *selem* means nothing else but the figures or statues which are erected. On the other hand, *demuth* denotes a likeness, that is, a perfect image. For example, when we speak of dead images, such as those on coins, we say: This is the image of Brutus, of Caesar; but that image does not express likeness, for it does not show all the characteristics. Therefore, when Moses says that man was made in the likeness of God, he emphasizes the fact that man not only reflects God in that he has an intellect and a will, but that he bears the likeness of God, that is, an intellect and a will by which he understands God and wants the things which God wants."[7]

22   This is the reason why the two words "image" and "likeness" of Gen. 1:26 are later included in one word, as in Gen. 5:1: "And God made man in the likeness of Elohim,"; this likeness, according to which Adam was made, is distinguished in v. 3 from the image and likeness which Adam by begetting children propagated in his sons. The Scriptures say: "Adam begot Seth in his own image and likeness,"; not in the image of God, but according to the image which was in him, i.e., in Adam himself at that time. What image? An image subject to sin, to the wrath of God, to the curse of the Law, and to temporal and eternal death.

23   (3)   The testimony of the Apostle Paul

In this connection we should add and evaluate the following two scriptural testimonies of the Apostle Paul.

In Eph. 4:24 we read: "Put on the new man, which after God is created in righteousness and true holiness,"; and in Col. 3:10: "You have put on the new man which is renewed in knowledge after the image of him that created him."

In these two passages we find two equivalent expressions, i.e., "after God" and "after the image of God," with which expressions is expounded the description of the new man, who is called "new" not because of a change of his essence, but because of new qualities, i.e., knowledge of God, righteousness, and true holiness. The image of God in man consists, then, in the fact that man was made "after God" and he is renewed "after the image of God." But man is re-

---

[7] *Super Genesim* 5:76; W.A. 42:247-8.

newed with respect to the knowledge of God, righteousness, and holiness, and with these qualities he was made "in the image of God." Therefore, in these same qualities is to be found the original image of God in man. . . .

30   These two apostolic utterances show what the Holy Spirit wants to teach us with regard to the true meaning of the image of God in man. We can draw from them two basic teachings.

31   The first is this: The apostle teaches that those who are born again are renewed in knowledge according to the image of him who created him. Therefore the image of God cannot be in man unless he is renewed by the Holy Spirit. Now, that which is supposed to be acquired through a renewal cannot be possessed previous to the renewal, and that which is obtained through the gift of regeneration cannot be possessed through carnal generation. In fact, if only that which is born of the Spirit is spirit, it follows that what is born of the flesh cannot be anything but flesh (John 3:6). As Tertullian rightly remarks, "Christians are not born, but they become Christian";[8] and Augustine says, "Not generation, but regeneration makes Christians."[9]

32   A corollary of this first teaching is that, according to the Scriptures, the image of God is not to be identified with the very essence of the living soul, for this is present also in men who are not regenerated. We must be renewed in the image of God because only then, when the soul is renewed in knowledge, is the image of God restored in the soul. In conclusion, the essence of the living soul is one thing and the image of God which is in the soul is another.

33   The other teaching is this: According to Col. 3:10, the image of God, according to which those who are born anew are renewed by the Holy Spirit, is restored through a "renewal in knowledge." Therefore the image of God cannot consist of those things which are essential also to the soul of men who are not born anew. For the knowledge which is brought about in those who are born anew by the illumination of the Holy Spirit is not a characteristic inherent in the human soul after the fall, but is a light coming from elsewhere, i.e., a light kindled through the light of the Holy Spirit and the

---

[8] *Apologeticus* 18; P.L. 1:378B.
[9] *De Peccatorum Meritis et Remissione* 3:9.17; P.L. 44:196A.

light of the Word. In Eph. 5:8 we read: "You were sometimes darkness, but now (i.e., through the benefit of regeneration and renovation) are ye light in the Lord"; in Eph. 1:17-18: "God gives the eyes of the heart enlightened through the Spirit of wisdom and revelation";[10] in John 8:12: "And I [Christ] am the light of the world"; in John 1:9: "The true light which enlightens every man coming into the world"; in John 9:39: "I am come into this world, that they which see not might see."

34   A corollary of this teaching is that, according to the Scriptures, the image of God is not to be identified with the soul insofar as it is spiritual, incorporeal, immortal, and endowed with the faculties of understanding and free will with respect to the choice of eternal and civil things; or insofar as it rules the body and thus surpasses in dignity all animated things. All these things, in fact, are characteristic also of the soul of the man who is not born anew.

35   (4)   The testimony of 2 Cor. 3:18

To the two scriptural statements of the Apostle Paul mentioned above, a third should be added: "We all, with open face beholding as in a glass the glory of the Lord, are changed (literally *transformed*) into the same image from glory to glory, even as by the Spirit of the Lord" (2 Cor. 3:18). Notice that the restoration of the divine image is to be brought about in us through a metamorphosis, or transformation, i.e., in such a way that the old form or image is laid aside, and we put on the new one. Therefore the essential nature of the divine image cannot and should not be sought in the very essence of the human soul. If such a transformation is performed in us by the Spirit of the Lord, it follows that the image of God resulting from it must not be identified with any of those things which are found also in the soul of unregenerate men.

36   Following the teaching of the Scriptures, we can expound the whole thing in this way: The image of God in man originally consisted of righteousness and true holiness. After the fall man must be renewed according to that original image. Therefore, if we want to follow the teachings of the Scriptures, we cannot say that the human soul reflects the image of God because of its very essence or because

---

[10] This is not a quotation but rather Gerhard's interpretation of the sense of the passage.

of those things which are by nature inherent in man's soul after the fall and hence are found also in men who are not born anew. The Apostle says: "Be renewed in the spirit of your mind; and . . . put on the new man, which after God is created in righteousness and true holiness" (Eph. 4:23-4). Here the new man is said to be created in a twofold respect, i.e., with regard to his first origin in Adam, who was created in the image of God, i.e., in righteousness and true holiness; and with regard to the second creation of the new man, which is brought about through the Holy Spirit and the ministry of the Word and the Sacraments. Regeneration is, in fact, a new and second creation accompanied by a renewal. In the man who is thus renewed there takes place the restoration of the image of God, which is begun in this life and completed in the life to come.

37   (5)   Righteousness and true holiness

What do righteousness and true holiness involve? The righteousness and true holiness which, according to the Apostle, constitute the image of God, include true knowledge of God in the mind, full conformity with the Law of God in the will, and the uprightness of the faculties of the soul. For man was created in such perfect innocence and purity of body and soul that the image of God would reflect in him as in a living mirror. Hence, the image of the divine wisdom was shining in the intellect of man: the image of goodness, patience, and tolerance in his soul; the image of divine love and mercy in the affections of the human heart; the image of divine righteousness, holiness, and purity in the will of man; the image of divine kindness and truth in his words and deeds; the image of the divine power in the dominion which was given to man over all animals.

38   As a result of all this man would be happy, blessed, and at peace, and would exult in God his Creator. No fear of any kind, no terror, no sorrow would be in him. In short, because of the divine image, the reason of man would be surrendered to God; his will to his reason; his feelings and all the other faculties to his will. Hence all the powers and faculties in man would constitute a perfect harmony.

39   God had manifested his power, wisdom, and goodness in the creatures in such a way that the whole cosmos should be truly a school and a teacher of the knowledge of God. However, in order

that man should not be urged to seek the knowledge of God outside of himself and from afar, God set his own image in man himself so that man, looking at it, might know what God was—righteous,
holy, merciful, pure, etc. After the creation of man, since no
animal was found similar to Adam with whom man could have
fellowship, friendship, and familiarity, God created Eve, a helper
similar to man. In like manner, after all the corporeal things had been
created, and there was yet no creature like God with whom God
himself might have fellowship and familiarity, he made man like
himself, in order that man might be the creature whom he might
love, whom he might make a partaker of his beatitude, and by
whom, in turn, he might be acknowledged, praised, and loved.
Hence that utterance of the Proverbs: "My delights were with the
sons of men" (Prov. 8:31.)[11]

43   After the fall, it was an innate power of the human mind to ignore
the essence and the will of God; it is an innate impulse of the
human will to run away from God; it is an innate quality of the
human heart to lean with all possible affection towards those things
which displease God. Before the fall, it was natural for man to
know God as the Creator, to fear him, to cling firmly to him, and
to be moved towards those things which please God, without any
conflict between man's superior and inferior parts. With the help
of a rough comparison, we can compare man before the fall to the
fabulous unicorn whose natural character, they say, is to follow
man and to cling caressingly to him. On the other hand, we can
compare man after the fall to the wolf, whose native character is

---

[11] In the sections of the text not translated here Gerhard expresses his
agreement with those theologians who distinguish two sides of God's image:
the material and the formal. The material side considers man's relation to God
the interior integrity and harmony of human nature in four stages: (1) the light
of wisdom in the mind, (2) the free conversion of the will to God (in volun-
tate libera ad Deum conversio), the ardent desire for God as supreme value,
and conformity to his will, (3) love of God in the heart, (4) conformity of
body and instincts to reason. The formal side implied the relation of God to man,
namely his pleasing acceptance of the human person and the gracious indwelling
of God (inhabitatio Dei gratiosa) (*Loci* II p. 97/98, sec. 40-42).

Some of the Orthodox Dogmaticians followed Gerhard in this point (Calov
and Quenstedt). Others (e.g. Hollaz) preferred to think that the indwelling of
the Trinity was not supernatural but natural to the first man.

to flee from man and to hate him. In the same way, the native character of man before the fall was to love God and to follow him, whereas his native character after the fall is to hate him and to flee from him.

44   (6) Conclusion

This, then, is the scriptural description of the image of God in the first man as he was before the fall. There was in him true righteousness and true holiness; with which words, as stated above, is expressed the perfect harmony of all the faculties of soul and body, that is, integrity and conformity with the divine law, complete perfection [12] of the whole man, and an innocence and purity confirmed by man's nudity. The first parents were naked. For why should they have shame, when there was no conflict in their members with the law of their reason? There was then in man no impulse toward which he should have a natural feeling of shame. In the words of Augustine: "They reckoned that nothing should be hidden because they felt nothing from which they should refrain."[13]

45   The very nature of Adam, then, was wholly untouched and upright. As we read in Ecclesiastes 7:29: "God hath made man upright." There was in him no infirmity, no deceitfulness, no conflict between the inferior and superior part, no tendency towards vices. What the Holy Spirit says about the work of the whole creation, "God saw everything that he had made, and behold, it was very good" (Gen. 1:31), ought to be said primarily about the nature of the first man and all the things which were by nature inherent in him. . . .

---

[12] Perfection is to be taken in the sense of integrity and inward harmony, not in the sense that there was no possibility of future growth and higher sanctity. The strong patristic emphasis on growth may be seen from Augustine's distinction between the first grace, i.e., the innocence of the first man before the fall, and the second and more powerful grace, i.e., the deeper sanctity of the true Christian. E.g., Augustine writes: "Did not Adam have the grace of God? Yes, truly he had it, but it was of a different kind. He was placed in the midst of benefits . . . in which he suffered absolutely no evil. But saints in this life, to whom pertains the grace of deliverance, are in the midst of evils out of which they cry to God . . ." (*De Correptione et Gratia* 11.29; P.L. 44:935D).

[13] *De Genesi ad Litteram* 11:1.3; P.L. 34:430C.

II

The Image of God
Not a Supernatural Gift

57   It should be well established that the original righteousness of man before the fall was an inward, essential perfection of the whole man who was made pure, untouched, and holy, without any stain of vicious concupiscence, without any inclination toward vice, and without any kind of weakness. This can be gathered also from the remnants of that original image and its propagation. The following are the arguments:

58   (a)   The Apostle Paul in Rom. 2:15 says that "the work of the law is written in the hearts of the Gentiles."[1] Now, if the remnants of the original divine image, i.e., some knowledge of the divine law, are written by nature in the hearts of men, it follows that the perfect knowledge of the divine law in man before the fall was natural also. When the whole and its parts are homogeneous, then the nature of the whole must be the same as the nature of its parts. It would be absurd to attribute a supernatural gift also to those who are not born anew.

59   (b)   In the same verse the Apostle states that for the Gentiles ". . . their consciences bear witness, their thoughts accusing or

---
[1] According to Gerhard's own free Latin translation.

41

excusing one another."[2] Hence we argue as follows: In the case of the Gentiles, the testimony of the conscience accusing or excusing is not and cannot be a supernatural gift, but is a natural characteristic of the soul and a small particle of the divine discernment in the minds of men. Therefore the uprightness of the first man was natural to him. Here also the logic of the consequence depends on the nature of the homogeneous parts.

60   (c) The things which are propagated by nature cannot but be natural. Now, had man persisted in the state of original integrity, the image of God in man before the fall would have been transmitted by nature, or naturally, to Adam's descendants. As Adam after the fall is said very significantly ". . . to have begotten a son . . ." in his own image and likeness (Gen. 5:3), and ". . . hence we all are by nature the children of wrath . . ." (Eph. 2:3), in the same manner Adam in the state of integrity would undoubtedly have begotten a son in the image of God. . . .

62   (d) According to Eccl. 7:30, "God hath made him upright." Therefore there was in man neither deceitfulness nor vicious concupiscence. God made him perfectly holy and righteous,[3] and God was pleased with such a work. . . .

---

[2] According to Gerhard's own free Latin translation.
[3] Cf. note 11, p. 23.

III

The Image of God
Not the Substance of Man

94   The image of God in the first man was neither some extraneous
supernatural[1] gift nor some kind of external ornament which could
be taken away without essential depravation of the very nature
of man. Actually, it was an uprightness, integrity, and perfection
inherent in the whole human nature and in all the faculties of the
human soul. However, the image of God as it was in man before
the fall cannot be identified with the very substance of man. For
if the image of God in man were the very substance of man, then
that image should be identified either with the whole man, or the
soul of man, or his body, or some essential part of the soul, or with
a substance different from the very substance of man. But none
of these five things can be identified with the image of God in man,

---

[1] The Roman Catholic teaching which is opposed here may be summarized
in two quotations from the *Baltimore Catechism:* "Sanctifying grace is a supernatural gift which is a sharing in the nature of God himself and which raises
men to the supernatural order, conferring on them powers entirely above those
proper to human nature" (explanation to q. 52). "God is not unjust in punish-
ing us on account of the sin of Adam, because original sin does not take away
from us anything to which we have a strict right as human beings, but only the
free gifts which God in his goodness would have bestowed on us if Adam had
not sinned" (answer to q. 61).

neither can there be a sixth alternative. Therefore it follows that the original image of God in man cannot and should not be identified with any kind of substance.

Let us prove each member of this negative assumption:

95   (1)   The image of God was not the whole man. This can be proved from the following considerations:

(a)   Only to the Son of God belongs this honor, that he is the exact and substantial image of the Father (Heb. 1:3).

(b)   If the image of God were the whole man, it would follow that the original sin, which succeeded in the place of the lost image of God, would be man himself[2] and, consequently, there would be no difference whatever between man and original sin. Now, such a conclusion, as we shall prove in its proper place, contradicts the teachings of Scripture and the articles of creation, incarnation, redemption, sanctification, and resurrection.

(c)   Man is described as made, or created, "in the image of God." By this phrase, that which is created in the image of God is distinguished from the image itself.

(d)   The Apostle defines the image of God as consisting in true holiness and righteousness. Now holiness and righteousness belong to man, not by essence but by inherence.[3] For God alone is so holy and righteous that he is by essence the very Righteousness and Holiness.

(e)   If the image of God were the whole man, it would follow that Adam, with regard to his essence, would after the fall be a man substantially different from what he was when he was first created. Hence neither would the concreated blessedness have belonged to the fallen Adam, nor would the misery which followed the fall have been inherent in Adam as he was originally made.

96   (2)   The image of God was neither the soul of man nor his body. This can be proved as follows:

The image of God was not the very soul of man. If it had been,

---

[2] This was the teaching of Matthias Flaccius.

[3] The word "inherence" (Latin, *inhaerentia*) designates those qualities possessed by a being which do not belong to the essence of that being. Cf. Thomas Aquinas, *Expositio in octo libros Physicorum* 3:5.1.

when the image of God was lost, either the soul of man would have perished or another soul would have replaced the one which was lost. Now, both these possible alternatives are absurd. Much less could the image of God be identified with Adam's body. For the body of Adam was far less noble than the soul, and yet it outlived the loss of the image of God.

(3) The image of God was not some part of the soul, and this can be proved with two arguments. First, if the image of God were some part of the soul, then, when the image of God was lost, a part of the soul also would have been lost. But this plainly contradicts the nature of that which is one single unit and, consequently, which has neither different parts nor one part distinct from the other.

Second, if the image of God were some part of the soul, then the original sin also would have been a part of the soul. The corruption brought about by the original sin would not have pervaded the whole nature of man, but would be located in one part of the soul only, while the remaining parts would have remained uncontaminated and sound.

97 (4) The image of God was not a substance different from the substance of man. This also can be proved with two arguments. First, if the image of God were a substance different from the original substance or essence of man, then original sin would also have been a substance different from the original substance of man. If so, who would have been the author of this new substance? God perhaps? But God cannot be the author of sin. The devil perhaps? But the devil cannot be the author or creator of a substance.

Second, if the image of God were a substance different from the original substance or essence of man, it would follow that not man himself was corrupted through sin, but rather something in man, namely, that substance actually distinct and different from man himself. Thus the sin of origin is in fact reduced by those who hold this opinion for the very purpose of stressing the great evil of original sin. . . .

IV

Immortality as a Part
of the Image of God

99   One aspect of the image of God in man before the fall was immortality. However, on this point there are different opinions in the church. More recently the Photinians[1] explicitly denied that "Adam was created in immortality."[2] Actually, they hold that "Adam could not even have known the way of immortality."[3] Apparently they have borrowed such an opinion from the Pelagians of old who, according to Augustine, taught that man was going to die even if he had not fallen into sin.[4] By the same error Eugubinus was seduced, writing that "with the fall of Adam, mankind incurred not the death

---

[1] The Photinians were a 4th century group whose main teaching was the denial of the full divinity of Christ. Gerhard uses this term to refer to the Socinians, whose teaching resembles that of the Photinians. The two quotations by which he characterizes the teachings of this group are from the Racovian Catechism, the basic statement of Socinian teachings. It was drafted by Faustus Socinus, the founder of the group, and was published in the Polish city of Racow in 1605. The rejection of the natural immortality of man is quite characteristic of Socinian teaching and fundamental to their doctrine of salvation.

[2] Racovian Catechism p. 21.

[3] *Ibid.*, p. 26.

[4] *De Haeresibus* 1:88; P.L. 42:48D; *Epistola* 186: 9:33; P.L. 33:828B.

of the body but the death of the soul, and men were to die even if they had not sinned."[5]

100   That the death of the body is not a necessary condition of human nature, but a punishment of sin, can be proved by the following scriptural arguments:

(a) In the Book of Wisdom 2:23 it is stated that "man was created by God ἐν ἀφθαρσία" [with immortality], that is, according to the Latin Vulgate, *inexterminabilis* [indestructible], or, as Tremellius[6] translates, *ad conditionem incorruptam* [in incorrupted condition], and therefore immortal and without corruptible evil condition. At this point it should not be objected that the Book of Wisdom is aprocryphal. For this testimony of the Book of Wisdom is in agreement with other utterances of canonical Scripture.

(b) According to Gen. 1:27, "man was made in the image of God." Now, the image of God must include in itself immortality also. For how could man reflect the image of the immortal God, if he himself were mortal? For this reason the author of Wisdom, having said that man was made immortal by God, gives, as it were, the ultimate reason for this by adding that God "made man in the image of his very nature" (Wisdom 2:23).

(c) That which is put to man as a threat cannot be a natural condition of man's nature. In Gen. 2:17, in fact, God is introduced as saying: "For in the day thou eatest thereof thou shalt surely die." Neither can it be argued that this should be understood as death of the soul only. The execution of the divine decree shows indeed that it must be understood as death of the body also. For in Gen. 3:19 we read: "In the sweat of thy face shalt thou eat bread, till thou return unto the ground; for out of it wast thou taken: for dust thou art, and unto dust shalt thou return." Hence Augustine[7] and Ambrose[8] rightly interpreted that threatening utterance of God as referring to both soul and body.

(d) In the Book of Wisdom 2:24 it is said that ". . . death came

---

[5] *Annotationes in Genesim* 2.

[6] An Orientalist of the 16th century, Johannes Immanuel Tremellius was famous for his translation of the Bible from Hebrew and Syriac into Latin.

[7] *De Civ. Dei* 13:12; P.L. 41:386A.

[8] *De Paradiso* 9; P.L. 14:294D.

into the world by the envy of the devil." Therefore death is not a condition of human nature as it was created by God.

(e)   In Rom. 5:12 we read that "death entered into the world because of the sin of our first parents";[9] in Rom. 6:23 that ". . . the wages of sin is death"; in Rom. 8:10 that ". . . the body is dead because of sin"; in 1 Cor. 15 that "by man came death" (v. 21), that "in Adam all die" (v. 22), and that "the sting of sin is death" (v. 56).[10] Therefore the death of man is not an essential condition of human nature.

(f)   According to Acts 3:21, in the life eternal there will be the ἀποκατάστασις πάντων, i.e., the restitution, or restoration, of all things. Now, according to Rev. 21:4, in the life eternal "there shall be no more death." Therefore, in the original state of integrity there was no death either. . . .

---

[9] According to Gerhard's own free Latin translation.
[10] According to Gerhard's own free Latin translation.

V

The Image of God
in Man's Body

104   Is the image of God to be found in man's body also? This question
is answered by Augustine as follows: "The fact that man is said to
have been made in the image of God must be understood not according to the body, but according to the mind, or intellect. However, it
can be said that even in the body man has a unique property which
somehow reflects the image of God. Such a property is the physical
constitution of man, whose body stands upright. By this he is warned
that he should not seek after earthly things, as the other animals do,
whose whole pleasure is out of the earth, and hence they are bent
and prostrated toward their belly."[1]

Along the same line, Bernard writes: "God made man upright
according to the soul, and not according to the earthly matter. For he
created him in his own image and likeness. You should know, therefore, that you ought to restore and keep the likeness of God in the
spiritual part of your being, and not in the mortal clay of your body.
For God is spirit, and those who wish to become or remain like him
must deal with this matter in spirit and in their hearts. Yet God
gave man an upright posture in order that the corporeal straight-

---

[1] *De Gen. ad Litt.* 6:12.22; P.L. 34:348C.

ness of the exterior and less worthy figure might be a warning to
the inward man, who was made in the image of God, that he should
keep his spiritual straightness; and thus the splendor of the body
might rebuke the deformity of the soul. In fact, what would be more
unbecoming in man than to carry his soul bent down while his
body is erect? It would be a perverse and ugly thing indeed, a
thing befitting only the clay out of which the body of man was made,
to have the eyes looking upwards and with them to look freely at
the sky above and be delighted with the lights of the heavens, while
the spiritual and celestial creature, that is, the spiritual part of man,
turns its eyes in the opposite direction, as it actually does when the
inward feelings and affections of man are bent downwards towards
the earth."[2]

So far Augustine and Bernard. Hence the Scholastics conclude
that, since God is incorporeal, there was properly speaking no image
of God in the body of man, but only as a sign. However, since, as
we have proved above, immortality of the body was a part of the
divine image, we rightly hold that in the body of man there is not
only some sign of the divine image, that is, the upright figure or
stature, but also an actual part, that is, immortality.[3]

According to Bucanus,[4] the image of God in man's body is expressed in three ways: (a) Insofar as the body joined with the
rational soul bears the image of God and in a sense contains in
itself the whole world, and hence man is said to be a microcosm in
which the Maker and Archetype of the universe shines. (b) Because
the various members of the body, such as eyes, ears, mouth, tongue,

[2] *In Canticam, Sermo* 24.5-6; P.L. 183:896D-897B. A Cistercian monk,
defender of orthodoxy, and mystical writer, Bernard of Clairvaux (1090-1153)
was the most powerful individual of the 12th century and its greatest represen-
tative of mystical piety.

[3] According to Gerhard only God possesses immortality properly speaking,
but man, by the grace of God is becoming immortal. Justin wrote: ". . . (the
soul) lives, not as being life, but as the partaker of life" (*Dialogus Cum
Tryphon Judaeo* 6; P.G. 6:489B); and Augustine: "The condition of the living body was mortal, yet immortal by the grace of the Creator" (*De Gen. Ad
Litt.* 6:25.36; P.L. 34:354B).

[4] *Institutiones Theologicae* 9. p. 86. Bucanus (Wilhelm du Buc), a Reformed theologian and professor of Theology at Lausanne 1591-1603, elaborated
the materials of Beza, Zanchius, Grynaeus and others of his predecessors within
the Reformed tradition.

and hands, reflect the spiritual members of God, that is, his spiritual perfections, such as wisdom, power, and all other divine attributes; in the same way as the tabernacle, the ark of the covenant, the sacrificial table, the vessels, and the victims were images of spiritual and celestial things (Heb. 8-10). (c) Because the qualities of the soul were reflecting their light through the body itself, in the same way as the light of a candle shines through the skin of a lantern; and the righteousness and holiness of the soul were overflowing in the members of the body, and thus through the body man was showing his dignity and eminence over all inferior things. He was bearing in his countenance a kind of majesty proper to a commander, and hence he was acknowledged by the beasts of the earth as a master and lord.

VI

The Image of God
in the Woman

105   Was the woman also made in the image of God? This question was discussed among the theologians of old in relation to what the Apostle Paul writes in 1 Cor. 11:7.

    The basis for the answer to this question is to be found in the fact that the word "image" can be applied in a different sense to the different parts in which the divine image actually consists. In fact, it can be applied in a primary and in a secondary sense.

106   In the primary sense, the image of God consisted in the perfect conformity of the living soul and its faculties to God and his law, the soul being so determined by righteousness, holiness, and truth that in the mind shone the light of wisdom and knowledge; in the will a constant impulse toward good; in the heart delight and approbation; in all other faculties a perfect subjection without any kind of opposition whatever. Together with this perfection of the soul was tranquility of conscience, cheerful quietness of the mind which was free from sorrow and rebellion, and perpetual soundness and integrity of all faculties.

107   To all these qualities and properties of the soul and of the body was added an external privilege, that is, the dominion over all

other living creatures. And on this point the image of God was shining less primarily, or, shall we say, secondarily. Thus, when the Apostle Paul says that ". . . the woman is the glory of the man and man, in turn, is the image and glory of God" (1 Cor. 11:7), he does not deny, with regard to the primary sense, that the woman also was made in the image and likeness of God. But he is concerned rather with the image of God in its secondary sense, i.e., with the dignity of dominion which belonged properly to man, while the woman was subject to his dominion. The Apostle Paul himself provides this explanation. For, he adds: "Man is not of the woman; but the woman of the man. Neither was the man created for the woman; but the woman for the man" (1 Cor. 11:8-9).

As God is the beginning and the end, the One by whom and for whom man was directly and immediately made, so the man is the beginning and the end of the woman, for she was made out of the man and for the man.[1]

---

[1] Augustine wrote somewhat differently: "For (Scripture) says that human nature itself, which is only complete in both sexes, was made in the image of God; it does not separate the woman from the image of God which it signifies" (*De Trinitate* 12:7; P.L. 42:1003C).

VII

The Dwelling
of the First Man

(1) The physical nature of Eden or Paradise

108 In order that nothing should be lacking to the blessedness of man, whom he had made in his own image, God provided him also with the most beautiful habitation. Hence it has been rightly remarked that man was given by God a threefold grace: the grace of the soul, that is, original righteousness; the grace of the body, that is, immortality; and the grace of place, that is, the dwelling of Paradise. . . .

109 The Mosaic description of Paradise clearly shows that it was a physical or corporeal garden. The following considerations about the nature of Paradise as it is described by Moses should prove this point beyond the shadow of doubt:

(a) According to Gen. 2:8, it was planted by God in a definite part of the earth, that is, in the eastern part.

(b) In this Garden planted by God was placed man, a corporeal being in need of a corporeal place.

(c) According to Gen. 2:9-10, in the Garden there were trees and rivers which irrigated it.

(d) Man was entrusted with the cultivation and care of that place (Gen. 2:15).

(e)   After the fall, the first parents hid themselves under the trees of that garden, and they sewed for themselves fig-leaves (Gen. 3:7-8).

(f)   After the fall, the first parents were driven out of the garden, and a Cherub was placed before it to prohibit entrance into it. (Gen. 3:23-24).

Along these lines, John Chrysostom writes: "For this reason Moses, describing Paradise, so carefully mentioned the name of the place in which it was located, that is, Eden; the eastern region which it was facing; and the names of the rivers, in order that it should not be allowed to those who like to deceive the simple to talk nonsense by saying that there was no Paradise on earth, but only in heaven.[1]

Peter Lombard mentions three opinions of the old theologians, as far as the nature of Paradise is concerned. He writes: "First, some thought of Paradise only as corporeal; others, only as spiritual; others, as both corporeal and spiritual."[2]

The second opinion mentioned by Lombard is that of Origen who, being committed to allegories more than is right, derived his comment about a spiritual paradise from the rabbinic dreams. The third is the opinion of Basil,[3] Augustine,[4] John Damascene,[5] and others who expounded the Mosaic text first according to the literal sense and then added spiritual allegories.

The earthly Paradise was indeed a preparation ($\pi a\iota\delta\epsilon\upsilon\tau\acute\eta\rho\iota o\nu$) for the heavenly Paradise. It was also some kind of mirror of the inward Paradise, that is, of the greatest tranquillity and happiness which our first parents were enjoying before the fall. However, we must

---

[1] *In Genesin Homilia* 13:3; P.G. 53; 108C.

[2] 2 *Sententiarum* 17:5; P.L. 192:686D. Peter of Lombard, a 12th century theologian, was famous for his *Four Books of Sentences*. The *Sentences,* an extensive summary of the Catholic faith with a great number of references to the Church Fathers, became the standard textbook of Catholic theology during the Middle Ages.

[3] *Oratio* 3; *De Paradiso;* P.G. 30. Basil the Great (c. 329-379) was the most important of the "Three Cappadocians." Next to Athanasius, he is the most important defender of the 4th century eastern church against heresies.

[4] *De Gen. ad Litt.* 8:1.1; P.L. 34:371D. "In the same way, the Paradise in which God placed man is nothing else than the place, where the earthly man lived, viz., the earth."

[5] *De Fide Orthodoxa* (2:11; P.G. 94:915C. John Damascenus (c. 676-c.749) was the last of the Greek Fathers. He is the most respected systematic theologian of the Greek Orthodox Church and is also considered a precursor of Scholasticism.

hold firmly that Moses describes, not a celestial and inward paradise, but an earthly one.

(2)   The location of Paradise

110   Where was that original and earthly Paradise located? Bellarmine
mentions four opinions: (a) The opinion of those who claimed that
Paradise was the whole earth. He attributes this opinion to Josephus
Flavius,[6] but not correctly. For Josephus, in fact, does hold that this
garden was located in the eastern part and that the first parents
were transferred from this region to another. Actually, he should
have attributed this opinion to Hugo of St. Victor.[7] (b) The
opinion of those who thought that Paradise was located outside
of the whole earth in which we dwell. They claimed that our earth
is surrounded by another earth far greater than ours, and this would
be the Mosaic Paradise. Such an opinion is simply a Jewish dream.
(c) The opinion of those who thought of Paradise as a place above
the earth, reaching the globe of the moon. This opinion is mentioned by Peter Lombard.[8] Actually, this is the opinion of Basil
who in his book, *De Paradiso*, writes that this place, that is, the
Mosaic Paradise, "stands higher than the whole earth"[9] and because
of its height contains no darkness. The same thing is repeated by
Damascenus,[10] Rupertus [11] and Marius Victor.[12] Bellarmine himself
tries to justify this opinion on the ground that "with such an hyper-
bolic altitude they wanted to stress the excellency of Paradise."[13]
However, this benevolent gloss, or explanation, is contrary to the
words and mind of those who expounded such an opinion. (d) The
opinion of those who thought that Paradise was in Mesopotamia

[6] *Antiquitates* 1:2. Josephus Flavius is the famous Jewish historian (c. 37-
100).

[7] Hugo of St. Victor (1096-1141) was a medieval philosopher, theologian
and mystical writer. He is considered by Harnack to be the most influential
theologian of the 12th century.

[8] 2 *Sent.* 17.5; P.L. 192:686D.

[9] *De Par.* 1; P.G. 30:63A.

[10] *De Fid. Orth.* 2:11; P.G. 94:914A.

[11] *In Gen.* 1:37; P.L. 167:223A.

[12] *Commentariorum in Genesim* 1; P.L. 61:943A. Claudius Marius Victor
(d. 425-450) was a rhetorician at Marseilles. He is known for the above work
(also entitled *Alēthia*), a 3-volume poem on the origins of mankind from creation to the destruction of Sodom and Gomorrah.

[13] *De Gratia Primi Hominis* 12.

and that it was destroyed afterwards by the waters of the deluge. This is actually the opinion of Augustine and others. Bellarmine himself does not approve this opinion.

As for our own opinion, we simply hold, according to the Mosaic text, that Paradise was a most pleasant place looking to the east. However, since the whole earth was utterly devastated by the deluge, its boundaries cannot be defined. . . .

VIII

The Propagation
of the Soul

116 (1) The soul is propagated

Thus far we have dealt with the happy condition of man before the fall. Man was then most blessed because of the qualities of his soul, body, and dwelling place. Had he persisted in the state of integrity in which he had been created, such an integrity would have been transmitted to his descendants also. Hence we deduce that the souls of those who were to be born from Adam and Eve were to be neither created nor generated, but propagated. This is proved by the following considerations:

(a) Since the image of God, which consisted in righteousness, holiness, and perfection, was concreated with the human soul and thus propagated by generation, it follows that the soul itself must also be propagated. . . .

(b) In Gen. 1:28, we read the divine command, "Be fruitful and multiply." Such a blessing was supposed to be efficacious for man as it was for all other animals. Neither can it be said that the fall of man enervated or weakened the efficacy of such a divine blessing. For in Gen. 9:7 we find the same blessing repeated, and in Gen. 5:3 we read: "Adam begat a son in his own likeness, after his

58

image," that is, "flesh out of the flesh" (John 3:6), indicating the whole unregenerate man and not only the body (Gal. 5:20). Therefore that image of Adam perverted by sins is to be found in the whole man, and not only in the body of the sons of Adam.

(c)   God did not create the soul of Eve, but he transferred it from Adam into Eve, and thus Eve was given a soul through Adam. Now, since the soul is all in the whole body and all in each part of it, the rib out of which Eve was formed was animated, and hence Eve received her soul by propagation from Adam, and not by the direct breathing of God or a new creation. The descendants of Eve are born animated out of animated parents.

Now, let us suppose that the souls of men were created every day by God and, consequently, breathed or inspired into man. I will ask: Would God create souls pure of any stain only to become corrupted afterwards because of the infusion into the imperfect vessel of the human body? Or would he create souls which are already stained with sin? The first cannot be said because the initial eruption of sins did not come from the body to the soul, but rather from the soul to the body. The second cannot be said either because God who is good can be the creator only of good; now, the original sin, by which the soul of man after the fall is stained, is not merely a privation, but a positive evil quality.

(d)   According to Gen. 2:2, on the seventh day God rested from the work of immediate creation. It cannot be objected that God rested only from creating new species and not from creating individuals. For the creation of individual souls made out of nothing, without the intervention of natural causes, would be a creation in the strict sense of the word.

(e)   We cannot exclude from man that which is proper of all animals, that is, the procreation according to one's likeness with regard to both body and soul. . . .

117   (2)   How the souls are propagated

As for the question concerning the manner in which the soul is propagated, we acknowledge that its investigation and explanation are very difficult. Following are various opinions:

(a)   Some hold that the soul of the children is enlightened out of the soul of the parents like light out of a light, or fire out of a fire.

(b)   Some maintain that the soul of the children is propagated out of the soul of the parents not separately or apart, but rather that the whole man is generated out of the whole. For, they say, the semen is endowed with the soul; however, not separately or apart from the seed of the other sex, but rather in the conjunction of the male and female as arranged for human generation by God himself.

(c)   Some hold that the human semen, besides the form, or causative power, as it is related to the nature of the organic body, has been endowed by God with a perfection and potentiality whereby it can produce the soul.

(d)   Some hold that the soul of the mother by its own activity produces the soul of the child in the same way and through the same process by which in growth it puts on new matter through nourishment.

(e)   Finally, some try to reconcile all the different and contrary opinions as follows: There are, they say, two kinds of production. One has to do with the potentiality or productive power of nature; this they call generation. The other has to do with the absolute power of God; this they call creation. In turn, they distinguish two kinds of creation; the one which proceeds out of nothing *(ex nihilo)*, which would be a creation in the proper sense; the other which proceeds indeed out of matter, neither necessarily, however, nor with a natural potentiality, but rather because of a so-called obediential potentiality. All this being presupposed, they maintain that God creates the new soul of the child out of the pre-existent soul of the parents according to the second manner of creation. Hence, they say, the human soul, since it has the matter out of Adam, partakes of Adam's guilt also. On the other hand, the human soul is produced by God; and thus they think that this opinion can escape the objections which possibly could be levelled against it.

As for us, we leave the philosophers to investigate the manner of the soul's propagation, for we see in the Scriptures no explanation concerning this matter. At the same time, we firmly hold that the human soul is propagated. For, although the manner of propagation is not clear, it does not follow that the propagation itself should be denied. There is something solemn in the divine mysteries. And yet Scripture teaches them, although it hesitates to explain them. . . .

IX

The Loss of the Divine Image
Through the Fall

129 Was the image of God lost in the fall? This question can be answered as follows:

(1) If the image of God refers to the very essence of the human soul, that is, to the intellect, will, and other faculties of the soul, then it cannot be said that the image of God was lost in consequence of the fall. For, as far as its essence is concerned, the soul of Adam remained after the fall essentially the same as it was before the fall.

(2) If the image of God refers to the general similarity which the human soul bears to some of the divine characteristics, such as incorporeity, spirituality, intelligence, and free will concerning the things which are under its control, then again it cannot be said that the image of God in the human soul was lost in the fall. All these things, in fact, belong to the soul of man even after the fall.

(3) If the image of God in man refers to the dominion over the other creatures, particularly animated creatures, in which dominion the image of God is to be found in a secondary sense, then again it cannot be said that in this sense and in this respect the image of God was completely lost. While the dignity of dominion over other creatures with which man was originally endowed was diminished

and in many ways weakened as a consequence of the fall, yet some vestiges of it did remain.

(4) If the image of God refers to some moral principles which are born in us and with us and which consist in some tiny remnants of the divine image in the mind and will of man, then too with regard to these most minute particles we maintain that the image of God was not utterly lost. In fact, the work of the Law is still written in the hearts of men, even of the unregenerate.

(5) But if, according to its scriptural understanding, the image of God refers primarily to that righteousness and holiness, integrity and uprightness of all faculties, in which man was originally created, then it must be said that the image of God was lost indeed through the fall.

130   The Holy Spirit bears witness of this whenever he speaks in the Scriptures of the original sin which was introduced in mankind by the fall of Adam. Actually, original sin is defined in the Scriptures as the lack of man's original righteousness and the corruption of the whole human nature, which corruption took the place of man's original integrity.

Along these lines we read in the Scriptures that we were before light in the Lord, but now we are darkness (Eph. 5:8); that formerly our will was conformed to the Law, but now there is in man the mind of the flesh, which is enmity against God (Rom. 8:7); that before there was in our members obedience to the spirit of the mind and to the Law of God, but now we see in our members another law warring against the law of our mind and bringing us into captivity (Rom. 7:23); that before we were beloved sons of God, but now we are by nature children of wrath (Eph. 2:3); that before we were partakers of the spiritual life which is from God, but now we are dead in trespasses and sins (Eph. 2:1). Hence to deny that the image of God was lost is the same as to deny the very reality of original sin.

131   Moreover, the very fact that we must be renewed through the Holy Spirit in such a way that he is restored in us proves that the Holy Spirit was lost. Now, we are to be renewed through the Holy Spirit in the image of God so that the image of God is restored in us by a new creation. Therefore the image of God was lost. The minor of

this syllogism[1] is confirmed by the Apostolic utterances of 2 Cor. 3:18, Eph. 4:23, Col. 3:10, in which the following emphases should be underlined:

(a) The restoration of the image of God is called a metamorphosis, consisting in the renewal of the spirit and in the putting on of a new man.

(b) Such a metamorphosis, or transformation, is brought about by the Spirit of God, that is, by the one who once created the first man in his own image.

(c) The image of God consists in righteousness, true holiness, and the true knowledge of God; all these things are such that nothing of their kind is left in the natural faculties of man and nothing of the kind can be expected from them.

132 In order that no doubt be left on this point, we must compare the first man as he was before the fall and as he is described after the fall. Moreover, we ought to examine how the descendants of Adam are described. Out of such a comparison it is clearly seen that man from being righteous and holy became impious and unrighteous; from rich, utterly poor; from healthy, sick; from living, dead; from free, a slave; from son of God, an enemy of God; from heir of life eternal, guilty of condemnation. Having lost the most beautiful image of God, man put on the dark specter of the devil. Hence the Apostle clearly states that we bear no longer the image of God and of the heavenly Adam, but the image of the earthly Adam (1 Cor. 15:49). Consequently we are by nature alienated from God, destitute of the innocence and righteousness in which we were created, and subject to calamities, diseases, death, and condemnation. . . .

137 Why did God want some remnants of that original divine image to be left in man after the fall?

(a) In order that they might be witnesses of the excellency of

---

[1] This hypothetical syllogism may be seen more clearly in the following form: *Major premise: If* the image of God is to be restored, *then* it must have been lost in the fall.
Minor premise: The image of God is to be restored (proved from Scripture).
Conclusion: Therefore the image of God must have been lost in the fall.

our nature as it was originally created by God, just as the old rubbish and ruins stand sometimes to bear witness to the dignity and excellency of a former edifice.

(b) In order that out of them we might learn the mercy of God toward us utterly undeserving sinners, and in the table of our hearts might read the goodness of God as expressed in the living letters of such remnants.

(c) In order that the knowledge coming to man out of those remnants might be a master of external discipline, of which discipline God makes use as some kind of pedagogy to restore in us his image, whose restoration was earned on our behalf by Jesus Christ.

(d) In order that the wicked might be left without excuse as long as they "hold the truth in unrighteousness" (Rom. 1:18) and "change the truth into a lie" (Rom. 1:25).

X

Definition and Application
of the Doctrine

138   (1) Practical deductions

As for the practical applications of the doctrine concerning the image of God in man, three deductions may be made.

(a)   It should lead us to recognize the goodness of God. To him alone we refer the fact that mankind is created in Adam after his own image; and to him alone we owe the glory of this divine gift which Christ has begun to restore in us and which will be perfected in the life to come.

(b)   It should lead us to acknowledge our misery. Having been endowed originally with a heavenly dignity, we are now born of parents who make us sinners even before we are born.

Esdras tells us that the elders who had seen the beauty of the first temple built by Solomon were moved to tears when they saw the new temple as it was restored by Zerubbabel after the Babylonian captivity. How much more reason for sorrow and tears should we have when we call to mind the first man as he was created in the image of God—as the most beautiful temple and dwelling of the most holy Trinity—and then look at him as he was horribly ravaged

65

65

by the infernal Chaldeans and robbed of all the divine gifts with which he had been first endowed.

(c)   It should lead us to strengthen our hope. The day of the last judgment will be a day of restoration of all things (Acts 3:20). The first temple of Jerusalem was not left devastated forever, but was rebuilt and restored; yea, at the coming of Christ it was made more glorious than ever before. In like manner, by the grace of God and the efficacy of the Holy Spirit, the former image of God, into which we begin to be transformed in this present life, will some day shine in us far more brightly and gloriously than it shone once in Adam. For he could die, but we shall not die.

(2)   Conclusion

139   From what has been said, the definition and description of the image of God can be summarized as follows:

The image of God in the first man consisted in the natural and highest perfection of the whole man, that is, in the uprightness of all the faculties of both soul and body, and in man's integrity and conformity to God, the archetype, without any conflict between flesh and spirit. The wisdom and the light of the divine knowledge shone in man's mind. Righteousness and holiness in his will were perfectly conformed to the Law of God. Hence he enjoyed the perfect harmony of all his members and all superior and inferior faculties, in perfect agreement with the will of God. He was made immortal and he had dominion over all the animals and creatures of the earth. And, had he persevered in the integrity in which he had been created, all these divine gifts would have been propagated unto all Adam's descendants.

140   We have discussed this subject as those who, being detained in a dark prison, try to inquire about the excellency of light. Honor and glory forever to God the Father, who created us in Adam after his own image; to the Son, who is the substantial image of God and who merited the restoration of God's image on our behalf; and to the Holy Spirit, through whom the image of God is restored in us!

PART TWO

Free
Will

by
Martin Chemnitz

Introduction

This topic is most comprehensive and embraces many questions for which an explanation is necessary. In order that this presentation may be both clear and instructive, therefore, we shall divide it into five parts.[1]

I. The first and most important thing in regard to this topic is to state the issue correctly so that foreign matters are not mixed in. For when this happens the fundamental problem can scarcely be discerned because it is so obscured by extraneous discussion. Therefore, not only will contradictory, opposing, and differing matters be mentioned, but also those that are similar, related, and connected. In this way we shall not only separate those things which diametrically oppose and contradict each other but, with much greater diligence, separate those things which seem related

---

[1] This introduction to Locus VI is divided into five sections, each of which discusses a particular question. The first section establishes the "state of the controversy"; it formulates the controversial question in distinction to other similar questions. The second section is concerned with "nominal definition," i.e., an explanation of the important terms. The third section consists of an attempt at "real definition," i.e., a descriptive characterization of free will itself according to its function. The fourth section is a discussion of the proper object of free will, i.e., the Law of God. The fifth section distinguishes between two ways of understanding free will: (a) in external actions, and (b) in spiritual pursuits.

because of their apparent similarity. For even the unwary are able to detect obviously contrary matters without too much effort. But for the sake of such readers we must carefully examine and distinguish matters which may be imposed on them because of some similarity which is actually only apparent. Many misleading statements arise from the confusion which exists because those things which are in some manner related have not been carefully distinguished and kept within their proper bounds.

In order that we may proceed even more carefully and wisely in discussions of this type, it is useful to cite examples. Many, who lacked neither ability nor industry, have not only engaged in idle talk but have often wandered far away from the fundamental question for the simple reason that they have not concentrated on the real issue. In their wandering they have buried, even perverted, the real question.

I mention the name of Lorenzo Valla,[2] who was by nature too fond of quarrels and did not love the plain truth expressed in simple language. He sought praise for his remarkable ability to make everything totter and fall as well as for his ingenuity in thinking up novel and paradoxical statements and clothing them with a certain appearance of probability. This led him to publish a certain composition on free will.[3] When he saw that papal and scholastic theology departed from the true doctrine of both the Apostles and the ancient Church Fathers, he proceeded in a different manner and built his position on the following principles: The foreknowledge of God foresees all things, whether they be good or bad, before they take place; God foresees what and in what manner things will be, nor can he be deceived in any way. For example, Judas, of his own will, to be sure, betrayed Christ. But this will existed of necessity since God had foreseen it; otherwise God's foreknowledge would be mendacious, and Valla says that it is useless to discuss whether God's foreknowledge makes for necessity, since in God will is always joined with foreknowledge. Because in God there is nothing acci-

---

[2] Lorenzo Valla was one of the most original of the Italian humanists of the 15th century.

[3] *De Libero Arbitrio* (c. 1440).

dental nor any diversity, but one simple essence, he sees the future for no other reason than that he has arranged and decided that things should so be. Even if it be said that he only permits things, nevertheless let it be added that he permits them because he so wills.

To clarify his position, Valla uses the following illustration: When Sextus Tarquinius[4] went to consult the oracle of Apollo, he received this response: "You will die a pauper and an exile, slain by an angry city." When Sextus strongly objected, Apollo answered: "Blame Jupiter if you like; both his will and his power govern the Fates. It is merely foreknowledge that I have, and the ability to prophesy."

"But why," said Sextus, "has Jupiter assigned me such a cruel fate? I do not deserve it."

Apollo answered, "The crimes you will commit, such as adultery, perjury, and the like, are to blame."

"But I swear to you," said Sextus, "that I will not commit the crimes you name. I shall pray that Jupiter will grant me a better mind."

"Then will my prediction be false?" asked Apollo.

Sextus answered, "Well, then, Apollo, is it impossible for me to restrain myself from crime? Am I unable to reform my mind?"

"So the matter stands," said Apollo. "Just as Jupiter created the wolf ravenous, the hare timid, the lion spirited, the ass dull, the dog fierce, and the sheep mild, so he has fashioned the heart of one man to be hard, and that of another to be soft. One man he has made so that it tends more toward crime, another more toward virtue. He has given to one man a corrigible character, but on you he has bestowed an evil mind that cannot be changed by any help from another."

By this demonstration Valla meant to make it clear that human actions are subject to a necessity which cannot be explained by the mere foreknowledge of God, but which must be referred to his will. Actually, what we see from Valla's example is simply this:

---

[4] Sextus Tarquinius was the brutal son of the last Tarquinian king of Rome (6th century B.C.).

When a mistake is made by shifting the sense of the premise, a proper conclusion cannot be deduced.[5]

Therefore discussions of contingency, foreknowledge, predestination, and the secret counsel of a God who governs all are to be excluded from this topic. For the issue here has to do with what power fallen man possesses to obey the Law. Since in the mind came darkness, in the will rejection of God, and in the heart inflexible stubbornness against the Law of God, and because God's Law demands not only external civil deeds but unceasing, perfect obedience of the whole man, the inquiry deals with what and how much the human will can do. "The Power of Man" is therefore a more appropriate title than "Free Will."

II. In this second section, something must be said about the term "free will," for many disputes have arisen about it.

Jerome says:[6] "What the Latins call 'free will' the Greeks call αὐτεξουσία or αὐτεξούσιον.[7] In the context of this weakness of nature, it is a quite arrogant term for it means man's power over himself, which is not subject to any command and which can be stopped or hindered by no one. It is an arrogant term, I say, since Paul complains even about the regenerate, who are led by the Spirit of God, 'The evil which I would not, that I do.' . . ." (Rom. 7:19).

Augustine often uses the terms "free will" and "the power of the will."[8] But it seems that the word "power" is taken from a passage

---

[5] The logical fallacy to which Chemnitz refers here is that of μετάβασις εἰς ἄλλο γένος, described above. The proper question in a discussion of free will is: What is the state of man concerning freedom of will? In what respect is man's will free or unfree? If his will is unfree, what in man is the cause of this loss of freedom? Instead of considering this proper question, Valla speculates about another question: What is God doing in man, what is his secret counsel about man? This improper question leads Valla to the unfounded assertion: Free will is not a natural possession of man. It is a gracious gift given only to those on whom God determines to show mercy and not to those whom God hardens.

[6] *Dialogus Contra Pelagianos* 3:7; P.L. 23:603C.

[7] Man's free will is one of the issues on which the Church Fathers seem to be unanimous. The following statement of Irenaeus' is typical of the general patristic position: ". . . man is possessed of free will from the beginning, and God is possessed of free will, in whose likeness man was made . . ." *Adversus Haereses* 4:37.4; P.G. 7:1102B.

[8] *De Libero Arbitrio* 3:3.7; P.L. 32:1224C.

in Paul: ". . . having no necessity, but hath power over his own will, and hath so decreed in his heart . . ." (1 Cor. 7:37).

The following passage offers a true description of free will which considers those matters over which the will has power: "All things are lawful for me, but I will not be brought under the power of any" (1 Cor. 6:12).

Irenaeus says, "In man as in the angels God has placed the power of choice."[9] Chrysostom makes power (of the will) the opposite of necessity.[10]

Moreover, in Scripture the word "freedom" is also used with this meaning: "If the Son therefore shall make you free, ye shall be free indeed" (John 8:36). "Where the Spirit of the Lord is, there is liberty" (2 Cor. 3:17). "Being then made free from sin, ye became the servants of righteousness" (Rom. 6:18). "The creature itself also shall be delivered from the bondage of corruption into the glorious liberty of the children of God" (Rom. 8:21). Furthermore, there are other meanings of freedom, which belong under the heading, "Christian Liberty."

From this we can develop the following distinctions:

(1) There is choice in regard to external civil works, which some call "freedom of nature." Peter calls it ἐξουσία.[11] For Christ is unwilling to attribute freedom to the unregenerate, nor does he use the term in that context: "Whosoever committeth sin is the servant of sin" (John 8:34).

(2) To those regenerated through the Holy Spirit, Scripture attributes "freedom" both of mind and will. For 2 Cor. 3:17 properly speaks of the freedom of mind and intellect, and John 8:36 and Rom. 6:18 of the freeing of the will. This freedom Christ calls "true freedom": "If the Son therefore shall make you free, ye shall be free indeed." For that freedom in externals which the unregenerate has is not true freedom. Paul refers to this in Rom. 6:20 as if to

---

[9] *Adv. Haer.* 4:37.1; P.L. 7:1099C.

[10] *In Matthaeum Homilia* 59; P.G. 58:575C-576D.

[11] By ἐξουσία Paul means power, right, or authority to do things. For example, he writes in 1 Cor. 9:4-5: "Have we not power to eat and to drink? Have we not power to lead about a sister, a wife, as well as other apostles, and as the brethren of the Lord, and Cephas?" This word does not necessarily mean "true freedom."

say: "Before you were regenerated you were free, so to speak, but free in regard to righteousness, yet slaves of sin." Paul calls this the "freedom of the Spirit" (2 Cor. 3:17). Others call it the "freedom of grace."

(3) Because the freedom just cited is not perfect in this life, but is held captive, Paul mentions that other full and perfect freedom after this life which he calls the "glorious liberty" (Rom. 8:21).

The term "free will" has given birth to many discussions. Pelagius argued as follows: "The church has always believed that man has free will. Even Augustine says: 'If anyone denies this, he is not catholic.'[12] But the term suggests that the will has equal power in either direction, whether it wishes to strive for evil or for good. For if without the help of God the will were free to do evil only, it would falsely be called free."

But when Augustine perceived that the real teaching of Scripture was being perverted by omission, he reconsidered the term in the light of the fountainheads of Scripture. And when Pelagius insisted on using the term "freedom" with respect to a will not even regenerate, Augustine cited other terms from Scripture to the contrary. "The free will is in captivity, and has no power except for sinning. It has no power for righteousness unless it is liberated and aided by God."[13] "If the help of God is utterly lacking, you will be able to do nothing good. Surely, you are acting of your own free will without God's help, but you are doing evil. For this, your so-called 'free will' is suited, and it becomes a damnable handmaid in wrongdoing. When I tell you that without God's help you do nothing, I mean nothing good. For you have the free will to do evil without God's help although such a will is not actually free. 'For of whom a man is overcome, to the same is he brought in bondage' (2 Peter 2:19); and 'Whosoever committeth sin is the servant of sin'" (John 8:34).[14] He also writes: "You wish to defend the position that man is perfected by his own will. May you rather contend that he is perfected by the gift of God, and not by his so-called free will,

---

[12] *Hypognosticon* (or *Hypomnesticon*) 3:10.18; P.L. 45:1631B. This work is judged by most to be spurious; it is probably written by a later disciple of Augustine.

[13] *Contra Duas Epistolas Pelagianorum* 3:8.24; P.L. 44:607B.

[14] *De Verbis Apostoli, Sermo* 156:11.12; P.L. 38:865B.

which is actually enslaved."[15] "By making evil use of his free will, man destroyed his very self. For when of his free will he sinned, sin was the victor and even free will was lost. 'For whatever overcomes a man, to that he is enslaved. . . .' "[16]

Let the weight of the words be observed which Augustine rightly spoke against the Pelagian praises of freedom: enslaved will, captive, destroyed, lost, damnable desire, handmaiden (in evil), arrogance. These descriptive terms are distinguished from certain others for this reason: When Augustine discusses the power of free will, he calls it captive, destroyed, lost, etc., as far as *spiritual* acts are concerned. But when it is a question of external conduct and the power of free will in that sphere, he uses different terms. He speaks of "an impoverished and damaged nature,"[17] and says: "They attribute much to a poor and disabled nature. . . . Man has become weak by sinning: he has been left half dead by robbers."[18]

Therefore these terms must be carefully distinguished. For the opposition likes to gather slogans of this type to deceive the simple, as if Augustine were saying that in spiritual matters free will is not removed nor lost, but only weakened.

Nevertheless, observe that those who came later, when the opinion of Augustine had begun to seem too harsh, generally spoke in these terms about free will. Lombard[19] speaks of a corruption and a suppression of the free will, a freedom corrupted, partially destroyed, an impaired and corrupted free will. . . .

III. In the third section we will try to give a characterization of free will. A full "real definition" does not seem possible, because the subject is too complex. No definition could embrace all of its various distinctions.

Augustine tried with the following definition: "Free will is that faculty of reason and will by which the good is chosen with the assistance of grace, or evil is chosen when grace is lacking."[20] But

---

[15] *Contra Julianum* 2:8.23; P.L. 44:689B.

[16] *Enchiridion* 1:30; P.L. 40:246D-247A.

[17] *De Verb. Ap., Serm.* 155:13.13; P.L. 38:848B.

[18] *Ibid. Serm.* 131:6.6; P.L. 38:732A.

[19] 2 *Sent.* 25.8; P.L. 192:707D.

[20] This is not a quotation, but rather Chemnitz's summary of Augustine's viewpoint.

because this definition cannot do justice to the individual sub-topics, it has originated many controversies. Therefore an exposition of the term is proposed, which is called a "nominal definition."

From the definition proposed above, we can deduce in what faculties of the soul free will resides, namely in the mind and will, when these join operations. For often the mind considers a matter independently and its consideration is followed by no desire. And often the will follows or flees something without previous consideration by the mind. Under such conditions it is not called "free will." But when mind and will are joined so that the will either conforms to or rebels against the judgment of the mind, and does not seek out nor reject things in random fashion, but only those things which have been demonstrated by the intellect—there is free will. . . .

Moreover in Biblical Hebrew a special word meaning "mind" does not exist, but only the word for "heart," viz., *lebh.* As for that which is written in Matt. 22:37, "Thou shalt love the Lord thy God with all thy . . . mind," Deut. 6:5 does not have a special word corresponding to "mind." The Hebrew says: "And you shall love the Lord your God with all your heart." So the Hebrew Scriptures are altogether lacking a word with which to designate the "seat of ideas," "the brain." But they include ideas and intellect in the term "heart," as in Deut. 29:4. "The Lord has not given you a heart to understand." The Apostles also speak thus: "(The Gentiles) became vain in their imaginations and their foolish heart was darkened" (Rom. 1:21). "Out of the heart proceed evil thoughts" (Matt. 15:19).

But the Greek language of the New Testament has both words, "mind" and "heart." Yet it does not always preserve that philosophical distinction by which ideas are attributed only to the mind and emotions to the heart.[21] Just as they often attribute ideas to the heart, so often they attribute desires to the mind. "Be renewed in the spirit of your mind . . . in righteousness and true holiness" (Eph. 4:23f.). Rom. 12:2 attributes judgment to the mind: "Be ye transformed by the renewing of your mind, that ye may prove what is . . . the will of God." Rom. 1:28 speaks of a "reprobate mind."

---

[21] A number of psychological textbooks attribute the discovery of emotions to Rousseau (18th cent.) and Romanticism. As we see here, however, the Orthodox Lutherans were clear in distinguishing "emotions" from reason and will.

According to the language of Scripture, therefore, free will is either in the mind and heart, or in the heart alone, or in the mind alone. This nominal definition is useful for two reasons.

First, the testimonies of Scripture from which the doctrine on this topic is drawn can rightly be divided under the following heads:

(1) What power the wounded mind still has; (2) of what powers or gifts the will has been deprived; (3) in what it is still half-alive; (4) what healing and help the grace of the Holy Spirit confers on the mind; (5) what [healing and help the Holy Spirit confers] on the will, in regeneration; (6) in what situations the will is not able to accommodate itself to those things which are shown it by a regenerate mind (Rom. 7:23).

Second, there are great differences among the writers of the church, some affirming free will, others denying it. Furthermore, Scripture also seems to say contradictory things about free will, sometimes affirming, sometimes denying it. This diversity can best be seen through an explanation of the meaning of the word itself. Thus the term free will is most commonly understood to mean that:

(1) Man is rational, i.e., he has a mind and will. (2) Beyond natural movements and actions, in which there is neither deliberation nor choice, man has voluntary movements, in which both the judgment of the mind and the desire of the will concur. (3) To be able to speak of vices and virtues and to call one action good and another bad, it is necessary to admit that there is a mind which knows and a will which either obeys or disobeys the judgment of the mind. But whether the powers of the soul have those faculties in all action by their own nature, and whence they have them, is another question.

Sometimes the Church Fathers use "free will" in reference to man's possibility of being converted according to God's plan and receiving the gifts of the Holy Spirit. Augustine says, "The possibility of having faith is given in nature."[22] He also declares, "Human nature has the capacity of being justified through the grace of the Holy Spirit."[23] "It is the nature of man to be able to have faith; but to have faith is an evidence of God's grace toward those who

---

[22] *De Praedestinatione Sanctorum* 5:10; P.L. 44:968C.
[23] *C. Jul.* 2:8.24; P.L. 44:690C.

believe."[24] Lombard is correct when he speaks about the ability of man to have faith, if his will is stimulated and helped by the Holy Spirit. A log does not have this faculty, nor does the devil.

In other cases writers consider the depravity of human nature in the fact that the mind of the flesh does not submit to God's Law (Rom. 8:7) and, indeed, cannot, since the Law is weakened in man by the resistance of the flesh. From this they conclude that there is not much sense in speaking about freedom of the will.

With this in mind we can use discrimination in considering the diversity of opinions among the ancient writers. Since the term "free will" is used with such variation of meaning, Soto[25] is arbitrary when he demands that we should simply affirm free will. In such linguistic ambiguities it is safest to put things clearly before our eyes as they actually are. Then it will be easy to judge these word battles.

IV. The object of free will is shown; but this is not discussed in a consistent manner. Valla asks whether it is within the power of man's will to move his foot, either the right one or the left. In Jerome's letter to Ctesiphon, Pelagius says: "If I will to bend my finger, must I always have the special help of God?"[26] In Augustine's *The Perfection of Man's Righteousness*, Celestius[27] cites 1 Cor. 7:36 about the one who has the gift of continence, of whom Paul says: "Let him do what he will." But Augustine answers: "As if to wish to marry is to be considered of great moment when we are painstakingly discussing the help of divine mercy!"[28]

Others say more correctly that good and evil things constitute the objects of free will. And because nature seeks some good things and recoils from certain evils without deliberation or choice by a certain natural instinct, these things do not pertain to free will.

---

[24] 2 *Sent.* 28.7; P.L. 192:718D; a quote from Augustine, *De Praedest. Sanct.* 3:7; P.L. 44:964B.

[25] Dominic Soto, a 16th century Roman Catholic theologian, was the Imperial Theologian at the Council of Trent.

[26] *Epistola* 133 (*ad Ctesiphontem*) 7; P.L. 22:1155B.

[27] An able theologian and one of the most important followers of Pelagius, Celestius precipitated the well-known Pelagian controversy when he attempted to get appointment as presbyter in Carthage and was excommunicated in 411-412.

[28] *De Perfectione Justitiae Hominis* 19:40.41; P.L. 44:313C-314B.

Concerning some other matters, however, we form judgments on the basis of deliberation, and in accordance therewith we either seek or flee them. These things do pertain to free will.

But it is stated more simply and plainly thus: The Law of God is the object of free will about which quest is made in the church. For the basic issues of this topic are arrived at by relating divine law to natural infirmity.

V. From such presuppositions, the necessary and most useful distinction follows between internal works of the Law and external observances.[29] Accordingly, attributed to free will are outward conduct, civil righteousness, activities of the flesh (thus speak the *Augsburg Confession* and the *Apology*), and the like, whatever terminology is used. Augustine calls them "outward things," works of the present life. But spiritual righteousness, worship from the heart, spiritual impulses and acts, divine matters, works which relate to God, these are attributed to the operation of the Holy Spirit through the Word. In the Schools they use the terms "naturally good" and "morally good," "essentially good" and "circumstantially good."[30] But these terms do not satisfactorily shed light on the real issue.[31]

The necessity of the useful distinction [between internal works

---

[29]The core of the problem is not whether man has some freedom of will in acts such as eating a meal, buying a house, etc. The real problem is whether my will is by itself free to desire what is truly good or what God wills. It is Augustine's opinion that Pelagius shifts the discussion of free will to external actions, thereby obscuring the real issue.

[30] "Naturally good" (Latin, *bonum naturale*) is a term applicable to a thing in the physical world such as a "good" apple. "Morally good" (Latin, *bonum morale*) applies to a human action or to the virtue which is the source of a human action. The Good Samaritan, or his action, may be described as *bonum morale*.

An action is "essentially good" (Latin, *bonum ex genere vel officio*) if it is directed toward its proper goal, if its aim is what it ought to be. An action, which might be either good or bad in itself, is judged to be "circumstantially good" (Latin, *bonum circumstantiis*) if it turns out to be good, not because of its primary motive, but because of special circumstances which were outside of the goal of the action itself. Cf. Thomas Aquinas, *Summa Theologiae* I-II: q. 18. a. 2-3.

[31] Chemnitz does not think that these divisions are important for the core problem. They pretend to explain something; but rather than solving the problem, they obscure it.

of the Law and external observances] can be understood when we consider that in all the writings on free will in which this distinction is not observed, many things are tangled together.

But as the writings of that period testify, it was a matter of great consternation in the papal Diet of Augsburg that this illuminating distinction had been written into the *Augsburg Confession.* The papists saw that by this distinction every occasion was cut off for the type of slander with which they had previously attempted to defame our writings. They realized that they could no longer defend their Pelagianism under that pretext. . . .

The Freedom of the Will in External Conduct

In this whole discussion we must carefully guard against the fallacy of unqualified generalization.[2] That is, just because in spiritual actions there is no freedom for a will not freed, let not the will be deprived of freedom in external matters in general. The following teaching is presented in respect to the liberty of the will in external conduct.

Right conduct consists in diligent control of external acts and restraint of external members in accordance with the precepts of the Decalogue, even if inward impulses either are not present or do not agree.

Here we bring more arguments to validate and clarify this distinction, for in this way matters will be better understood.

(1) It has been stated that free will involves both mind and will. Therefore we must consider the mind, to which the Scripture attributes darkness, blindness, and uncertainty in spiritual actions before its renewal by the Spirit. But in externals, Paul attributes

---

[1] Chapter I is omitted, being mainly quotations from the Fathers.

[2] The reference here is to the logical fallacy: *a dicto secundum quid ad dictum simpliciter.* This fallacy occurs when one makes an unconditional statement where the statement is given only conditionally. Chemnitz has in mind the Pelagian argument: the will is not free *in spiritual matters* (conditional statement); therefore, the will is not free (unconditional statement).

even to the unregenerate mind thought, comprehension, truth, etc. (Rom. 1:20 f.). It is very clear that the mind was not simply deprived of all understanding by the fall. There remains even in unregenerate men a certain faculty of the mind for perceiving and considering those things which are subject to reason and the senses, e.g., that which is involved in the various branches of research and learning: in economics, politics, ethics, in careful deliberative bodies, etc. For this faculty constitutes the difference between rational man and irrational animals. When we consider morons, insane persons, maniacs, and others similarly afflicted who are without that faculty, i.e., judgment of the mind, it is evident what a tremendous good it is that the use of reason is granted even to the unregenerate.

Let us learn to look reverently at these remnants, of whatever sort they be, because although human nature was deprived of the true gifts of intelligence[3] by the fall, nevertheless God wanted some portion of his gifts to remain in the mind by which man might recognize both what God is and what sort he is. God desired this, furthermore, in order that there might be a preparation toward Christ, an instruction that is not in devils. This gift of intelligence in the unregenerate is surely related to the general activity of God. Nevertheless it is not blasphemous to say that distinguished artists, in the realms of invention and the creative arts, are stimulated with a certain peculiar divine power. For Scripture also speaks thus about Bezalel and Oholiab (Exod. 31:3 and 35:34). Is. 54:16 says, "Behold, I have created the smith who blows the fire of coals, and produces a weapon for its purpose." That which God has manifested to the Gentiles, Paul calls "truth" (Rom. 1:18). Therefore those gifts of God must be revered, even in the unregenerate.

As far as the will is concerned, everyday experience testifies that even the unregenerate have this faculty. They can make their own choice in regard to the things which they have been shown by their intellect, either accepting or rejecting. The stories of many dis-

---

[3] What is lost in the fall is not the natural understanding but a higher understanding of spiritual matters. However, according to Orthodox Lutheran theologians, the loss is not complete; some small amount of spiritual understanding remains.

tinguished men bear witness to this, men who have governed their conduct with some care.

Justin in his *Apology*[4] makes this distinction: "Some things move without judgment, as a stone moves downward. Some move with judgment that is not free; a sheep seeing a wolf decides it must flee and does so by instinct, not by deliberation. It cannot choose whether or not it should flee. But through the power of intelligence man judges that something is either to be fled from or followed. And because he chooses his acts by a concentration of his reasoning powers, and not as a sheep, he is said to have free will. Therefore the acts of a man are voluntary and not comparable to the movement of a stone, the flight of a sheep, etc." Also worthy of consideration is what Paul says in Rom. 1:28: "God gave them up to a reprobate mind, to do those things which are not proper." Therefore in a certain marvelous way God generally restrains and controls the wills even of the unregenerate, as by a bridle, that there may be some discipline lest they burst forth into all manner of crimes. And he does this that the pious, who live in the world as sheep among wolves, "may lead a quiet and peaceable life, in all godliness and honesty." (1 Tim. 2:2).

Here the distinction is relevant which delineates two types of acts in the unregenerate:[5] (1) forced acts, when the movements in the members are ruled by the authority of the will, whether the inner feelings agree or not; (2) voluntary acts, when the will with deep feeling prefers that which is morally good. Either type proves that there is some freedom of the will in externals.

(2) Next, Paul argues that there is some righteousness of the flesh.[6] Let us note from what passages such testimony is to be sought. "(Gentiles) . . . do by nature the things contained in the law" (Rom. 2:14), that is, by their natural powers, without the renewal of the

---

[4] This passage from the *Apology* is not a quotation; still, it is a correct rendering of Justin's views. Cf. *Apology* I:28; P.G. 6:372C; 10; P.G. 6:342A; and especially 69; P.G. 6:394A, B.

[5] Chemnitz has *renatus* here, but the context refers to the unregenerate. We consider this to be a misprint.

[6] I.e., that the morality of the unconverted natural man has some value but is too imperfect to stand before God's judgment.

Spirit. Romans 10:3 speaks of the Jews who are without Christ: "Being ignorant of God's righteousness, and going about to establish their own. . . ." In Phil. 3:6 Paul says that before his conversion he was living according to the righteousness which is in the Law, blameless. He grants, therefore, a certain righteousness to those who are outside of Christ. But whatever is not of the Spirit is flesh. Therefore it is rightly called the righteousness of the flesh. And thus Paul speaks: "If any other man thinketh that he hath whereof he might trust in the flesh, I more" (Phil. 3:4).

(3) Paul further contends that law is the object of free will even among the unrighteous (1 Tim. 1:9), that is, that the Law is given the unregenerate to control their will and the feelings of their heart in externals. For he uses the word "lies," that is, the Law lies, pressing like a yoke, forcing the jaws like a bit, so that they are either compelled by fear or restrained by shame. Relevant here is the quotation from Augustine's *City of God:* "God rewards external discipline, even in the unregenerate with temporal gifts."[7] But he takes this from Matt. 6:5, where it is stated that the hypocrites have received their reward because they are honored by men. Augustine says: "The Romans received wages for their careful discipline: a flourishing empire comprising the whole world, brilliant successes,"[8] etc. In Ezekiel 29:19 we read that Nebuchadrezzar and his army had not yet received wages. "I will give the land of Egypt unto Nebuchadrezzar . . . and it shall be the wages for his army" (v. 19).

These are the main arguments. There are certain sayings, however, which are cited against this position, especially the passage from Jeremiah (10:23): "O Lord, I know that the way of man is not in himself: it is not in man that walketh to direct his steps." We shall now note certain interpretations based on the context and background of the text. Through these it will become clear that, whatever interpretation is given (provided it is in harmony with the text), this passage does not altogether take away freedom in external action, nor does it establish the absolute necessity of all things.

(1) Some interpret it thus: When the prophet with great urgency

[7] *De Civ. Dei* 5:15; P.L. 41:160B.
[8] *Ibid.* 5:16; P.L. 41:160D.

was exhorting men to repent, as appears from the beginning of the chapter, and when he saw that there was no amendment of life among the wicked, finally he cried out: "O Lord, I know . . ." as if he were about to say: "It is not in the power of man, even when God's Word has been heard, to begin spiritual activity unless God teaches within through the Spirit." Therefore he adds, "O Lord, correct me, but with judgment" (Jer. 10:24). If the passage is so understood, it does not contradict the teaching on external freedom.

(2) From the context and background of the passage the following interpretation also is given: Jeremiah had said, "The shepherds are stupid and do not inquire of the Lord; therefore they shall not prosper, and all their flock shall be scattered" (Jer. 10:21). There is a story in 2 Kings 24 and 25 about the time when Jehoiakim and Zedekiah rebelled against the king of Babylon, contrary to treaties. For they thought that thus with a strong hand they could vindicate themselves for freedom. But Jeremiah says, "O Lord, I know that the way of man is not in himself; it is not in man that walketh to direct his steps." That is, many mistakes are made, although the greatest effort is put forth that plans may not go wrong. Man's efforts are useless unless they are governed and helped by God. The Prophet mentions two things: (1) "the way" means wisdom, counsel, effort; and (2) "to direct his steps" means to control outcomes and successes. And he distinguishes between mere human beings and real men.[9] It is known that when these words are in juxtaposition, by the latter are meant heroes who have been endowed with special gifts beyond mere human beings, that is, men of the common sort. Therefore he says not only that ordinary people are often wishful in their planning, but that even for those endowed with the most outstanding gifts of wisdom, things do not always come out as they plan. This interpretation seems very apt.

(3) Some interpreters of the Hebrew text state the following connection: At first they call attention to the fact that in the preceding verse of Jeremiah God directs Nebuchadrezzar to devastate the cities of Judah. Then in Ezek. 21:16 the prophet sees the sword

---

[9] This distinction may be made in several languages. For a mere human being, Latin uses *homo;* Greek, ἄνθρωπος; and Hebrew *adham.* For a real man Latin uses *vir;* Greek, ἀνήρ; and Hebrew, *zaqen, gibbor,* and *adhon.*

cutting to the right and to the left. God interprets this vision to mean that the king of Babylon at the beginning of his campaign was not certain whether to attack the Ammonites or the Jews first. However, he invaded Judea first. Hebrew scholars presume that this led the prophet Jeremiah to exclaim: "O Lord, I know that the ways of man are not in himself (do not belong to him) . . ." (Jer. 10:23).

Such a statement seems to rule out any possibility of free choice even in external matters. However, as we shall see in discussing contingency, external freedom does not mean such an independence that God could not hinder or change it. Jeremiah does not intend to say that God impelled the king to commit robbery. The king came in order to plunder and kill because he desired to destroy. He stood at the crossroads, uncertain whom to attack first. Because God wanted to punish the crimes of his people, he hindered the king from attacking the Ammonites in order that he might invade Judea. Jeremiah relates that Nebuchadrezzar destroyed everything without being punished, without effective resistance from anyone. Jeremiah then explains that the reason for this is not to be found in the strength of Nebuchadrezzar but in God's wrath against Israel. He abandoned her and permitted the king to do what he did.

This can be clarified by a consideration of the meaning of the word "way." First, there is the *way of divine ordinances* (Latin, *mandatorum*). Cf. Ps. 119:32. This is also called the *way of the Lord* in Ps. 25:4 and the *way of the righteous* in Ps. 1:6. There is no contingency, no free choice, in this first "way." Second, there is the *way of man*. By this is meant man's free choice and efforts in external things, as in Ps. 37:5: "Commit thy way unto the Lord. . . ." In regard to this "way" there is some freedom. However, if the decisions and efforts of man are not directed and aided by God, this "way" may become "dark and slippery" (Ps. 35:6). Man may err in thinking and acting, with tragic and unpredictable consequences. Third, there is the *way of sinners*. Cf. Ps. 1:1; Ps. 119:29. This "way" is in direct opposition to the will of God.

Proverbs 20:24 explains how God directs the *way of man* and how man is to understand this "way." Man has preserved his gift of free choice in civil affairs; but man cannot see everything, he cannot guard against losing himself in fantasy and wishful thinking. For this divine help is needed, not only for success in a good action, but even for the choice of the action itself. In this way we can interpret the above-mentioned Scripture passages and others like them. . . .

II[1]

The Bondage of the Will

After the doctrine of the freedom of the will in external conduct has been explained, this reminder must be added immediately: The Law of God speaks not only of external conduct, but of complete obedience and fulfillment. Furthermore, the will does not have the freedom to put aside the depravity with which we are born, but is in that regard captive. Now we must consider why that reminder is immediately inserted, for thus the matter will be better understood.

The scholastic writers broke through the true limits of impaired freedom and fashioned certain strange paradoxes with too great an admiration for external conduct; their conclusions contradict holy Scripture and cover up the blessed work of God's Son. The first axiom of the scholastics is this: Free will by its own strength, that is, without the renewal of Spirit, is able to fulfill the commandments of God as far as the substance of the act is concerned. Lest they attribute nothing to the Holy Spirit, they say that to the substance of the act is added the circumstances, viz., the work of the Holy

---
[1] Chapter III is omitted but content is covered in text and footnotes of Chapter IV.

Spirit, which renews man and creates the possibility of earning merit. The Spirit does nothing in the regenerate concerning the substance of the act, but only adds to the acts such a new relation[2] that the acts of the natural powers become meritorious.[3] Against this falsification we put the true statement: The Law of God speaks not only of external conduct, but demands complete obedience of the heart, spoken of in Rom. 8:3. Rom. 8:7 says it is impossible: "Neither can it be." Acts 15:10 calls this commandment ". . . a yoke . . . which neither our fathers nor we were able to bear." Martin Luther correctly refutes the Scholastic falsehood in this way: Christ says that the commandments of God are summed up in this part of the first table: "Thou shalt love the Lord thy God with all thy heart," etc. Even the saner Scholastics also admit that this is impossible for an unregenerate man. Therefore all these speculations about the "substance of the act" must be discarded. Accordingly, Augustine says of perfect righteousness: The substance of all the negative commandments is: "Thou shalt not covet."[4] Therefore, because that act is not possible even for the regenerate in this life, the axiom of the Scholastics is false.

We must clearly explain, therefore, what and how much the will can do, since the fulfillment of the Law is impossible for man's nature. We must consider, in order, what works in the various commandments pertain to external conduct. For instance, in the First Commandment, to love God above all things does not pertain to external conduct. But to know something about God, to think out some external act of worship—this is possible for anyone.

Augustine writes thus about faith: "Hold this most firmly and do not doubt it in the least, that any man can either read the words of

---

[2] The text has *revelationem vel respectum*, but this is obviously a misprint. Our corrected reading is *relationem vel respectum*, these two terms being synonymous in Scholastic usage.

[3] The particular viewpoint against which Chemnitz polemizes here is not characteristic of high Scholasticism. E.g., Thomas Aquinas clearly denies that man can, by his own natural abilities, fulfill the commandments of God without grace (Cf. *S. Th.* I-II: q. 109 a. 4.).

[4] These references to Luther and Augustine are not treated as quotations in the Chemnitz text; rather they seem to be summaries of the respective viewpoints.

the Holy Law and the Gospel or hear them from the mouth of a preacher unless ignorance of the language, some handicap, or adversity prevents his doing so. But that he should also perceive in his heart what he hears with his body, and will it and be able to do it—no one can do this except the man whom God has prepared by His grace."[5]

Confusion of external conduct with complete obedience to the Law is no new device. Pelagius argued on the basis of Phil. 3:6: "Paul before his conversion was blameless as far as the righteousness of the Law was concerned. Therefore man without grace can fulfill the demands of the Law." But Augustine refutes the argument of Pelagius on this basis: "It is one thing to perform the external works of the Law and quite another to be perfectly obedient from the heart."[6]

The second axiom of the Scholastics is this: An unregenerate man, without faith and the Holy Spirit, who does the works of the commandments by his free will alone, does not sin. This axiom is no less false than the former. For the hearts of the unregenerate are without the Holy Spirit, without fear of God, and without faith toward God, and they do not believe that they are heard or that their sins are forgiven. Therefore they are wicked. "Nor can a corrupt tree bring forth good fruit" (Matt. 7:18). "Without faith it is impossible to please Him" (Heb. 11:6). "Whatsoever is not of faith is sin" (Rom. 14:23). But it is surely true that God punishes the violation of His will even in the unregenerate. And of those who observe his will externally Christ says, "They have their reward" (Matt. 6:2, 5, 16). But because of that external conduct a person is not accepted by God, he does not merit grace. To say it in a word: in the article of justification, external discipline is sin.[7]

This point must be the more carefully held because from this second axiom the Schoolmen have constructed the doctrine of

---

[5] *De Fide ad Petrum* 32; P.L. 40:775C. This work is considered by most authorities to be spurious.

[6] *C. Duas Epp. Pelag.* 1:9.15; P.L. 44:558B.

[7] This does not mean that by disciplining themselves men commit an actual sin against God. The meaning is that man's outwardly good conduct is still sinful; even moral discipline is unable to overcome those sinful characteristics.

"fitting merit,"[8] the merit which is fit for God's goodness, the teaching that to an unregenerate man doing what is in his power, God does not deny his grace. Erasmus says: In this way the soul is approved and made more fit to receive grace. For although the philosophers did honorable works without faith, nevertheless they did not sin as they would have if they had poisoned their mother or violated their sister. But the answer is plain. Although there are degrees of sin (for all sins are not equal, as Jovinian[9] held), nevertheless a person neither becomes acceptable to God nor merits his grace because of external conduct. "Whatsoever is not of faith is sin" (Rom. 14:24).

We must note that the Pelagians have impugned the grace of God with the same argument, saying that the Gentiles, strangers to faith and without the help of grace, have abounded in virtues only because of the good of nature. They are found to be merciful, chaste, and sober by the power of their innate freedom alone. These are the words of Julian.[10] But Augustine refutes this argument at length in *Against Julian*, Book 4, where he says, "Some good things can be done, when those who do them are not acting from good motives."[11]

He treats the same question in *The City of God*[12] when he says that such deeds are more truly vices than virtues. Therefore external conduct and good works are in a class by themselves as Augustine

---

[8] The Scholastics distinguished two kinds of merit: (a) "worthy merit" (Latin, *meritum condigni*), a reward which the receiver rightfully deserves; and (b) "fitting merit" (Latin, *meritum congrui*), a reward which is received not because the receiver has any proper right to it but because the giver has imposed on himself the duty of giving the reward if some conditions are attained.

[9] A controversial theologian of the 4th century, he has been called the "Christian Epicurean." The Church Father Jerome was one of his main opponents (Cf. Adversus Jovinianum; P.L. 23:2214.). Among his characteristic viewpoints are the contentions that all sins are equal and that the heavenly reward is the same for all.

[10] A 5th century Pelagian bishop and critic of Augustine.

[11] *C. Jul.* 4:1.22; P.L. 44:749C. The meaning of this quotation may be seen quite clearly from the two sentences which immediately follow in Augustine's work: "It is good to help a man in danger, especially an innocent man. However, if a man acts while loving his own glory more than the glory of God, he does a good thing but not in a good way because he is not good when his deed is not done in a good way."

[12] *De Civ. Dei* 19:25; P.L. 41:656B.

also says: "Good works do not profit the wicked as far as eternal salvation is concerned; it would be very difficult not to find some good works in the life of the worst man imaginable."[13] But because the person is without faith, it is impossible that his works shall please God. This statement of truth, however, did not please the scholastic doctors. For they say that it seems too harsh to affirm that unbelievers sin when they give alms. Ambrosius Spiera[14] cites this statement from Lombard: "The entire life of unbelievers is sin."[15] He says that this opinion is too harsh. I remind you of these things in order that, when we have considered those struggles, we may better understand these reminders.

The third axiom of the Scholastics is this: man existing in mortal flesh without faith and the Holy Spirit is able to avoid committing any mortal sin. Here they depart from the sentence of Lombard: "Man before the restoration of grace is not able not to commit sin, both venial and mortal."[16] Notice, however, what errors there are in that axiom; first, in what we said about contingency.[17] While it is true that an unregenerate man can in some manner either choose or not choose, and thus avoid sins contrary to right external conduct, he does *not* have the freedom to do away with inner depravity, that is, those faults or sins with which he is born.

Secondly, we maintain that for the unregenerate all sins are mortal. Therefore it is not right to say that a man can "avoid any mortal sin." If "mortal" were to be defined simply as that which is incom-

---

[13] *De Spiritu et Littera* 28:48; P.L. 44:230D.

[14] A Roman Catholic theologian, Ambrosius Spiera or Spera (d. 1454) was known for his great doctrinal erudition but also for his crudeness in commenting on Lombard's *Sentences*.

[15] 2 *Sent.* 41.1; P.L. 192:749D.

[16] 2 *Sent.* 25.6; P.L. 192:707B.

[17] Contingency in Scholastic usage is the opposite of necessity. It is a state in which an event can occur but it is not certain whether or not the event will occur. In the case of contingency, only the possibility of the event is given. In the case of necessity, however, the reality of the event is guaranteed, i.e., the event must occur. Another shade of contingency is the question, not of whether an event occurs, but of the way in which it occurs, i.e., whether exactly in one way or somewhat differently. Chemnitz, in this regard, presents the following definition from Aristotle's *Rhetorica:* Necessary events are those which could not occur in a different manner; contingent events are those which could occur in a different manner and which are in our power.

patible with right external conduct, the axiom would be true in a way. But they themselves speak thus to support their doctrine of fitting merit. They reason that if he avoids mortal sin, a man is not under the wrath of God, but is pleasing to God and merits grace.

Thirdly, because of the hindrances to freedom mentioned above, a man cannot always avoid even the kind of mortal sin which is contrary to right external conduct. For we see that some of the finest men have slipped most shamefully although they tried to live honorably. Therefore in the sins of the unregenerate we find both contingency and necessity:[18] contingency because man is able in some way to avoid the sins contrary to right external conduct; necessity for a twofold reason: (1) He is not able not to sin because he cannot put off the inner depravity. (2) His heart lacks fear of God because he is not reconciled by faith. Therefore even in external deeds of conduct, man is not able not to sin, as has been said.

If these things are distinguished with reasonable care, the matter will be without ambiguity, and it will be possible to understand many passages in Augustine's disputations against Pelagius: "The power of the corrupted will is too little to keep from sinning unless the grace of God cleanses."[19] "There are some so presumptuous about free will that they think that once freedom of the will has been granted to our very nature, we do not need help from God to keep from sinning; from this it follows that we ought not to pray 'lead us not into temptation.' "[20]

In a letter to Innocent I, Augustine cites 2 Cor. 13:7 ("We pray to God that ye do no evil!") and comments, "From this word it is sufficiently clear that although the existence of freedom of the will for not sinning, that is, not doing evil, is not to be doubted, yet its power does not suffice unless its weakness receives aid."[21]

---

[18] Chemnitz looks on this problem dialectically, i.e., from two opposite sides. He states the following paradox about the unregenerate: (a) On the one hand, their sins are contingent and not necessary; they are not forced to sin by an external power. (b) On the other hand, their sins are necessary in that they must sin because of their corrupted will.

[19] *De Perf. Just. Hom.* 2:3; P.L. 44:294A.

[20] *De Baptismo* 2:2.2; P.L. 44:151D.

[21] *Epistola* 177:4; P.L. 33:766C. Innocent I was a powerful and able Pope (402-417).

The Canon of the Council of Mileve [22] declares: "Whoever says: 'The grace of God by which we are justified through Christ our Lord avails for remission of past sins, but is not able to help so that sins should not be committed,' let him be anathema."

From what has been said we can discover the extent to which there is any possibility of not sinning, and to what extent the will is captive to sin. For Augustine affirms both, although not distinctly enough. And from these sentences of Augustine we have noticed that Pelagius also once extended the possibility of not sinning to all sins, just as the Scholastics have afterward done.

---

[22] This council was held in 416 against Pelagius in the Numidian city of Mileve. From this Council there is extant only the Synodical Letter to Innocent I, which is *Epistola 176* of the Augustinian epistles. Cf. P.L. 33:763B. In the pseudo-Isidorian Decretals there are 27 canons which supposedly come from this council; however, it is now agreed by scholars that all of these canons are spurious. The quotation which follows in the Chemnitz text is Canon No. 3 of the spurious canons. Cf. Mansi's *Sacrorum Conciliorum Nova et Amplissima Collectio* 4:327.

III

Concerning Spiritual Powers[1] in Man

The principal point in the doctrine of free will is that the human will of its own powers cannot without the Holy Spirit initiate inner spiritual impulses.[2] It cannot perform the inner obedience of the heart; nor can it persevere in, accomplish, and complete a course of action which has been undertaken.

We speak of spiritual powers or activities because in Rom. 7:14 the Law is described as "spiritual." That is, it is not content with certain outward, civil activities which the unregenerate flesh can perform. Rather, the Law demands such impulses and activities as cannot be accomplished without the working of the Holy Spirit. These the flesh cannot perform, for the flesh hinders the Holy Spirit in his work, not only by evil desires (Rom. 7:8), but also by the wisdom of the flesh (Rom. 8:7). Frequently when we speak of spiritual impulses, we think of the knowledge, fear, faith, and love of God. For it is characteristic of these affections that they cannot be produced by the flesh. However, in the case of other virtues, such as temperance, chastity, bravery, freedom, etc., the distinction is not so clear; even human reason has such virtues.[3] But we must

---

[1] Latin, *actionibus*.

[2] Latin, *motus*.

[3] These virtues may be based on sound common sense, guided by reason. However, they may not always be based on the deeper Christian foundations of faith and love.

distinguish on the basis of causes and goals.[4] For example, the chastity of Joseph had a different cause from that of Scipio.

The whole force of our argument rests upon the testimony of Scripture, upon which the correct teaching regarding the bondage of the human will is based. But in a work on dogmatics not all passages of Scripture are mentioned; only the method of gathering correct and applicable passages is indicated. Therefore it will be useful to present the Scripture passages in a certain order, so that one can see the entire matter clearly.[5]

I. Inasmuch as both the mind and will of man are embraced under the term Free Will, we shall first present those passages of Scripture which speak of the mind of unregenerate man in spiritual matters. But the mind includes the understanding, the evaluation, the judgment, the ideas, and the thoughts of unregenerate man.

Concerning each of these there are passages from Scripture. "Ye were sometimes darkness, but now are ye light in the Lord" (Eph. 5:8); i.e., without Christ men are only darkness, for they are "light" only "in the Lord." Let none imagine that the mind can be enlightened either by its own acumen in seeking the truth or by the teachings of philosophy. "The light shineth in darkness" (John 1:5); "to turn them from darkness to light" (Acts 26:18); "to give light to them that sit in darkness and in the shadow of death" (Luke 1:79). In Ephesians 4:17-19 Paul explains how unregenerate men are in darkness. They "walk in the vanity of their mind, having the understanding darkened . . . through the ignorance that is in them," i.e., the ignorance that clings to their nature. . . ."[6] Also in 1 Cor.

---

[4] By causes are meant those things which produce virtues; by goals, that toward which the virtue is directed.

[5] This fifth chapter is divided into four sections. The first section describes the mind of the unregenerate man; the second, the will of the unregenerate man concerning spiritual matters. The third section then recounts the gifts of grace mentioned in Scripture for the renewal of the mind and will of the unregenerate. The fourth section consists of special word studies concerning the captivity of the unregenerate mind and the illumination and conversion of it.

[6] Chemnitz also cites the following Scripture passages: 2 Cor. 3:5; Rom. 1:27; Matt. 16:17; Deut. 29:3-4; 1 Tim. 6:5; 2 Tim. 3:8; 2 Cor. 4:4; Is. 53:6; and Acts 17:30.

2:14 he writes, "The natural (Greek, ψυχικός; Latin, *animalis*) man receiveth not the things of the Spirit of God."

This last passage, which is the most extraordinary, should be considered more fully than the others. Emser[7] foolishly says that, just as we speak of animal spirits or animal emotions, so the part of man which he has in common with the brutes is called the animal part. Thus he wants the term translated, "the brutish man." But it is clear that the term *animalis* is used with reference to the soul, as in Jas. 3:15, "sensuous wisdom," ψυχική, and in Jude 19, "sensual, ψυχικοί, not having the Spirit." Therefore he is "natural man," *animalis*, who without the renewal of the Holy Spirit possesses only his own natural powers and abilities. Further, Paul calls man "natural," ψυχικός, because he does not wish to be understood as speaking in the Epicurean sense of a herd of beasts, which in 2 Pet. 2:12 are called "natural brute beasts"; he is speaking rather of those who possess the most important part of man, namely a soul. In 1 Cor. 2:6, Paul calls them "the princes of this world," that is, those who are outstanding in wisdom. Paul says that in this respect the natural man does not understand spiritual matters "because they are spiritually discerned," that is, unless the Spirit enlightens the mind, spiritual things are regarded as "foolishness." Moreover, he uses two terms, γνῶναι, "know," and δέχεται, "receive."[8] Thus, more is necessary than merely understanding; one must accept with firm conviction.

Therefore Paul says two things: 1) the natural man cannot recognize and understand the things of the Spirit of God. For none of the princes of this world knows the wisdom of the Gospel (1 Cor. 2:6). Flesh and blood have not revealed it, but the Holy Spirit has revealed it in the Word (Matt. 16:17). 2) When God in his Word sets forth and explains the doctrine of the Gospel, although natural man may read, hear, and understand it, he nevertheless does not receive it with certainty, either its threats or its promises. "Who knoweth the power of thine anger?" (Ps. 90:11). Thus David knew from the Word of God, "Thou shalt not commit adultery"; but be-

---

[7] Hieronymus Emser (1477-1527) was a pioneer of classical humanism in Germany and was a bitter literary opponent of Martin Luther.

[8] Chemnitz cites the following Scripture passages as examples of this usage of δέχεται: Acts 8:14; 17:11; 1 Thess. 2:13.

cause he drove out the Holy Spirit, he did not receive the things of the Spirit of God. Otherwise he would have repented before the preaching of Nathan.

II.   Secondly, we shall cite passages which describe the will of man, showing what it is like without the renewal of the Holy Spirit and his inner spiritual impulses. Eph. 2:1 and Col. 2:13 call men "dead in trespasses and sins," Rom. 6:20, "free from righteousness," and John 8:34, "the servants of sin." Moreover, we have already mentioned that sin dwells particularly in the will. "The carnal mind is enmity against God: for it is not subject to the Law of God" (Rom. 8:7). φρόνημα, mind, indicates the most strenuous efforts of the flesh or the unregenerate will. "The imagination of man's heart is evil from his youth" (Gen. 8:21); "fulfilling the desires of the flesh and of the mind, and we were by nature the children of wrath" (Eph. 2:3); we were born "not of the will of the flesh nor of the will of man, but of God" (John 1:13).

In Rom. 3:10ff., Paul locates human corruption not only in the mind and will, but in the whole man, and describes how sin dwells even in the individual parts of man. 1) In the mind, man does not understand. 2) In the will, man does not seek God. 3) Both negatively and positively, man is not righteous; he does not do good, is unprofitable, is gone out of the way, etc. 4) In the individual parts of man: "their throat is an open sepulchre, the poison of asps is under their lips, with their tongues they have used deceit, their mouth is full of cursing, their feet are swift to shed blood" (Rom. 3:13-15).

III.   Thirdly, we shall cite passages which describe the grace of the Son of God which he bestows upon the mind and will of man through the Spirit of regeneration. For in the darkness of this world we cannot better understand of what gifts the mind and will of man have been deprived than from those passages of Scripture. in which are described how the mind of the regenerate man is enlightened by the Holy Spirit, how the heart is converted, how the will is renewed, and how the new man is created in Christ Jesus according to God. Likewise, the words of the holy Fathers testify clearly to the bondage of the will. Augustine asks, "What is more foolish than to pray that you may do what you have within your power?"[9] Likewise in his Epistle 217 he says, "In short, we do not really pray to God, but only imagine that we are praying if we think that we can do the things for which we pray. Again, we do not really thank God, but only imagine that we are thanking him, if we think that he does not do the things for which we thank him."[10] There are also many Scripture passages which are applicable here.[11]

In John 15:5 Jesus says, "Without me ye can do nothing." He is not speaking about the universal presence of God in the affairs of this life, for Paul in Eph. 2:12 says of unregenerate gentiles, "Ye were without Christ, without God." Rather, Jesus here is speaking of spiritual fruits, among which he includes also the observance of God's commands: "Without me ye can do nothing." Nor does he speak this way in a Pelagian sense, as it is popularly said, "A knowledge of art without a natural inclination cannot produce good artists." For Christ declares that as the branch cannot bear fruit of itself, but draws its life and strength from the vine and withers apart from it, so also "without me ye can do nothing." Augustine carefully analyzes each word: "Christ does not say, 'Without me ye can do little,' nor does he say, 'Ye cannot do anything difficult without me,' or 'Without me ye will do the task with great difficulty,' but, 'Without me ye can do nothing.' Nor does he say, 'Without me ye cannot complete it,' but 'Ye can do nothing without me.' "[12] Note Solomon's prayer in 1 Kings 3:9; 8:58, and also Ps. 51:10, "Create in me a clean heart." Note also from the introductions and conclusions of St. Paul's Epistles how he prays for the churches and what he hopes for the believers.

IV.   Fourthly, it is also useful to set down together the shades and meanings of the words showing (1) how they describe the bondage of unregenerate man: darkness (Eph. 5:8); darkened understanding (Eph. 4:18); blinded minds (2 Cor. 4:4); corrupt minds (2

---

[9] *De Natura et Gratia, contra Pelagium* 18:20; P.L. 44:256B.

[10] *Epistola* 217:2.7; P.L. 33:981A.

[11] Chemnitz cites the following: Eph. 1:7; 2:5; 4:7; Acts 26:18; 2 Cor. 4:6; Is. 11:2; Ps. 119:34; Jer. 31:33; 1 Cor. 12:3; and John 15:5.

[12] *Contra Duas Epistolas Pelagianorum* 2:8.18; P.L. 44:584B.

Tim. 3:8); vain imaginings and darkened, foolish hearts (Rom. 1:21); erring hearts (Heb. 3:10); foolish (Tit. 3:3); fools and slow of heart (Luke 24:25); liars (Rom. 3:4); seeing and not perceiving (Acts 28:26-27); hard and impenitent hearts (Rom. 2:5); stony hearts (Ezek. 36:26); obstinate (Is. 48:4); blind hearts (Eph. 4:18); being past feeling (Eph. 4:19); hardened hearts (Mark 6:52); dead in trespasses (Eph. 2:1); without Christ and without God (Eph. 2:12).

(2) The following words also describe the enlightenment of the mind and the conversion of the will and the healing of each through Christ. For thus the Holy Spirit speaks in Eph. 1:18: "The eyes of your understanding being enlightened"; and in 2 Cor. 4:6, "God hath shined in our hearts, to give the light of the knowledge of the glory of God."

Moreover, we must observe the stronger emphasis of Scripture: it speaks not only of the enlightenment of the eyes, but in Acts 26:18 says, "To open their eyes, and to turn them from darkness to light." Note especially Deut. 29:4, "Unless God shall have given eyes to see and a heart to perceive, the word is heard in vain, and signs are seen in vain";[13] likewise Ps. 119:34, "Give me understanding, Lord." Augustine has also made this observation: "The grace of enlightenment is no less necessary for the mind than light for the eyes; rather, we ourselves open the eyes to see the light; however, the eyes of the mind, unless they are opened by God, remain closed."[14]

Finally, we observe an even stronger emphasis in the following passages: in 1 Sam. 10:26, God touches the heart; in 2 Sam. 19:14, he sways the hearts of men; in Job 12:24, he changes the heart. Thus Scripture speaks concerning external matters. But in regard to spiritual matters it declares: "Because thou hast heard the words of the book, thy heart is tender" (2 Chron. 34:27). "The Lord will circumcise thy heart" (Deut. 30:6). "I have broken their heart that was faithless, and revolted from me" (Ezek. 6:9).[15] "They have

---

[13] According to Chemnitz's own Latin translation.
[14] *De Peccatorum Meritis et Remissione* 2:55; P.L. 44:153D-154A.
[15] According to the Douai version of the Bible.

brought a heart of stone, and I will give them a new heart" (Ezek. 11:19; 36:26). "Create in me a clean heart" (Ps. 51:10).[16]

Note that in outward matters God can touch and sway the hearts of men, but in spiritual things our infirmity cannot be healed so simply. Rather, God softens, converts, and opens the heart. But because our hearts are hard beyond measure, he wounds, circumcises, and even breaks them. When this avails nothing he takes the heart completely away, gives it new life, and even creates a new heart.

Thus in Ps. 41:4 we read, "Heal my soul"; in Eph. 5:14, "Arise from the dead"; in Eph. 2:5, "When we were dead in sins he hath quickened us"; in 2 Cor. 4:16, "The inward man is renewed"; in Tit. 3:5, "The renewing of the Holy Ghost"; in 1 Pet. 3:3, "He hath begotten us again unto a lively hope"; in John 3:3, "Except a man be born again, he cannot see the kingdom of God"; in Eph. 2:10, "We are his workmanship, created in Christ Jesus"; in Eph. 4:24, "The new man which after God is created. . . ." Observe that God heals the weak nature of man and applies remedies to it: "I will bind up that which was broken" (Ezek. 34:16). The heart must be renewed, raised from the dead, regenerated, so that it is born again. This is not only a healing, but a complete rebirth, a work of no small value, an actual creation. Therefore, each of these activities must be ascribed to God.

---

[16] Chemnitz also cites the following passages: Acts 16:14; Luke 1:7; Ezra 6:22; Song of Sol. 4:9; Ps. 51:17; 2 Cor. 4:16; Rom. 6:6; Is. 57:15; Eph. 4:23; and Acts 15:9.

IV

Augustine's Distinctions in the Doctrine of Grace

Now surely the entire doctrine of the free will is established on the passages cited; nor should it be necessary to add anything further. For against those who imagine that the free will has only been weakened in regard to spiritual activities we can properly pit the great weight of evidence which we have examined.

But because by various deceptions the simple understanding of this doctrine has been so skillfully perverted that the uninformed can scarcely comprehend the matter, I do not think it out of place to point out Augustine's distinctions regarding prevenient, subsequent, operating, and cooperating grace. For by these distinctions he clearly uncovered in his own day the snares of the Pelagians, and brought to light their subterfuges, beautifully setting forth the true teaching of Scripture. If we follow his clear distinction the doctrine is not so liable to corruption.

For even Lombard has retained this distinction and, insofar as he has followed this course, he has not dealt badly with the matter.

But afterward the writers of "Sentences" plainly corrupted this distinction, although for some time they kept the same terminology. Indeed, it is conceded even by all the more sensible scholastics that the free will does not suffice for carrying on spiritual activities without the aid of the Holy Spirit. Even the Papists wish to be seen with their mouths overflowing as they preach about the necessity of grace, which they understand as the aid of the Holy Spirit.

At one time even Pelagius began to speak in this way, as we see in Augustine's treatise, *Against Two Epistles of the Pelagians:* "Pelagius says that grace aids everyone to complete his good works; however, it does not arouse a zeal for virtue in the reluctant, nor does it inspire a desire for good in the unwilling."[1] Pelagius also says, "In every good work man is always aided by grace." To this Augustine responds, "We would accept this statement without difficulty if we did not know the intention of those who say it."[2] However, we see what Pelagius means by the statement: "Man by his own powers can desire and long for conversion and thus obtain the grace of the Holy Spirit."[3] Augustine cites the following Pelagian argument: When the desire to come to Christ flows out of free will, then the Holy Spirit is given to those who seek him.[4] Again, when of our own free will we run to God and desire to be ruled by him, then the Holy Spirit is given. In *Against Two Epistles of the Pelagians,* Augustine says: "Why do you not say that a man is aroused by God's grace to good works? You say rather that he is always aided by grace in a good work, as if by his own will, and without any grace of God, man undertakes a good work, and then is divinely helped for the first time only in the actual work itself?"[6] Although Pelagius toned down this statement afterward, saying that a man of his free will certainly had a desire for good, but only an imperfect desire, yet Augustine resisted him strongly.

Here I wish to point out that in these controversies with Pelagius

---

[1] *Contra Duas Epistolas Pelagianorum* 4:2.2; P.L. 44:610C.

[2] *Ibid.* 1:19.37; P.L. 44:567C.

[3] *Ibid.* 2:8.17-18; P.L. 44:583C-584D.

[4] *De Gratia Christi et de Peccato Originali* 1:14.15;P.L. 44:368. This is not a quotation but a paraphrase.

[5] *Ibid.* 1:23.24; P.L. 44:372C. This is not a quotation but a paraphrase. According to Pelagius, the possibility of coming to God belongs to the nature of man, and also in some way to Grace (because Grace aids the human possibility). Still, the coming itself belongs to the will of man; it is man himself who comes.

[6] *C. Duas Epp. Pel.* 1:19.37; P.L. 44:567C.

we have the very image of our own times. And it is worthy of note that Jerome, in his disputes with the Pelagians, reduced the whole problem to this one aspect alone.[7] In his *Dialogues Against the Pelagians,* he says, "The conclusion of this long controversy is that God in our specific acts aids and sustains us according to his grace by which he has given us a free will."[8] Also in his letter to Ctesiphon he says, "In this respect we differ from brute animals, not simply that we are endowed with a free will, but the free will itself depends upon the help of God and stands in need of his help in every case."[9] Again, "What we will is not of our own power, but of the mercy of God, if he will aid our will."[10]

Note that Jerome concedes that the free will by nature has some strength and can do something, which, however, it cannot carry to completion if not divinely aided. However, he does not distinguish between the external works of the Law and spiritual activities; nor does he make a difference between the general and the spiritual acts of God. Augustine cites the statement of Ambrose: "And so you see that in every case the power of God cooperates with human effort. No one can build anything without God."[11] But under these vague generalizations Pelagius could hide the roots of his error. Therefore Augustine examined Pelagius very closely and first set forth the difference between works of this present life and those which pertain to God.[12] Since Pelagius was even beginning to talk about God's help, Augustine defined the point of controversy as follows: Can the human will by its own natural powers apply itself to spiritual activities? Can it, even though it is too weak to proceed to any action, still do something if aided by the Holy Spirit? Can nature and human skill join with the Holy Spirit to produce this excellent condition in man?

In order to explain the point of controversy in such a way as to draw his opponents into the light and show them up as enemies of

[7] Jerome discussed only the question of whether there is free will in any sense. He did not discuss the question of where the will is free (in outward actions) and where it is not (in spiritual matters).
[8] *Dialogus adversus Pelagianos* 3:6; P.L. 23:601D.
[9] *Epistola 133 (ad Ctesiphontem)* 10; P.L. 22:1158B.
[10] *Dial. adv. Pel.* 2:6; P.L. 23:567B.
[11] *De Grat. Chr. et de Pec. Orig.* 1:44.48; P.L. 44:382A.
[12] *Hypognosticon* (or *Hypomnesticon*) 3:4.5; P.L. 45:1623D-1624A.

the grace of God who are trying to hide their errors, Augustine clearly and effectively sets up the various degrees or steps of spiritual impulses and activities . . . in terms of their beginning and completion, designating "completion" by the terms "persevering" and "completing." To each of these steps he assigns their characteristics and names, so that the distinction may be more clearly seen. Hence, in the Augsburg Confession and in our other writings we use the terms "begin" and "accomplish." I have reviewed the cause and origin of the distinction because I believe it sheds light on this controversy. The necessary use of this distinction can thereby be understood. Now let us briefly consider the degrees themselves.[13]

I. The First Degree—Prevenient Grace: Regarding the origin of our conversion, the ancient Fathers before the rise of the Pelagian controversy almost all spoke in this way:

Jerome says, "It is for us to begin, for God to complete; for us to offer what we can, for him to fill in what we cannot do."[14]

Chrysostom says that, just as unaided we can never do anything right, so unless we contribute what is ours to give, we can never receive divine favor.[15]

Hilary[16] wrote to Augustine that many in Gaul felt that in the nature of man, although it is weakened, there remains such ability that it can by its own efforts seek the physician, i.e., make a beginning. And regarding natural gifts, they interpreted the statement of Paul, "What hast thou, that thou didst not receive?" (1 Cor.

---

[13] It should not be thought that this division of five degrees of grace is ontological. There are not five graces, but one and the same grace in different functions according to different needs of man. The basis of this distinction is twofold: (a) Holy Scripture and (b) practical psychology, i.e., Augustine's personal observations in his own life and in his pastoral activities.

[14] *Dial. adv. Pel.* 3:1; P.L. 23:596C.

[15] *In Genesin Homilia* 52; P.G. 54:456-463. This is not a quotation but a summary of the content of this particular sermon.

[16] This is not the Church Father, Hilary of Poitiers (315-367). Neither is it Hilary of Arles, able and respected bishop and admirer of Augustine in spite of their differences of opinion on predestination.

The letter to which Chemnitz refers (Cf. *Epistola* 226; P.L. 33:1006.) is written by another Hilary, probably an unknown Gaul. His standpoint on this particular question is less polemical than that of Hilary of Arles, but he still expresses some embarrassment about Augustine's attitude, which he considers too radical.

4:7), by adding that unless such ability is found in our nature, God cannot be defended against the charge of being a respecter of persons. And thus the scholastics often spoke in later times. But Augustine refuted this opinion in his treatise, *On the Predestination of the Saints.*[17]

Augustine even says that he himself had formerly stated that "it is for us to believe and will, but for God to give to those who believe and will the ability to do it."[18] But he confesses that while he was still holding this opinion, the force of 2 Cor. 3:5 came home to him, when he had more carefully studied it: "Not that we are sufficient of ourselves to think anything as of ourselves. . . ." "To think," he concludes, is even less than to decide or to strive for or to begin. "He which hath begun a good work in you will perfect it . . ." (Phil. 1:6). "You, who have begun before, . . . Now therefore perform the doing of it" (2 Cor. 8:10-11). This passage may seem to attribute the beginning of an act to the free will. But in Phil. 2:13 Paul says, "It is God which worketh in you both to will and to do"; and in 1 Cor. 4:7, "What hast thou that thou didst not receive?" Augustine shows from the context that Paul is not speaking of natural gifts, as the Gauls at that time were contending, but of spiritual activities, as in John 15:5, "Without me ye can do nothing." He does not here say "complete," but simply "do."[19]

Therefore, from these Scripture passages Augustine correctly and truthfully maintains against the Pelagians that it is not in our power to begin a good work, nor does the origin of a good will toward God arise from our own efforts. Rather, holy thinking, good intentions, the desire and longing for the good, are all by grace, the gift and work of the Holy Spirit.[20] And for the sake of instruction or

---

[17] *De Praedestinatione Sanctorum* 1:5; P.L. 44:967-8.

[18] *Ibid.* 1:3.7; P.L. 44:965A.

[19] *De Praedest. Sanct.* 1:5.9; P.L. 44:967D.

[20] *De Ecclesiasticis Dogmatibus* P.L. 42:1217D. This work is obviously not written by Augustine, though it is referred to by some important theologians (Cf. Peter Lombard, III *Sent.* 35.2; P.L. 192:735.). Among the probable authors of this work are Gennadius of Constantinople, Gennadius of Marseille, and Faustus of Maxilio. The text used by Chemnitz was obviously much larger than that found in Migne, P.L. 42:1213-1222 as an appendix to Augustine's proper works. Chemnitz's reference corresponds approximately to chapter 21 of this work, P.L. 42:1217D.

definition he calls this prevenient, preceding, or anticipating grace.
. . . Augustine says: "Subsequent grace certainly aids a good intention, but the intention itself would not occur unless grace had pre-
ceded. That zeal of man which is called good, when it begins to
appear, is aided by grace, but it is inspired by him of whom we read
in Phil. 2:13, 'It is God which worketh in you both to will and to do
of his good pleasure.'"[21] In the same connection Augustine says,
"Faith is given to him who wants to believe, rather the very will
itself is incited from above, so that one becomes willing even if he is
persecuting the faith, as Saul was."[22] Also, "Faith is given when it
is not sought, even as other things are given when they are sought";[23]
and, "From the Law, if it is used properly, we flee to grace. But
who would flee unless the steps of men are directed by God? And
thus even to ask for the help of grace is the beginning of grace."[24]

We must always hold to the rule that the Holy Spirit is efficacious
through the Word of the Gospel which is heard or known, nor must
we seek violent raptures or enthusiastic emotions. Also we must
note that Pelagius very cunningly corrupted this rule. For he supposed that the Holy Spirit works in us to will simply by showing
us through the Word what ought to be done; but that he does not
also move us efficaciously from within nor impel our will, nor inspire holy thoughts and good purpose. . . . When the heavenly doctrine is offered to man by the ministry of the Word, the human will
by itself has the ability to produce spiritual desires and to make
good decisions.

Furthermore, just as Pelagius in his day laid his snares with the
word "aid," so the Papists in the *Interim Book*[25] made their deceptions with the word "arouse," saying that as a man is aroused from

[21] *C. Duas Epp. Pel.* 2:10.22; P.L. 44:587B. In Migne Augustine quotes
2 Cor. 8:16 rather than Phil. 2:13.
[22] *Ibid.* 1:19.37; P.L. 44:568A.
[23] *De Gratia et Libero Arbitrio* 14.28; P.L. 44:897D.
[24] *De Correptione et Gratia* 1:2; P.L. 44:917B.
[25] By "Interim" is meant a doctrinal formula which will serve as a temporary
settlement of religious differences until the next general council. During the
Reformation there were three Interims drawn up, all unsuccessful, resulting
from colloquies called by Emperor Charles V to settle Protestant-Catholic
differences. Of these three (Ratisbon, 1541; Augsburg, 1548; and Leipzig,
1548), Chemnitz is probably referring to the Augsburg Interim.

sleep, so the will has the ability to work in spiritual matters. It can be aroused, since it is only inactive, dull and sleepy. But this is a sophistic and Pelagian trick. For the Scripture passage, "Awake thou that sleepest," can only mean "Arise from the dead" (Eph. 5:14).

They also inject certain passages, the explanation of which we ought to consider. For example, Rom. 7:18, "To will is present with me, but how to perform that which is good I find not." This passage troubles many, as Augustine confesses of himself, until it becomes clear to them that Paul is speaking, not of the will of the natural man, but of the will of the regenerate man who is led by the Spirit.

"The preparations of the heart in man, and the answer of the tongue, is from the Lord," says Prov. 16:1. This speaks of the thoughts, plans, and emotions in those matters which are subject to reason and our senses.

"We are redeemed, that we might receive the promise of the Spirit through faith" (Gal. 3:14). If the Spirit is received by faith, then they say faith precedes and comes before the work of the Holy Spirit[26] and man can without his aid begin those activities which pertain to salvation. . . . Malvenda at Ratisbon[27] pointed to the following antinomy in Scripture: "The fruit of the Spirit is faith" (Gal. 5:22), as against ". . . that by faith we might receive the Spirit" (Gal. 3:14). There are many answers sought to this question, of which I shall mention a few, in order that the true explanation of this most consoling verse may be more diligently considered.

Some say that in Gal. 5:22 the word "faith" should be taken, not in the sense of justifying faith, or trust, the correlative of which is a promise, but it should be taken in the sense of faithfulness in agreements, of candor; thus there is no contradiction, since the term "faith" is used in two different senses.[28] But this answer does not solve

---

[26] According to Augustine, the holy desires and moral decisions are not man's own achievements of his autonomous will. Rather they are inspired or infused by the Holy Spirit, i.e., given as gifts by the work of the Holy Spirit.

[27] Malvenda was the leading Catholic theologian at the last of several Protestant-Catholic colloquies at Ratisbon, held in 1546 just before the outbreak of the Smalkaldic War.

[28] Literally, "since there are four terms. . . ." The reference here is to the "fallacy of four terms." This fallacy occurs when the middle term of a syllogism appears in a different sense in each of the premises, making impossible the linking of the subject and predicate of the conclusion. (Cf. Vulgate of Gal. 5:22.)

the problem. For whatever word we use for "faith" in Gal. 5:22, it is still certain from many other passages that faith is not conceived or kindled by our own natural powers, but only by the operation of the Holy Spirit. And thus the question still remains: How is the Holy Spirit received by faith?

Others answer that Paul in Gal. 3:14 is speaking only of those visible gifts of the Holy Spirit which are often mentioned in the Book of Acts, where it says that the Holy Spirit was poured out or fell upon the believers, that is, the visible gifts of the Holy Spirit. But this answer certainly takes the consolation of this passage away from us, as if it pertained only to the brief period of the primitive church, while it is perfectly clear that Paul is speaking in general terms of the promise of the efficacy of the Holy Spirit. For he explains the promise given to Abraham, which certainly ought not and cannot be restricted to that short period in which the visible gifts of the Holy Spirit were given. Therefore there are two other explanations which come closer to Paul's meaning.

There is no doubt that the gifts of the Holy Spirit are varied, and that they increase and are augmented. This agrees with Scripture, which says that when we receive a new or increased gift of the Spirit, then we receive the Holy Spirit. In Acts, for instance, this often occurs; and in John 20:22, where Christ says to his apostles, "Receive ye the Holy Spirit," there is no doubt that the Holy Spirit had dwelt in the apostles previously. Thus it is true that faith is a work of the Holy Spirit. And because many gifts are bestowed upon believers and those given earlier are increased, we can rightly say that faith which is kindled by the Holy Spirit also receives the Holy Spirit, that is, it receives many other gifts or an increase of gifts. These things are certainly true, but I am not sure that Paul wants to discuss that matter here.

Therefore the simplest and best explanation is this: In Gal. 3:14 Paul is making the same point as in 2 Cor. 3:6: the Gospel is the ministry of the Spirit. Paul has often said that faith is a gift of God, and that the Holy Spirit wishes to work and accomplish it. And in Gal. 3:14 he wants to explain how the Holy Spirit reveals his efficacy, when and in whom He works—when, in other words, the Gospel is the ministry of the Spirit, and how the Holy Spirit is received by faith. For the Word of the Gospel and faith are correlated and faith includes assent and trust. To assent belong hearing and meditation upon the Word, and to trust belongs the fact that the heart sustains itself in its struggle by means of the Word, and desires a fuller trust. Therefore when we read, hear, or meditate upon the Word of the Gospel, when the conscience supports itself in its struggle by means of the Word and has a desire for faith, in keeping with the statement of Mark 9:24, "Help thou mine unbelief," there is no doubt that the Holy Spirit precedes us with his grace and exercises the efficacy of which the Scripture speaks.

"But," you object, "I do not have faith, and the Holy Spirit is received by faith." I reply that faith comes by hearing, and the preaching of the Gospel is the ministration of the Spirit. Thus we receive the Holy Spirit by faith at the time when we hear and meditate upon the Word of the Gospel. Paul does not want these two concepts separated, as if we first feel the operation of the Spirit and then afterward there follows the hearing, meditation upon the Word, prayer, etc. Nor should we think that the Holy Spirit is obtained by our meditation or desire; rather, by faith we receive the promise of the Spirit, and faith comes by hearing. The Holy Spirit prepares our will, but this happens only when we begin with the Word. Therefore, if we ask in our hearts whether we have that grace which Augustine calls prevenient grace, we ought not consider our experience, as to how we feel. For faith comes by hearing, and by faith we receive the promise of the Spirit, and the grace, efficacy, work, and gift of the Holy Spirit. I have discussed this statement of Paul at some length now because with this understanding of it we can rightly guard against both Pelagianism and enthusiasm. This explanation also pertains to the subsequent grades of grace.

This same interpretation applies to that most beautiful verse, "Your heavenly Father shall give the Holy Spirit to them that ask him" (Luke 11:13). Not without the Spirit are we able to pray by our own natural powers and by our prayer to call down the Spirit. For in Zech. 12:10 he is called the "Spirit of supplications," and without faith, which is a gift of the Holy Spirit, no one can pray. But Scripture speaks in this way for two reasons.

The first reason is that we are not to expect perceptible and violent emotions, by which we can judge if the Spirit is present, even though we are struggling against the Word and indulging in wicked thoughts and passions. But when I have a desire, even though the voice [of the Spirit] reveals itself with an inaudible groan, I must be certain that the Holy Spirit is then present and operative.

The second is that we are not to give up, even though his first workings are dimly discerned and obscure, but rather keep on seeking. For the Lord gives his Holy Spirit to those who seek him. Note here Phil. 1:6, "Being confident of this very thing, that he who hath begun a good work in you will perform it." We ought to consider these two passages carefully, for they contain the true explanation of this doctrine which we are treating.

The opponents bring up certain examples by way of objection, e.g., Cornelius in Acts 10:1, Zaccheus in Luke 19:2, and the Prodigal Son in Luke 15:17. Augustine answers these objections very well: "Whatever good works Cornelius did before he believed, while he was coming to faith and after he had come to faith, must all be given to God's credit, lest any one exalt himself."[29] And although he was praying and giving alms and doing other good works before he had a clear understanding of Christ, yet not without faith was he praying and giving. For, "How shall they call on him whom they have not believed?" (Rom. 10:14). "Without faith it is impossible to please God" (Heb. 11:6). But Cornelius' works of mercy had been accepted by God. Thus he had been endowed with faith. Augustine says of the Prodigal Son, "He would not have had this knowledge ('I will arise and go to my father'), unless a most merciful God had created it in him secretly."[30] Concerning Zacchaeus Augustine says further, "We must clearly believe that this remarkable faith of Zacchaeus, who wanted to see Jesus, was not there by nature but given by the bounty of divine grace."[31] Again

---

[29] *De Praedest. Sanct.* 1:7.12; P.L. 44:970B.

[30] *Epistola* 186:2.5; P.L. 33:818A.

[31] *De Eccl. Dog.* 51; P.L. 42. This quotation is not to be found in Migne. See note 20, p. 23. For an analogical Augustinian interpretation of Zacchaeus, see the polemics of Prosper Aquitanus against Cassianus (*Contra Collatorem* 6:19; P.L. 42:1810).

Augustine declares, "In certain cases there is the grace of faith such as does not suffice for gaining the kingdom of God, as in the case of Cornelius. Thus the beginning of their conversion is something like conception. But it is necessary not only to be conceived but also to be born. However, none of these acts occurs without the gracious mercy of God."[32]

Finally, we must consider also that objection which can disturb our minds against the doctrine of prevenient grace. It is manifest that unregenerate men think about God (Rom. 1:20); that they can read the Scripture (2 Cor. 3:2); that they can talk about the Word of God (Ps. 50:16); that they can hear sermons as the Athenians in Acts 17:19. Indeed they can conceive an historic faith,[33] as James says of the devils (James 2:19); and this is manifest in regard to hypocrites. Paul himself attributes to the unregenerate effort and zeal, indeed a zeal not only in regard to the civil works of the Second Table of the Law but even in religion. "Ye were carried away unto these dumb idols" (I Cor. 12:2). "I bear them record that they have a zeal of God, but not according to knowledge" (Rom. 10:2). "Israel followed after the law of righteousness" (Rom. 9:31), and not only to be seen by men. Since this is the case, how do we establish the doctrine of prevenient grace against the Pelagians?

I reply, we must call to mind the distinction between acts of external discipline and spiritual impulses. And here there is a clear difference in the thoughts of the unregenerate in those matters which pertain to God. "They became vain in their imaginations. . . . Professing themselves to be wise, they became fools" (Rom. 1:21-22); "For until this day remaineth the same veil untaken away in the reading of the Old Testament; which veil is done away in Christ" (2 Cor. 3:14); "Ye shall hear and shall not understand" (Matt. 13:14); "The Lord hath not given you eyes to see" (Deut. 29:4). What Israel seeks, not only with eagerness, but even with zeal, he does not obtain, but rather is hardened (Rom. 11:7).[34]

---

[32]*De Diversis Quaestionibus ad Simplicianum* 1:2.2; P.L. 40:112A.

[33] *Fides historica,* "mere recognition and crediting of that which is promised, while the person may be inwardly indifferent towards it" (H. Schmid, *The Doctrinal Theology of the Evangelical Lutheran Church,* p. 417).

[34] This is not a quotation but rather Chemnitz's interpretation of the sense of the passage.

Thus the flesh has thoughts about God, but these are not the beginning of conversion, though a reprobate mind follows them (Rom. 1:28). The flesh has an eagerness; it tries, it even has a zeal for God. But it is not said about them: You have only to will something and God runs ahead to provide it; but actually a hardening follows (Rom. 11:8). Augustine, to be sure, in disputing about prevenient grace, speaks of thoughts of this kind, which are not vain before God, of which Phil. 1:6 speaks, "He which hath begun a good work in you will perform it. . . ."

Augustine very clearly illustrates this matter in an example from his own experience. In his *Confessions* he tells that he had come upon the *Hortensius* of Cicero, which included a piece in praise of wisdom and an exhortation to seek wisdom. "By this speech," he says, "I was excited and aroused and my heart burned incredibly to seek wisdom. I undertook to turn my mind to the Holy Scripture, but it seemed unworthy of comparison with Tully."[35] And he adds that because of this contempt for Scripture he fell into the Manichean heresy, which deluded him for nine years. But afterwards, he tells how he was inspired by the preaching of Ambrose with a desire which led to his conversion to Christianity, as we shall note later. Thus Augustine conceived a desire of his own free will, but it only led him into the Manichean heresy. However, it is something entirely different when in Luke 24:13ff. we read of the case of the two men going to Emmaus who by hearing and meditating on the Word of the Gospel were inspired by the Holy Spirit with a desire for grace. For there is fulfilled the saying, "He precedes the unwilling, so that he becomes willing: he follows the willing so that he does not will in vain."

From these remarks I believe that similar arguments may easily be settled. We have spoken at great length regarding the first degree of grace because of the many disputes by which this doctrine has been corrupted. We shall refer only briefly to the others.

II. The Second Degree—Preparatory Grace: Among the Scholastics this statement from Augustine is quoted, "We have the begin-

---

[35] *Confessiones* 3:4.8; P.L. 32:686B and 3:5.9; P.L. 32:686C.

ning of our salvation by the mercy of God, but that we consent to be saved by the working of the Spirit is of our own power."[36] Indeed, Augustine in *On the Spirit and the Letter* discusses at length the idea that to consent to the call of God is of our own will.[37] But in *On the Predestination of the Saints* he eloquently confesses that he had erred in thinking that the grace of God consists only in that the Gospel is preached to us, but that our consenting to the Gospel when it is preached is of our own power and will.[38] And in his *Epistle* 217 he sharply rebukes Vitales because he had said, "God works so that we are willing when his preaching is made known to us; but to consent to the Word is of our own ability."[39]

Bernard even declares, "This is the whole work of the free will that it consents, not indeed that this very consent is of itself, since we are not able even to think (which is less than our consenting) as of ourselves."[40] These, however, are the fundamentals, namely, that to acquiesce or to consent pertains to faith; but this without any argument does not belong to our natural ability, but is a gift of God. "For unto you it is given . . . to believe on him" (Phil. 1:29); "For by grace are ye saved through faith; and that not of yourselves, it is the gift of God" (Eph. 2:8); "Peace be to the brethren, and love with faith from God the Father" (Eph. 6:23); I obtained mercy, that I might be faithful (1 Tim. 1:13, 12);[41] "According as God has dealt to every man the measure of faith" (Rom. 12:3); "Having the spirit of faith" (2 Cor. 4:13); "No man can come to me, except the Father draw him" (John 6:44). Afterwards Christ explains regarding faith, for he knew who were the believers, "Therefore I said unto you, that no man can come unto me, except it were given unto him of my Father" (John 6:65).

This grace, for the sake of distinction and teaching, Augustine calls preparatory grace. For both the mind and the will are prepared by the Lord, so that they do not struggle against the Holy

---

[36] *De Eccl. Dogm.* 21; P.L. 42:1217A.

[37] *De Spiritu et Littera* 33.57-34.60; P.L. 44:237-241A.

[38] *De Praedest. Sanct.* 1:3.7; P.L. 44:964-5.

[39] *Epistola* 217:1.1; P.L. 33:978C.

[40] *Tractatus de Gratia et Libero Arbitrio* 14.46; P.L. 182:1026B.

[41] This is not a quotation, but it is rather Chemnitz's paraphrase of the content of the two verses.

Spirit, but assent and obey. As that clear testimony of Acts 16:14 says of Lydia, who was, says Luke, worshipping God: She had the beginning, the resolution, and the desire, but the Lord opened her heart, "that she attended unto the things which were spoken by Paul."

III. The Third Degree—Operating Grace: After the Holy Spirit has aroused a pious resolution, the desire, the effort, is not in our own power to change our will for the better (Augustine had at one time spoken in this way, but he retracted it[42]); but God works in us to will (Phil. 2:13). However, he does not work in us, as the Pelagians teach, only by showing his will in the Word, but as it says in Ezek. 36:26-27, "I will take away the stony heart out of your flesh, and I will give you a heart of flesh, and I will put my Spirit within you, and cause you to walk in my statutes, and ye shall keep my judgments, and do them."

This grace Augustine calls operating grace and distinguishes it from that which he calls cooperating grace, because it belongs to God alone to take away a stony heart and give a new one. To this pertains (1) the enlightenment of mind and intellect; (2) the renewal of the will, so that "ye may prove what is that good and acceptable will of God" (Rom. 12:2); and (3) the ability to obey God from the heart (Rom. 6:17).[43]

IV. The Fourth Degree—Cooperating Grace: The captive will is not freed in such a way that after its liberation or renewal it no longer stands in need of the help of its liberator, but as we have heard, John 15:5, "Without me ye can do nothing." So the Psalmist says, "Thou hast been my help; leave me not" (27:9). And Augustine speaks of this in his *On Admonition and Grace*.[44]

Bernard [45] tells us that he was censured by some monks because after he had received the grace of renewal, he still continued to pray for the help of God. He was right in opposing them, because

---

[42] Cf. *Epistola* 217.
[43] *De Grat. et Lib. Arb.* 17.33; P.L. 44:901C.
[44] *De Corrept. et Grat.* 1.2; P.L. 44:917C.
[45] *Vita et Res Gestae* 1:3.13; P.L. 185:234C.

Paul does not say, "When God has begun the work in you, you will be able to complete it," but rather, "He which hath begun a good work in you will perform it" (Phil. 1:6). Therefore we must cling to that most comforting statement of Augustine: "If in so much weakness of this life the renewed will alone remained for the regenerate that they might, if they willed, continue in the help of God, but God should not work in them to make them willing, amidst so many and so great temptations their will itself would give way because of its own weakness. Therefore aid is given to the infirmity of the human will, so that it works inseparably with divine grace and thus, although weak, it does not fail and is not overcome by any adversity."[46] In the *Hypognosticon* 3 Augustine very beautifully applies the parable of the man who had been robbed and beaten, who immediately after his wounds were bound up was not entirely healed but was under constant care (Luke 10:35).[47]

This Augustine calls cooperating, subsequent and helping grace. For after our renewal we consent to the Law of God (Rom. 7:22), approve what is the good will of God (Rom. 12:2), and obey from the heart (Rom. 6:17), that is, when as new creatures we do something good, there is always and constantly a need for the grace and help of the Holy Spirit, who aids the efforts of the regenerate so that they neither fall away nor err, but rather grow in holiness (Eph. 4:13). When we run, he follows after us, so that we do not fall but continue on until we "obtain" (1 Cor. 9:24; Phil. 3:12). He directs and rules our course, so that we do not go astray (Ps. 143:10); just as a driver steers a horse.[48] He raises up the falling and encourages the broken (Ps. 146:8). On this basis Augustine quite rightly speaks of cooperating, subsequent, helping, or directing grace. Concerning the grace of Christ St. Paul says, "My strength is made perfect in weakness" (2 Cor. 12:9). Thus in those who after their renewal do not realize the greatness of their weakness, on account of which they constantly need the grace and truth of God, there is indeed a beginning of strength, but it is not brought to perfection, because God's "strength is made perfect in weakness."

---

[46] *De Corrept. et Grat.* 12.38; P.L. 44:939D-940A.

[47] *Hypognosticon* (or *Hypomnesticon*) 3:8.11-13; P.L. 45:1627D-1629C.

[48] Cf. *ibid.* 3:11.20; P.L. 45:1632B.

V. Fifth Degree—Persevering Grace: In regard to the gift of perseverance, Peter says, "Ye are kept by the power of God through faith unto salvation" (1 Pet. 1:5), and in Rom. 14:4 we read, "He shall be holden up: for God is able to make him stand." Note the significance of the words by which Peter in his First Epistle (5:9-10) describes the gift of perseverance; for after he has said, "Resist the devil, steadfast in the faith," he adds, "But the God of all grace, who hath called us unto his eternal glory by Christ Jesus, after ye have suffered a while, make you perfect, stablish, strengthen, settle you."

I believe that these remarks regarding the degrees of spiritual activities and impulses are profitable, first, so that we may recognize that the Pelagian controversy belongs entirely under the article of the free will, and, second, that we may learn to see more clearly there the gracious benefits of the Son of God in each individual step.

Further, this doctrine, which deprives human powers of every ability to consider, desire, begin, carry on, or accomplish anything in the way of spiritual impulses or actions, is not taught in order that slothfulness, contempt, security, insolence, or similar vices, which by nature cling to the hearts of all men, should be encouraged and aided. And because the world shamefully misuses this doctrine, the Fathers concealed it as a mystery; and to drive slothfulness from the human heart, they spoke eloquently and more fully about human powers than the Holy Scripture did.[49] But we must not teach evil that good may come of it. Peter says in his Second Epistle 3:16, "They that are unlearned and unstable wrest" the whole Scripture and especially the Epistles of Paul. For that reason, however, Paul does not change the form of true and sound doctrine. Because they assail this doctrine and pervert it, they go to their own destruction, as Peter in the same passage points out.

But we should consider and diligently set forth the reasons for which this doctrine was first revealed and ought always to be taught in the church. Therefore, we shall note some of them.

(1) The magnitude of the blessings of God's Son, our Mediator,

---

[49] The Fathers did not "trespass"; they simply asserted without good basis, not noticing the disharmony with Holy Scripture.

cannot be sufficiently understood unless we recognize that human powers have been not only wounded but totally deprived of strength.

(2)   Moreover, when we have such gifts as holy thoughts, pious desires, and similar salutary impulses, we should not glory because of our own powers and efforts, but recognize that it is a gracious gift of the Spirit's working, and give thanks to him and from whom we have received sufficiency to think something good (2 Cor. 3:4) and who has worked in us to will the good (Phil. 2:13).

(3)   When we confess that holy thoughts do not arise out of the speculations of our reason, but that the Holy Spirit by his prevenient grace has begun in us the work of salvation, we will show ourselves more obedient to this work of his, so that we do not despise or drive out these holy thoughts and desires.

(4)   We will also have that consolation in the face of the helplessness of our flesh, even in the rebellion of the law of sin which is in our members, because not the flesh but the Holy Spirit has begun the good work in us, and therefore he will perfect it (Phil. 1:6).

(5)   This doctrine is profitable also so that we do not become secure, when we have the beginnings of faith, love, and repentance, as if we could not lose them but by our own powers could hold and increase them; but rather that we may cling the more closely to him who has called us. Because not of our own free will can we call forth that which is lacking in our spiritual gifts or preserve what we have received, but we are able through him without whom we can do nothing, as Augustine says. "If any of you lack wisdom, let him ask of God" (James 1:5).

(6)   When we cast away such gifts or bury them in the ground, let us bear in mind that we are not doing injury to our own nature, but we are actually struggling against the very working of the Holy Spirit within us. We are destroying his work (Rom. 14:20). Therefore, from this doctrine there is kindled in us faith, prayer, fear of God, and a diligence in keeping these divine gifts.

V

Is the Will Purely Passive in Conversion?

This question can easily be settled from what has already been said; but, because of the two extremes of Pelagianism and Enthusiasm,[1] men often deviate from the sound middle way. For it occurs, as Basil says to Maximus the philosopher regarding tree grafters, "When they are anxious to straighten the crookedness of a tender tree, they err by too much bending in the opposite direction."[2] Erasmus in his *Heavy-Armed Soldier*[3] collects contradictions from the writings of Luther by which he tries to show that Luther was not consistent when debating the problem of free will. Because, he declares, sometimes Luther says that man can neither consider nor do anything good or evil, but that all things happen of absolute necessity; and at other times he says that the free will is strong only towards doing evil. He sometimes says that in externals it can do all things with the aid of grace. But Paul would contradict himself in the same way when he says, "The Gentiles . . . do by nature

---

[1] Chemnitz is probably referring to the Swiss reformers, viz., the Zwinglians and especially the Calvinists.

[2] *Epistola* 9; P.G. 32:270A.

[3] *Hyperaspistes Diatribae adversus Servum Arbitrium Martini Lutheri.*

the things contained in the law" (Rom. 2:14); "Not that we are sufficient of ourselves to think anything as of ourselves" (2 Cor. 3:5); and "I can do all things through Christ which strengtheneth me" (Phil. 4:13).

Even our own people, who believe the same thing, often do not appear to be saying the same thing, because while one wants to oppose Pelagianism, another struggles against Enthusiasm. And on this account contradictions and unnecessary controversies frequently arise. All in all, however, we must tread cautiously and prudently between the Pelagians and the Enthusiasts, lest while we wish to avoid Scylla we are dashed against Charybdis.

Therefore I shall make three observations, which in a simple manner will show the true principles of this matter and will throw light on many things which seem perplexing.

In the first place, noteworthy and useful is that distinction between the four phases of the free will: (1) before the fall in the uncorrupted state; (2) after the fall in the natural corruption before regeneration; (3) after the restoration of the fallen nature through the Son of God and the renewal of the Holy Spirit (we have said before that this is to be called the liberty of grace, when our strength is made perfect in weakness, according to 2 Cor. 12:9); (4) after our glorification, when there will be no weakness, no flesh which struggles against the Spirit, but we shall be equal to the angels (Matt. 22:30). Yea, God will be all in all (1 Cor. 15:28). This is the "glorious liberty of the children of God" (Rom. 8:21).

From these points we derive a plain and simple answer. Regarding the first and fourth categories there is no dispute. But if, relative to the second category, the question is raised as to what the free will can of itself accomplish in the way of spiritual activities, by its own nature, of its own powers, and apart from the grace of renewal, we must answer correctly that it can do nothing, as we have shown above. For a dead nature does nothing. Likewise in regard to the second category, if one asks whether the free will of its own natural powers contributes any ability or activity toward conversion and renewal which can be called either a partial cause or by a name similar to that, we can truthfully answer that the will remains merely passive. And thus it has been said that Augustine did not want to call the first movement toward conversion cooperating grace, but rather operating grace.

When, therefore, one asks in regard to the third category whether there is actually any liberty belonging to the now liberated will, the Scripture answers very pointedly, "Where the Spirit of the Lord is, there is liberty" (2 Cor. 3:17). "If the Son shall make you free, ye shall be free indeed" (John 8:36); "Being then made free from sin, ye became the servants of righteousness" (Rom. 6:18). Thus it is manifest that in this state the will is not inactive. "For this purpose the Son of God was manifested, that he might destroy the works of the devil" (1 John 3:8), in order that he might free us from the bondage of sin (Rom. 6:18), and that he might quicken us from the dead (Eph. 2:5).

Augustine also uses this distinction in response to the statement of 2 Tim. 2:21 ("If a man therefore purge himself from these, he shall be a vessel unto honor, sanctified and meet for the master's use"), saying that the reason of the man who does not yet believe is one thing; that of the man enlightened and restored by grace is quite another.[4] And we must note that in the time of Augustine there were certain teachers who, because of the points in dispute against the Pelagians regarding the slavery and bondage of the human will, held that even after regeneration and even with the aid of the Holy Spirit, there was no freedom or action of the will now liberated. But the will received this renewal just as a stone or piece of wax receives a certain impression. On account of these disputations of the Enthusiasts Augustine wrote a special book,[5] just as before he had written against the Pelagians in regard to nature and grace.[6] Against the Enthusiasts he says, "When one does something according to God's command, this does not deprive him of his own will."[7] And later in the same work, "It is certain that we do the willing when we will something, but he who works in us to will causes us to be willing. Further, it is certain that we do the acting when we do something, but he causes us to act by giving his most

---

[4] *Hypognosticon* (or *Hypomnesticon*) 3:9.15; P.L. 45:1630A. This is not a quotation but a paraphrase.

[5] *De Gratia et Libero Arbitrio;* P.L. 44:881ff.

[6] *De Natura et Gratia;* P.L. 44:247ff.

[7] *De Grat. et Lib. Arb.* 2.4; P.L. 44:884B.

efficacious power to our will, as he says in Ezek. 36:27, 'I will put my spirit within you, and cause you to walk in my statutes, and ye shall keep my judgments and do them.' "⁸

We must diligently teach this doctrine of the liberty of the new creature: (1) in order that we may learn to know what and how great is the blessing of renewal; (2) "lest any man fail of the grace of God" (Heb. 12:15); (3) so that we do not grieve the Holy Spirit who wishes to help us. For thus Paul urges the Corinthians in 2 Cor. 6:1, "that ye receive not the grace of God in vain." But always we must add that this is not a full liberty, but his strength is made perfect in our weakness (2 Cor. 12:9).

Further, if someone asks whether in this state the will is purely passive or is active, Augustine gives a remarkable reply: "They will understand, if they are the children of God, that they are led by the Spirit of God, so that they do what should be done, and when they have done it, they thank him by whom they are led. For they are led in order that they may do something, not so that they may do nothing."⁹ Thus also Paul refers in 2 Cor. 13:3 to "Christ speaking in me."

In the second place, conversion or renewal is not such a change as is completed and finished instantaneously, in one moment, in all its parts. But it has its beginnings and its steps by which it is completed in great weakness. It must not be supposed that I should wait expectantly with a secure and listless will for conversion or renewal to take place according to the above-mentioned steps by the operation of the Holy Spirit, entirely without activity on my part. For it cannot be shown at what mathematical point the freed will begins to be active. But when prevenient grace, that is, the beginning of faith and conversion, is given to man, then straightway the struggle between flesh and Spirit begins, and it is manifest that this struggle does not occur without any activity of our will. For the Holy Spirit struggled against the flesh in Moses while he was yet alive in a different way than Michael struggled with the devil over the dead body of Moses (Jude 9). Likewise, in the first stages of renewal our desire is very uncertain, our assent frail, our obedience

---
⁸ *Ibid.* 16.32; P.L. 44:900D, 901A.
⁹ *De Corrept. et Grat.* 2.3; P.L. 44:918B.

wavering, and these gifts must increase. Further, they increase, in us, not in the manner of a tree trunk being transported by great force, or as lilies which grow without effort and without care, but they increase in us by effort, by struggles, by searching, by seeking, by strenuous battle, and all of this is not of ourselves but a gift of God. In Luke 19:13, giving his servants the talents, the master says, "Occupy till I come." He does not say, "Hide them in the ground" (Matt. 25:25). And Paul uses an intensely illustrative word in 2 Tim. 1:6, "I put thee in remembrance, that thou stir up[10] the gift of God, which is in thee."

What we have said regarding prevenient, preparatory, and oper-ating grace therefore has this meaning, that the earlier stages of conversion are not our own, but God through the Word and through divine leading precedes us by moving and impelling our will. More-over, after this divinely caused movement of the will has taken place, the human will does not keep itself purely passive, but moved and helped by the Holy Spirit it does not resist, but assents and becomes a co-worker[11] with God. A similar statement occurs in Augustine's writings: "God works in us so that what he wills, we will and do, nor does he permit any sluggishness to dwell in us. He has given us what we must exercise ourselves in and not neglect, so that we become co-workers with the grace of God, and if we see anything lacking in ourselves because of our own failures, we anxiously run to him who cleanses all our disease, and he orders us to pray, 'Lead us not into temptation.' "[12]

Furthermore, Augustine furnishes an excellent example of this in his own conversion, in which we are permitted to see a living ex-ample of this event,[13] showing how among the feeble sparks and small beginnings of prevenient grace the will is not sluggish but begins the struggle between the flesh and the Spirit. These struggles ought to be most evident to the individual observer, not from idle disputations or from examples about other people, but from the serious practice of personal repentance. But because many people

---

[10] Greek, ἀναζωπυρεῖν.

[11] Greek, συνεργός.

[12] *De Eccl. Dog.* 32; P.L. 42. This quotation is not to be found in Migne. See note 20, p. 23.

[13] Latin, *quaestionis.*

live without any practice of faith or prayer, many errors have arisen
regarding matters which are not understood. Thus it will be useful
to consider the example of Augustine's conversion.

We have already mentioned that Augustine, while reading Cicero's
Hortensius, by the powers of his free will had conceived a desire
for truth, but that, the Bible having begun to sicken him, he had embraced the Manichean heresy. But the beginning of his true conversion, because he was anticipated by God's grace, he describes
thus, in his *Confessions:* "I used to listen very attentively to Ambrose
as he disputed with the people, not with the purpose which I should
have had, but as one studying his eloquence. I stood apart, indifferent to his subject matter and despising it. But along with his
words which I loved, there came into my mind gradually matters
which I had been disregarding. For at first it began to seem to
me that the Catholic doctrine could be defended, although it did
not yet seem overwhelming in its force. But then I paid closer
attention to see if I could by the correct fundamentals convict the
Manicheans of error. Thus in a wavering manner I determined that
I must leave the Manicheans, and I decided gradually to become
a catechumen in the Catholic Church, until something definite
should manifest itself."[14] In the same work he writes: "And so I
eagerly took up the venerable pen of the Spirit of God, especially
the Apostle Paul, and thus those questions disappeared in which
Paul had formerly seemed to me to contradict himself and to dis-
agree with the testimony of the Law. I began to read, and I discovered that what I read in the Scripture was true; and I learned
this only by the help of grace; so that if anyone sees, let him not
glory in this, as if he had not received from grace both what he sees
and the fact that he sees at all."[15]

In the third place, the Spirit anticipates, moves, and impels the
will in conversion, not as in a general activity, by changing and up-
setting the plans of the wicked who do not consider any such things,
as has been mentioned previously, but rather through the Word of
the Gospel. However, this does not happen in such a way as to kill
the wicked by the Spirit of his mouth (2 Thess. 2:8, Is. 11:4) even

[14] *Conf.* 5:13-14. 23-25; P.L. 32:717B-718C.
[15] *Ibid.* 7:21.27; P.L. 32:747C.

if such a person does not hear, read, or think of the Word, but rather despises and persecutes it.

But "faith cometh by hearing" (Rom. 10:17). Therefore, the Spirit is efficacious through the Word of the Gospel as it is heard or considered, and prevenient grace takes its beginning from the Word.

It is correctly stated that there are three causes of good works: (1) the Word of God, (2) the Holy Spirit, (3) the will of man, if only this latter is correctly and properly understood.

For the human will does not cooperate in such a way as if of its own powers it aided spiritual activities, as if in a good character these three causes worked together, namely, natural impulses, teaching, and exercise. For this is a Pelagian opinion. But the human will is included among the causes of good works: (1) because it can resist the Holy Spirit (Acts 7:51) and destroy the work of God (Rom. 14:20). For Saul had the Word, and the good Spirit of God led him; that is, two of the causes were present with him. But because Saul set up a contrary act of his will in opposition, the Holy Spirit departed from him (1 Sam. 16:14). Thus also Jesus said, I wished to gather you through my Word, but "ye would not" (Matt. 22:37). (2) The human will is also included in this way, that the sons of God are led by the Holy Spirit, not so that they may believe or do good works in ignorance and unwillingness. In this manner Balaam blessed, and the ass spoke (Num. 22); Caiaphas prophesied (John 11:51). But grace makes willing men out of unwilling, because it causes them to be willing. "I delight in the law of God. . . . to will is present with me" (Rom. 7:22).[16]

Thus the human will indeed does cooperate in a good work, but not as a captive and dead will as it was of itself and by its own nature, as it is described in Eph. 2:1, but as a will freed and living through the Holy Spirit. Augustine therefore says correctly: It is certain that our will is required for this that we do good works, but we do not have this will of our own powers, but God works in us so that we are willing.[17] And in his work *On Admonition and Grace*

---

[16] Chemnitz also cites the following Scripture passages: 1 Cor. 9:17; 2 Cor. 8:11; 1 Pet. 5:2; Rom. 6:14; Philemon 14; Ps. 1:2; Ps. 54:6.

[17] *De Grat. et Lib. Arb.* 16:32; 17.33; P.L. 44:900D, 901D. This is a paraphrase of several passages.

he says, "Only by the Holy Spirit is the will of the regenerate kindled, so that they can do God's will because they are willing, and they are thus willing because God causes them to be willing."[18]

And finally, we should note that feeling and experience do not precede faith, but it must all come out of the Word. Therefore we must not dispute about experience in this way, "I do not *feel* this movement and impulse of the will with which the Holy Spirit must anticipate us, therefore I will not hear, or meditate, or seek, or struggle, or contend, or try." But rather when the mind hears and meditates upon the Word, sustains itself, and does not resist;[19] rather when it seriously contends, as we have seen in the case of Augustine, it is certain that then the Holy Spirit is moving, impelling, and aiding the will. Therefore one should seek, beg, contend. Sometimes indeed the heart plainly senses that which it grasps in the promise, but often, to be sure most often, it experiences that the Holy Spirit conceals his aid with groanings "which cannot be uttered" (Rom. 8:26). Thus you should not inquire whether you feel something, because his strength is made perfect in weakness; but by faith you must rest in God according to his promise, even though you feel nothing, yea even though you feel the very contrary. Augustine says, "If you are not drawn, pray that you may be drawn."[20]

And we must note that in Augustine's time there were those who wanted to teach that the man who did not feel the new emotions inspired within him by God should not be admonished but only prayed for. Augustine refuted this notion in a special treatise, *On Admonition and Grace*, saying that the Word by its teachings, exhortations, and admonitions was the very means by which the Holy Spirit anticipated the will.[21]

These observations contain many warnings, showing that when the refutations which Augustine brought against the Pelagians were

---

[18] *De Corrept. et Grat.* 12.38; P.L. 44:939D.

[19] By the phrase "does not resist" is meant conscious and wilful resistance. However, there might be very strong interior resistance out of subconscious sources. Augustine gives a very remarkable picture of his own interior conflict at the time of his conversion. Cf. *Confessiones* 8:5ff., esp. 5.18-29.

[20] *In Joannis Evangelium tractatus* 26.2; P.L. 35:1607C.

[21] *De Corrept. et Grat.* 2.3; P.L. 44:918A.

not correctly understood, other errors arose which he had to refute and thus more clearly explain his own position. From these remarks can be understood the question of the activities of the will, whether it keeps itself purely passive in conversion or whether it is merely sluggish in spiritual matters. . . .[22]

---

[22] Here are omitted Chapter VIII on the Manicheans, Enthusiasts, Pelagians and others who err in this doctrine and Chapter IX, refutations of errors.

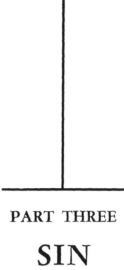

PART THREE

SIN

by

Martin Chemnitz

Introduction

Although all nations see the fearful confusion, crimes, and distressing calamities of the human race, and feel the burden of sin, yet only the church of God teaches both from whence it comes and what sin actually is; and it takes heed to the Word of God regarding divine wrath and present and eternal punishment. And although human wisdom teaches us to govern our behavior and disapproves and punishes works contrary to reason, yet it does not recognize that which is essential in the consideration of sin, namely, our guilt before God or the wrath of God.

The church, however, points to the wrath of God and teaches that sin is a much greater evil than human reason thinks. The church not only denounces external acts which are contrary to the Law of God or reason, as philosophy does; it also censures the origin and fruits (of sin), the inner darkness of the mind, the doubts regarding the will of God, the stubbornness of the heart against God's Law, and the turning of the human will away from God. It also exposes ignorance of and contempt for the Son of God. These are disastrous and atrocious evils, the magnitude of which cannot be expressed in words. Thus Christ says that the Holy Spirit shall "reprove the world of sin . . . because they believe not on me, of righteousness,

131

because I go to my Father, and of judgment because the prince of this world is already judged" (John 16:8-11).

This is a declaration entirely alien to civil judgments. Therefore, Christ says, I have reproved the world by the Holy Ghost, by the word of the Gospel, not by human and civil judgments; and I have reproved the world of the sin of despising the Son of God, because men spurn the Gospel and the blessings of Christ; nor do they approach God through faith in the Son of God, but remain in perpetual doubt and flee God, or with unspeakable boldness create false religions and idols.

In the next place, he says he will also reprove the world "of righteousness." For the wise think that righteousness is a kind of discipline or universal obedience, as they call it, to the laws. But the Gospel asserts that righteousness is something far different. Human discipline removes neither sin nor death; but the righteousness before God, by which God regards us as just, accepted, and heirs of eternal life, removes sin and death; as he says: This is my going to the Father, that is, my offering and satisfaction for you, and my going to the kingdom in which I am an everlasting mediator for you; I sanctify and renew you for life eternal, I take away your sin and death. This going to the Father and this kingdom of Christ justifies us.

In the third place, he adds, "of judgment." The world always stirs up and will stir up strong arguments against this doctrine, and condemns and will condemn the Son of God; and the devil arouses his instruments to blasphemous judgments and barbarity, such as the heresies, blasphemies, and savagery of every period demonstrate. But these ravings of the devil will not destroy the church. For the Holy Spirit will always strengthen the church, so that it may take a stand against these impious judgments; and the church will finally conquer because the devil has been condemned. Wherefore God confounds his judgments and ravings.

When therefore the Holy Spirit by the ministering voice of the Gospel reproves the world and shows whence sin comes and what it is and how great an evil it is, it is necessary to heed the teaching of the Holy Spirit. The benefits of Christ cannot be understood if the nature of sin is not known. Rather, for this very reason God, both by the voice of the ministry and by great disasters, proclaims it to his church, so that we might recognize his wrath against sin and seek refuge in his Son, our Mediator. Christ epitomizes the doctrine of the church thus: Go preaching repentance and remission of sins in my name (Luke 24:47). He includes also the knowledge of sin, that is, the terrors of conscience which arise from a knowledge of God's wrath against sin. Paul in his Epistle to the Romans deals particularly with this matter, in order that he may point out these three topics: what sin is, what the Law accomplishes, and what the grace of Christ is and does. Therefore we should know that the teaching of these doctrines must stand forth clear, pure, and explicit in the church.

Furthermore, it is customary in teaching to begin with definitions. Therefore a definition of sin must also first be drawn up. But I see that the writers who edited the questions in Lombard[1] have not given us one common definition suited to original sin and actual sin; perhaps because they did not think a common definition could be given. For actual sin convicts us on account of our deeds, while

---

[1] The "Sentence writers," Sententiarii.

The original meaning of "Sentences" was a topically organized collection of Bible verses and quotations from the Church Fathers. Such are the Sentences of Prosper of Aquitania, Isidor of Seville, and Tajus of Saragosa (7th century).

These selections developed into more independent and systematic summaries of the entire theology, such as the "books of sentences" of Anselm of Laon and William of Champeaux.

The really important book of Sentences was written by the "Master of Sentences," Peter Lombard (c. 1100-60) between 1148 and 1150. It became a standard theological textbook which was frequently interpreted and elaborated.

From the 13th century a more popular name for a systematic work of theology was *Summa*.

Chemnitz calls by the general name of "Sentence writers" the scholastics from the Dominican and Franciscan schools from 1200-1350, who had been too much under the influence of the semipelagian Cassianus (vide Loci I, p. 190). The first and oldest of these is Alexander of Hales (c. 1170-1245). Among other works he wrote glosses (commentaries) on the Sentences of Peter Lombard. Probably this is the work Chemnitz has in mind here.

While the attitude of Martin Luther and the Lutheran Orthodoxy to Peter Lombard can be called respectfully critical, their attitude is different toward his successors (e.g., Loci I. 11, 196, etc.). The main objections of the Lutheran theologians to them are the semipelagian tendencies in the interpretation of the freedom of the will, inadequate understanding of original sin, and a shallow optimism concerning human nature.

original sin holds us guilty both because of the fall of another and on account of our own uncleanness, which is born in us.

Next, they also devise this, that the Law of God condemns only actual sin, which is shown to be false from the seventh chapter of Romans.

The meaning of the term in Scripture is plain, namely, that sin properly signifies a certain guilt and condemnation by God, unless there is remission. This general description applies both to original sin and actual sin. But because mention is made only of a relationship (toward God), namely, that of guilt, the mind also seeks the reason for man's guilt. Therefore I use this definition and would have hoped that some definition existed in the church, composed by the wisdom of many learned and pious men: Sin is a defect, or inclination, or action opposing the Law of God, offending God, condemned by God, making men guilty of eternal wrath and worthy of eternal punishments, unless forgiveness is granted. In this definition there are terms, such as "defect" and "inclination," which pertain to original sin. "Action" includes all actual sins, both secret and open.

The term, "opposing the Law of God," is common (to both kinds of sin). For the Law not only speaks about actions, as the adversaries say, but also condemns the dark shadows, the defects, and the perverse inclination in man's nature, as Paul most emphatically contends in Rom. 7.

Then we add the characteristic marks of sin, namely, "condemned by God," "offending God," and "making men guilty of wrath and punishment." The church stresses especially these characteristic marks of sin. For reason understands that vicious deeds are against the Law of God, but it makes light of the wrath of God which follows. Therefore this characteristic of sin must be particularly considered whenever sin is named, in order that we may be able to understand something about the guilt and punishment of God.

Further, this definition is taken from these words, "Cursed is he who does not continue in all things which are written in the law." This defines sin as disobedience cursed by God. And disobedience must be understood not only as actual sin, but also as something universal which in man's nature is opposed to God. Moreover, there is the horrifying addition that sin is said to be cursed by God, that is, something which an angry God rejects and on account of which he casts out the creature into horrible punishments.

Paul's words in Romans also agree with this definition: "For the wrath of God is revealed from heaven against all ungodliness. . . ." In Romans 7 Paul says, "That sin by the commandment might become exceeding sinful," that is, the Law shows the wrath of God; and through this knowledge we understand that our impurity is not a small evil, but is something which renders us guilty, damned, cursed by God, accompanied by terrible punishments. Therefore, as often as "sin" is named, it must be distinguished in the church from the philosophical term "vice." For the church warns of judgment and of the wrath of God.

If anyone imagines that original sin is only a guilt on account of the fall of Adam, without any depravity in us, he is in error. Further, if anyone contends that we are born guilty both on account of Adam's fall and on account of the depravity born in us, I would not hinder him from adding this bit to the definition, that sin is both guilt on account of Adam's fall and a defect or inclination or action opposed to the Law of God. But I am not willing to diminish any part of this doctrine in the least degree. This stands firm, that on account of the fall of Adam there is lacking to his posterity that light which shines in a pure nature, and uprightness of will and heart. On account of these evils we are born guilty. Of this there is no doubt. . . .[2]

---

[2] Here is omitted a brief section on the relation between Original Sin and Free Will. "The two doctrines are closely related, so that one cannot be understood or explained without the other. If one doctrine is corrupted, violence is done to the other. From the free will are taken away the natural powers to begin or accomplish spiritual movements and actions. But why and how they are taken away is explained in the Locus on Original Sin."

I

A Comparison
of the Doctrines

It is useful to consider the differences between the teaching of the church regarding sin, and the disputations of the philosophers regarding vices. No nation is so savage and uncivilized that it does not know something about vices or sins and does not speak about them. All the books of the poets, the historians, the philosophers, and the lawyers are filled with such matters. Even wicked men cry out and accuse one another (Rom. 2:15). The knowledge of sin is so engrafted, as it were, in their very children that as soon as they begin to have some use of reason, they immediately know how to devise some kind of excuse to sin.

Because the church teaches about matters which are above and beyond the realm of reason (wherefore the doctrine of the church is called wisdom, *sapientia,* which the princes of this world do not understand), it follows of necessity that there is a difference between the doctrine of sin which the Holy Spirit reveals in the Word and the natural knowledge of the disputations of the philosophers regarding vices.

This difference between the kinds of sin is taken up for consideration in the first part of the Locus, and this for important reasons.

It is recognized that political laws punish only outward deeds and outward attempts. But the philosophers have proceeded further, and speak about how these very instincts are to be moderated and bridled. However, many even among ecclesiastical writers have restricted the doctrine of the church regarding sin to the boundaries of the philosophers. And when the doctrine of sin has been adulterated, there follows corruption of the article on the benefits of the Son of God in justification.

We see that the difference consists chiefly in these four points:[1]

(1) Regarding the efficient or working or originating cause (causa efficiens). Although philosophy is to be admired, yet it ignores the fact that even those who try to rule their instincts with some degree of diligence often have the most grievous lapses. Theology, however, sets forth and explains the cause of sin, namely, the depravity of nature and the tyranny of Satan working in the sons of disobedience (Eph. 2:2).

(2) Regarding the material cause, or the object. Philosophy teaches that vice is that which contends with the judgment of right reason. But Scripture tells us that there is another rule for recognizing and judging sins, namely, the norm of the divine Law as it is revealed in the written Word.

(3) Regarding the formal cause. Reason recognizes only those sins which consist either in the external actions or in the excess of wicked desires, that is, it understands the fruits of sin to some extent. But Scripture shows the root itself, that is, it charges the entire natural man with sin (Rom. 6:6, "the body of sin"; Col. 3:5, "the members which are upon the earth") which is called original sin. Further, the Holy Spirit charges with sin even the most praiseworthy works which are done on earth without faith and apart from Christ (John 16:8-9; Rom. 14:23; Heb. 11:6).

(4) Regarding the final cause, or consequences. Political laws speak of civil punishments. The philosophers also speak of the torments of conscience. Poets dream something about punishments after this life. But only the teaching of the church shows what is

---

[1] The distinction of four causes, frequent in the Scholastic and Orthodox texts is taken from Aristotle (especially from *Analytica Posteriora*).

most significant in a consideration of sin, namely, being guilty of the wrath of God, condemned to punishments both physical and eternal, unless there is forgiveness for the sake of Christ the Mediator. Thus it is said, "The wrath of God abideth on him" (John 3:36); "For which things' sake the wrath of God cometh" (Col. 3:6); "Tribulation and anguish upon every soul of man that doeth evil" (Rom. 2:9); and "their fire is not quenched, their worm dieth not" (Mark 9:44).

This comparison also illustrates the Locus on sin and shows with what attitude we must read the writings of many who write about sin only as philosophers.

II

The Classification of Sin[1]

The next section shows the distinction between original sin and actual sin. . . .

The sources from which this distinction is drawn are well known. To this pertains the entire fifth chapter of Romans. "Death," says Paul in v. 12, "reigned over all, because all have sinned." Likewise in v. 19, "For as by one man's disobedience many were made sinners." And he distinctly adds in v. 14, "Even those who had not sinned after the similitude of Adam's transgression," because it is beyond debate that it was an actual sin. Therefore, because not all have actual sins, and yet all are sinners, having sin, it therefore follows of necessity that there is another kind of sin than only actual sin.

James 1:15 says, "When lust hath conceived, it bringeth forth sin"; and Rom. 7:17 and 20, "Sin dwelling in me worked concupiscence." But it is plain that sin is one thing in Romans 7 and another in James 1.

Eph. 5:5 and Col. 3:6 teach that the wrath of God comes because of our walking in fornication, avarice, etc.; and Eph. 2:3 says, "We are by nature the children of wrath."

---

[1] Chapters II and III in Chemnitz are omitted. They deal with the words for "sin" in Scripture and with the definition of sin in the Fathers.

Furthermore, Scripture plainly distinguishes between a bad tree and its fruit, between the root and the branch, between flesh and works. Therefore Scripture does not speak about sin in general and without distinction; but as we have shown by clear and definite testimony, the Scripture teaches this distinction, that actual sin is one thing and original sin another.

I wanted to point out these things in general about sin and its names, its definition and its distinctions. We shall now come point by point and in detail to an explanation of the doctrine of original sin.

ORIGINAL SIN

Original sin is the lack of the original righteousness which ought to be present in us. This short and incomplete definition, however, requires greater elaboration. For it is necessary to inquire what the term "original righteousness" means. Therefore we must add that original righteousness was the acceptance of the human race before God and in man's very nature the light in his mind by which he could strongly give assent to the Word of God. Furthermore, it was the turning of the will toward God and the obedience of the heart in agreement with the judgment of the Law of God which had been engrafted into his mind.

That original righteousness embraced all of this can be understood from this statement: "Man was created in the image and likeness of God." Paul interprets it thus and teaches that the image of God was a mind which knew God and a will free, righteous and concurring with the Law of God, as he says in Eph. 4, "Man was created in righteousness and true holiness." True sanctification he calls all virtues directed by a true heart to this end, that obedience to God be shown forth, and that God be loved and honored. Therefore, after it has been determined what "original righteousness" means, then the opposing lack of it can also be defined.

Original sin is the lack of original righteousness, that is, there is in men born of the seed of man a loss of light in the mind, a turning away of the will from God, a stubbornness of the heart, so that they cannot obey the Law of God, following the fall of Adam. On account of this corruption they are born guilty and the sons of wrath; they are condemned by God unless there is forgiveness. If one wishes to add that men are born guilty on account of Adam's fall, I will not object. Furthermore, it has truly been the age-long opinion of the church, of the prophets, apostles, and ancient writers, that original sin is not only an imputation but also in the very nature of man a blindness and a depravity, as I have said. . . .

III

Regarding Testimonies or Proof Passages[1]

All the passages which could be referred to this subject have not been gathered, but certain more select ones are cited and so explained that one may see the true and logical reason for considering these passages in other places. (1) We shall so seek the natural meaning of the testimonies of Scripture that we may show how they can be used for the confirmation of the true doctrine and the refutation of all corruptions. (2) Since often the entire doctrine of a Locus, as it applies to its individual parts, cannot be gathered out of one single testimony, that which appears either briefly or incompletely in one passage will be explained more clearly in another. (3) We will show how a comparison of the testimonies of the Old and New Testaments is to be made.

The other passages which deal with this subject and shed some light upon it can be taken from the Locus on the Free Will, where we have arranged them in the order which can well be accommodated to this subject: (1) How the Holy Spirit describes the cor-

---

[1] This is Chapter III in Chemnitz. Omitted are Chapters I and II on names and definitions of original sin.

ruption of the mind. (2) How he describes the depravity of the will. (3) The disobedience of all human powers. (4) What the Holy Spirit in renewal takes away from the mind and heart and what gifts He bestows upon the new man.

In certain passages of Scripture mention is made in passing of a certain article of doctrine; in other passages, however, it is so clearly treated and established that there in its own setting it has its *sedes* or basis.

There is a proper basis for the doctrine of original sin in the fifth chapter of Romans, where the apostle among other things writes: "By one man sin entered into the world, and death by sin, and so death passed upon all men, for that all have sinned" (Rom. 5:12). And it is common practice that such passages of Scripture, before any others, are torn apart and distorted. Therefore, I will cite some of the controversies of antiquity regarding this verse, so that we may teach and retain more correctly the true explanation of the passage.

There is a grammatical question which greatly bothered Augustine and other good men. ἐφ' ᾧ in the Latin translation is *in quo*, "in which." Augustine tortured himself a long time as to its meaning. Because there are two antecedents ("through man sin entered"), he tried at first to explain it thus: "In which sin all have sinned," as it afterwards is said, "from one offense upon all. . . ." But the grammar does not permit this explanation. Therefore, he suggested another: "In whom (in quo), namely, in the first man," and he constructed out of this the true, good, and pious teaching which Anselm later developed, namely, that God bestowed upon Adam his image, that is, those gifts with which he wished to adorn the whole human race, on this condition, that if he would guard these gifts, he would pass them on to his entire posterity. But if he lost or corrupted them, it would come to pass that he would beget sons in his own image or likeness (Gen. 5:3). Thus we have all sinned in Adam and lost the image and glory of God. This is the true doctrine. . . .

But it is safer and better to seek the true interpretation from the grammar. For it is plain that ἐφ' ᾧ to the Greeks indicated the return to the cause.[2] Luther translates it *dieweil*, because.

---

[2] Chemnitz accepts the teaching of Augustine but is not in full accord with his linguistic interpretation of ἐφ' ᾧ. He has the same view as most of our

The second question was whether sin indicates an action. Because Paul says, "All have sinned," it must be understood of actual sins.

Reply: Among the Hebrews words often meant, not so much an act, as an attitude, and the rule is verified by grammatical examples. But if one asks whether in that quotation of Paul the word "sin" indicates an act or an attitude, there is very good reason to take the meaning from the context. For after Paul uses the term "They have sinned," he explains it by saying, "They have been made sinners," and says they have not sinned "after the similitude of Adam's transgression." And Adam sinned by act. Therefore, "to sin" in that passage of Paul does not mean a simple act. These are true and correct conclusions. Thus in the German translation it is rendered, "Sie sind Sünder," "they are sinners."

The meaning of this passage (Rom. 5:12) can very simply be taught and grasped if we divide it into parts.

(1) We see first the working cause *(causa efficiens)* of original sin, namely, the first man of his own free will turning himself away from God.

(2) We see the subject, which not only clung to Adam, but also passes into the world, that is, to all men who come into this world.

(3) The condition of the guilty man is described, which consists not only in bodily death, but in the reign of death, the judgment of condemnation, etc. Those are the words of Paul. For in that passage he makes the connection: Wherever death is, there of necessity is sin. But death rules in infants. Therefore it follows that they have sin. They do not have it in the likeness of Adam's sin. Therefore they have original sin.

(4) The guilt must not be understood as only on account of another's (i.e. Adam's) sin, without any guilt of one's own. Paul affirms that the world is guilty from the one sin of the first man; and because all have sinned, they have all become sinners.

---

contemporary New Testament exegetes. Such an interpretation has this advantage that man has not only sinned in the past "in Adam" as a part of humanity, but he is individually a sinner now, a sinful being both in his heart and in his life.

(5) What kind of sin it is he points out when he says that they also have original sin who have not sinned by an act, as Adam did.

(6) He describes the way in which original sin is propagated: "Through one man," he says. And because posterity is reckoned through men, carnal propagation is understood, as Mal. 2:15 says, "He made one, and what did the one seek except the seed of God?" and Acts 17:26, "And he hath made of one blood all nations of men."

In the next place, we cite proof passages from Romans 7 and 8 and Ephesians 2. Notice that the matters which are found in Rom. 5 in a brief and unclear way are in these passages more fully and clearly illustrated. For Paul had previously stated what original sin is ("who had not sinned after the similitude of Adam's transgression"). But since this is somewhat too general, he takes up for fuller explanation in Romans 7 and 8 that part of the subject which deals with the adult regenerate man. For where the Spirit lusts against the flesh, original sin can be more clearly seen. Thus the matter is stated negatively *(privative)*: "How to perform that which is good I find not; for the good that I would, I do not" (Rom. 7:18-19); "The carnal mind is not subject to the Law of God" (Rom. 8:7); and positively: "I see another law in my members warring against the law of my mind" (Rom. 7:23).

The witness of Eph. 2:3 is one of the best. For it sheds light on what Romans 5 says in a brief and unclear way regarding the propagation of original sin; namely, that the original contagion is contracted, not by imitation, but by our nature which is propagated by human birth. For he says, "We were by nature the children of wrath," that is, we are born with sin in the very moment of our conception, when we receive a human nature; together with our human nature is born in us such a weakness or frailty of nature that we because of this are the children of wrath.[3] . . .

---

[3] Chemnitz continues: "The term φύσει is used for those things which are present by nature and are innate, as opposed to θέσει, custom, habit, imitation. Note Aristotle's *Ethics* bk. 2, "None of the moral virtues, such as knowledge, occurs by nature. . . ." "The gentiles do by nature, φύσει, the things contained in the law" (Rom. 2:14). "We are Jews by nature, φύσει, born Jews, *geborne Jüden*, not gentiles" (Gal. 2:15). Erasmus observed that Paul by this comparison shows what nature is. For he says, "By grace are ye saved," "by nature the children of wrath." That is, nature is whatever is in man without,

Finally we are making a comparison of Old Testament and New Testament proofs. Especially significant is the statement of Psalm 51, and it most beautifully illustrates the statement of Eph. 2:3 that "we are by nature ($\phi\acute{v}\sigma\epsilon\iota$) the children of wrath." For David, as he laments his sin of murder and adultery, progresses in his knowledge of sin to the point where he not only says that he is a sinner and guilty because of his crime, but he goes further. Infants themselves have sin, and that not only when they are born and come into the light. The very mass from which man at his conception begins to be formed is totally corrupt with sin; while he is carried in the womb, while he is still being formed, he has sin; so that his mother with her own blood nourishes this sinner while still in her womb, even before she has brought forth her child. Thus Luther explains this passage. In this connection the passage in Job 14:4 is important, "Who will cleanse that which is conceived by unclean seed?"[4]

These passages illustrate the three parts of the doctrine, namely, (1) that adults, even the regenerate, have defects and depraved inclinations, that is, original sin; (2) that even infants themselves, who are not yet able to sin in the likeness of Adam's sin, by nature are born sinners and the children of wrath; (3) that the very unformed substance of human nature, while it is being conceived and is still in the womb, is full of sin and is a mass of perdition.

The passages of Moses in Gen. 6:5 and 8:21 are accurately and learnedly explained by Luther. . . . Gen. 8:21 speaks more properly

---

before, besides grace, and which has so contaminated him that he is worthy of the wrath of God. Let us look at the entire section in Paul. For he not only speaks about our guilt, as if nature, namely, that which has been created by God, is so evil; but he also shows what there is in our nature that makes us the children of wrath, namely, trespasses, sins, death, the tyranny of the devil, the lusts of the flesh, wilful thoughts, as can be seen in Eph. 2:1-3. And thus the subject of original sin is even more fully expounded. Rom. 5:12 says that sin came into the world and upon all men. Rom. 7:18, 23-25 and 8:8-10 teach that sin is in the flesh, the body, the members; and Eph. 2:3 shows that it is in the mind, the will, and in our nature. Further, Paul says, "And we also, namely, the Jews." For he had said in Rom. 11:16, "If the root be holy, so are the branches." Therefore, lest it be thought that the Jews were by nature holy, he says, "And we Jews also are the children of wrath, even as the others." But holiness (Rom. 11:16 and 1 Cor. 7:14) pertains to the grace of adoption and the promise, so that one is grafted into the church (Acts 2:39).

[4] Chemnitz's own translation.

of original sin than does Gen. 6, which however can correctly be accommodated to this doctrine. . . . (1) For it is certain that Gen. 8:21 is speaking, not of the ungodly people who lived before the flood, but of the whole human race. (2) There were not at that time any other men on earth than Noah the righteous with his family, and yet even of them he says, "The imagination of the thoughts of the human heart is corrupt."[5] (3) He clearly shows that the human heart is corrupted by bad examples and that it contracts wickedness by imitation, but from "youth," as that word has been explained before. (4) He speaks not only of the thought, but of the imagination of man's heart. For the word *yasar* means "to form" something, such as figures from clay, and secondly, "to conceive" something with the mind.

Three interpretations are shown here, not to make one's opinion confused, but rather to illustrate the matter more clearly. (1) The imagination of the heart is the corrupt mass (Chemnitz reads Ps. 103:14: "He knows our imagination, *figmentum*, since we are dust"). (2) Often in Scripture we join "imagination" with "thoughts." This seems to point to first impulses and instincts, since the thoughts are not yet clarified by deliberation. Therefore, he says, not only the thoughts, but the very imagination is evil. (3) Luther explains it thus: The thoughts which are devised with the most careful deliberation and greatest wisdom are still evil. . . .

Finally, we must say a few things regarding the proof text in Jer. 17:9, so that the corruption may be refuted and the right emphasis put where it belongs. Some argue that the prophet was speaking only about manifest wickedness and about men of open impiety. But the context of the prophet's sermon plainly shows the reason for Jeremiah's complaint. For he says in v. 5, "Cursed be the man that trusteth in man," and in v. 7, "And blessed is the man that trusteth in the Lord." But then he adds in v. 9-10, that so corrupt and unsearchable is man's heart that it does not wish to appear not to trust in God; but God, he says, "searches the heart, and tries the reins." And lest anyone think the prophet by this statement is touching only hypocrites, he includes himself. For he adds in v. 14,

---

[5] Chemnitz's own translation.

"Heal me, Lord, and I shall be healed; save me, and I shall be saved." Thus the prophet shows by this one important statement how corrupt the best part of man is, namely, the heart. And this is the case not only with the godless and hypocrites, but with the regenerate themselves, that is, with all men as they are by nature. . . .

IV

Regarding Questions
of Method

Having determined the true doctrine of original sin and having established its Biblical basis, we may now turn to the way in which, as with other doctrines, we may apply logical research methods correctly and purposefully toward a fuller statement of the doctrine. For when the causes and effects have been set up in order, then the matters themselves unfold in parts, and we can present in context each individual aspect of the matter for careful investigation. For truth can be more easily put in opposition to error, if the argument is carried on methodically, accurately, and judiciously.

Therefore the first question concerns the efficient or working cause. When we have considered the arguments, the explanation will be easier. The Manicheans blasphemously claim that God is the efficient cause of original sin. He created the first sin and to this day creates it in individuals. It is correctly said that the devil and the will of man are the efficient cause of sin. The Pelagians sophistically reject this. They affirm that the will of each individual is so much the efficient cause of every sin that Adam was a cause only in an accidental way, that is, by showing a bad example, which his posterity imitated and thus by its own will also contracted sin. Therefore

149

we must explain more lucidly and distinctly what the efficient cause of original sin is.

The will of Adam and Eve was the cause of the first fall, because of their own free will they turned themselves from the will of God. This same human will is the efficient cause of original sin in all men, but for a different reason, namely, not because of example and imitation, as Pelagius held, but because our first parents deserved both for themselves and for their posterity the corruption of nature which followed the fall.

Furthermore, to the efficient cause pertains the important question whether the soul exists by human reproduction. This question was under discussion in Luther's last disputation. The point is that just as in reproduction the flesh of the child is essentially derived from the seed of the father, so also the soul of the child in essence is derived from the soul of the father; just as a stalk brings forth the ear from the seed, the beard, the ear, etc., or as a candle is lit from another candle.

Now another question, deeper and more difficult, arises out of the controversies of the ancients, who had as yet not argued pointedly, because the Pelagian controversy had not yet arisen. Is the body alone transmitted by procreation, and not the soul? The Pelagians argued thus: If original sin is produced by carnal propagation; if the soul, however, is not transmitted, but only the body, then the soul is free and untainted with original sin.

Many fine statements of Augustine about this question are extant, a few of which could well be committed to memory. To Jerome he says, "Regarding the soul I firmly hold this: (1) it is a created thing, not part of the essence of God; (2) it is not corporeal; (3) it inherits the original fall; (4) it fell into sin without any guilt on God's part; (5) it cannot be freed from original sin except by the grace of Christ, and no soul in the human race can be liberated except through Christ; (6) the souls which leave this world without being born again are in punishment. I hold firmly to these points. But it is a more difficult question to determine how, when, and from whence the soul becomes sinful."[1] . . .

About the time of Lombard, the Romanists made it an article of

---

[1] Ep. 116:1:3, 4; P.L. 33 p. 721.

faith, that souls do not come into existence by reproduction but that they are infused by creation and created by infusion. And this rash pronouncement on an obscure and futile question was the main cause, or certainly one of the main causes, for the corruption of the doctrine of original sin. For they imagine that original sin inheres in the flesh, because it is by transmission, and that the soul by union with the flesh is caused to sin only in those lusts which occur through the organs of the body. But in the higher powers, which are not organic, they say that the soul is free from original sin, because it is created by God so good that it cannot be led into sin by the body in respect to those higher powers. And these notions have brought with them the ruin of some very important articles of faith.

Therefore Luther in his discussion concluded that he wished to say nothing publicly about this question, but privately among his own followers he said that he held to traducianism. Further, he said that the Romanists were very blameworthy because in an obscure matter, without any clear Scripture passages and with rash boldness, they had established an article of faith which overturned the pure doctrine of original sin.

The second question concerns the subject of sin, and where it is located. This question is one of those which has come into controversy in our day, and its explanation is absolutely necessary for maintaining the correct understanding of the doctrine of this article.

The Romanists say there is a weakness in the body and in that power of the soul which is in touch with the body, namely, sensuality. But the higher powers of the soul, they claim, are pure in themselves, so that they are only tempted and attacked by sensuality, but sometimes they can actually tear themselves away from sensuality and even fight back. These ideas are pleasing to philosophers, because they agree with the principles of physical philosophy.

Lombard first posed this question, whether original sin is in the soul or in the body. And because of the question of traducianism he says that original sin properly and in a primary sense is in the body, but in a secondary sense in the soul, because it is led into sin by union with the sinful flesh. And even Lombard did not say that the higher powers were immune to original sin, but the later scholastics imagined this. For a small error in the beginning grows as it progresses.

Augustine, however, does not speak this way, but says that original sin is in man, in his nature, in the human mass. He clearly points out that the seat of sin is in the soul, and for this reason he rejects the question about the origin of the soul, as we have indicated.

Anselm also clearly says that since there is a lack of righteousness, it necessarily is in the soul, because righteousness is in the most important and highest powers of the soul. And the condition of righteousness and its opposite, the loss of righteousness, pertain to the same subject. This argument moves even the scholastics. That which has the faculty of virtue, grace, vice, or sin properly cannot be in the body but in the soul. Since, therefore, original evil is not sin figuratively but essentially, therefore, of necessity, its subject is in the soul.

The passages from Scripture which point out the subject of original sin have been cited previously in this and the preceding Locus. Relevant also are the passages regarding the names given to it. For they are eloquently called "man," "flesh," "the body," "the member," "the eyes" (1 John 2:16), "the tongue" (James 3:5), "the feet," "the throat," "the lips" (Rom. 3:13 and 15); and I Pet. 1:22 speaks of "souls" and "purified souls." Hence we find the terms "spiritual man," "the mind," "the thoughts," "the heart," "the will," "the desires."

Thus the subject of original sin is the entire true man in body and soul, in individual members as well as powers. Furthermore, most of these are called the powers of the soul, because in them especially original sin is sensed. Moreover, we must consider what it is which deceived the Sentence-writers, so that they imagine the mind and higher faculties to be so free of the corruption of original sin that by their own natural powers they can struggle against the evil which is inherent in sensuality. Paul uses the terms "flesh," "body," "members," etc., and the scholastics understood this to mean that body and flesh are different from the soul, while actually it is certain that by this expression of Scripture the whole unregenerate man is indicated, with body and soul and all his powers, opposed to the Spirit (John 3:6, "That which is born of the flesh is flesh").

Rom. 8:6-7 attributes it to the mind, φρόνημα. Gal. 5:20-21 includes among the works of the flesh heresies, hatreds, envy. And in 1 Cor. 2:14 man is called unspiritual. So it is in Rom. 7:23, "The law in my members warring against the law of my mind"; in v. 25, "With the mind I myself serve the law of God, but with the flesh the law of sin"; in Jas. 4:1, "Lust wars in your members against the soul."[2]

The Scholastics understood the term "mind" as referring to the higher powers of the unregenerate soul, although it is certain in each case that Paul is speaking about the regenerate man whose heart is made pure, as in Eph. 4:23: "Be renewed in the spirit of your mind"; also in Rom. 12:2 and Col. 2:12. And Paul also pictures the mind of unregenerate man as most dark (Eph. 4:18. Note also the other passages mentioned under the free will).

Furthermore, they have received encouragement in their error from Augustine, who in disputing about original sin often exemplifies it by that which is most crass and thus best known to all, namely, lust for bodily pleasure and sexual desire. The Scholastics understand this as if it were the only ground and power of original sin, while they openly reject so many clear testimonies from Scripture. For Paul, in explaining how the flesh lusts against the Spirit, names not only sexual lust, but also heresies. Likewise, original righteousness, the lack of which is concupiscence, did not consist only of continence and chastity, and the like. And when original sin is cleansed, not only is the libido restrained, but men are renewed with newness of mind according to the promise of God, "I will give a new heart that ye may walk in my precepts."[3,4]

---

[2] Chemnitz's own translation.
[3] From Ez. 36:26, 27, abridged.
[4] Chemnitz continues: "The third question concerns the form and matter of original sin. . . . There is a two-fold form of original sin, as considered from the standpoint of quality and of consequence. In Baptism the form of consequence is removed by full forgiveness. The form of quality begins in Baptism to be removed and cleansed, but it is not entirely removed. For that the disease and defects remain, that is, the form of quality, is plain from passages of Scripture.
The fourth question regarding the effects of original sin is simple: only let Augustine's distinction be observed: "The particular effects of original sin are punishments. At the same time certain penalties are also sins."

V

The Chief Perversions
of the Doctrine

It is profitable to examine the principal perversions by which the true teaching of this doctrine is either obscured or corrupted. When and by whom have these perversions been spread abroad? And what sound teachers has God raised up against these perversions to rekindle the light of the true teaching? We shall examine, as if upon a placard, the zealous efforts of the enemy, who delights in imposing the tares upon the good seed while men are sleeping. This he does not only once, but many times and by various devices. Our study should then make us more diligent to learn and more faithful to guard a sound doctrine of original sin. For since this doctrine is fundamental, its overthrow would surely cause the corruption of the doctrines of free will, of justification, of the Law, and of the gifts of the Holy Spirit.

Philosophers outside the church have often handed down conflicting opinions concerning the causes of sin because they were entirely ignorant of this doctrine. Julian, writing against Augustine,[1] amasses many opinions from the principal philosophers concerning

---

[1] *Ad Turbantium,* a four-volume work against Augustine's doctrine of original sin and especially against Augustine's *De Nuptiis et Concupiscentia.*

the superiority and worth of human nature. But Augustine answers briefly: "What wisdom have those been able to lay down in this matter, who have neither known nor read this: 'Through one man sin entered into the world'?"[2] Cicero writes in the *Tusculan Disputations:* "There are innate seeds of virtue in our spirits; if these were permitted to mature, they would lead us through to a blessed life. However, as soon as we have been brought to the light of day and acknowledged, we move about continually in every corruption and in the consummate perversity of opinions, so that we seem almost to have sucked in error with the nurse's milk. But when we have been returned to our parents or delivered to teachers, then we are imbued with such various errors that truth yields to emptiness and nature itself to the established opinion."[3]

Elsewhere he argues that certain sparks of virtue have been implanted in nature, which, if stirred up by study and practice, will grow by divine help into an established habit. In a certain manner these things are true concerning external discipline. Seneca writes: "You err if you think that vices are born with us; they have entered into us."[4]

Aristotle argues that neither virtue nor vice is generated by nature. It is no wonder that the philosophers have produced fantasies in this matter: The corruption of nature was unknown to reason, because reason itself was so obscured by this general corruption that it could not recognize it. Nevertheless they saw something in their darkness, namely, that a most excellent creature is not hurled before other creatures into such great calamities without a cause.

Augustine cites the *Hortensius* of Cicero to show that disasters in human life are the results of divine judgment: "For seers who have had visions of the origins of things sacred have maintained that we are born to undergo punishment for misdeeds committed in a former life. We find a statement in Aristotle that we are afflicted with a punishment like one given to some men who fell into the hands of Etruscan robbers and were slaughtered with exquisite

---

[2] *C. Jul.* 4:15.77; P.L. 44:778AB.

[3] *Tusculanae Disputationes* 3:1.2.

[4] *Epistola* 96.

cruelty. Their bodies were neatly piled up, the living with the dead. So our souls are united with our bodies just as the living were joined together with the dead."[5] I write down this opinion more fully because Origen liked the same thought pattern: All souls were created in the beginning simultaneously, and those which sinned in that former age were thrust down on earth into bodies, etc. Scholastics have defended the latter opinion, that the soul is defiled by the body.

Nevertheless it is helpful to consider the opinions of the philosophers because they demonstrate to us the judgment of reason in the things which can be properly illuminated only by divine revelation. The Jews, too, have their peculiar interpretation of evil. And even among the Pharisees this doctrine did not exist in a pure form. For in John 9:34 they say of the one born blind, "Thou wast altogether born in sins." It follows that they had judged concerning others that they were not wholly born in sins. But I shall speak only concerning those disputes which have arisen within the church regarding this doctrine.

I.   Here belong first the things mentioned in the preceding Locus concerning the contentions of the Manicheans.[6] There were three principal errors in their doctrine of original sin.

(1)   They erred regarding the originating cause.[7] They did not distinguish between nature itself, which is both good and the work of God, and the corruption of nature, which passed upon all through one man. Instead they taught that sin had not entered the world

---

[5] *C. Jul.* 4:15.78; P.L. 44:778C.

[6] This sect was founded by the prophet Mani or Manicheus (c. 216-277) in Persia. It is not a Christian heresy but an independent, syncretistic religion, composed of Christian, Zoroastrian, Gnostic, and Buddhist elements. It combines the belief in the eternal conflict of the forces of Good or Light and Evil or Darkness with an extreme asceticism. During the 3rd and 4th centuries it spread from the East into Egypt, Rome, and Africa; and it even for a time won the Church Father Augustine to its ranks.

[7] Literally, the "efficient cause." Aristotle held that there are four varieties of causes present in any thing or process: the "material cause" (that of which a thing is composed); the "formal cause" (the essence of a thing, the pattern which is to be embodied in the thing); the "efficient cause" (the energy or motivating force which brings a thing into being); and the "final cause" (the end or purpose for which the thing exists).

through one man, but was in the beginning created by a certain evil deity, and that those now being born do not contract sin by carnal propagation, but sin itself in man is the work of a creating deity.

(2) They held further that only certain men, namely the earthy, were born in sin, but that others were born pure of all vice, since they were of the nature of light.

(3) They taught that some men had been so completely born in sin that they could not even be set free through Christ. These they called unreleased.[8] But among their so-called elect they imagined that no remnants of sin were left after cleansing and liberation (as they called it) in this life, but that even here below such remnants were completely removed from the nature of man. The fathers were violently opposed to these absurd speculations.

II. Secondly, since they undertook to refute only the Manicheans (the Pelagian controversy had not yet begun), the Fathers wrote treatises on the doctrine of original sin which were less than thorough. Origen, whose doctrines were taught in the well-known School of Alexandria, neither employed the title "Original Sin" nor treated the matter anywhere directly and expressly.

Basil said (just as Julian objected to Augustine) that sin could easily be separated from human nature so that no signs of evil should remain.[9]

Chrysostom on Ephesians 1 declares, "From nature herself we have seeds of virtue, but malice is contrary to nature."[10] Concerning Romans 7 he says, "Passions in themselves are not sin, but their unbridled immodesties are; so concupiscence is not sin, but adultery is."[11]

Julian cites an opinion of Chrysostom: "We baptize infants although they have no sins."[12]

Various questionable statements by the Fathers have been noted above. Even though on occasion they felt and spoke correctly con-

---

[8] Greek, ἄλυτος.
[9] *C. Jul.* 1:5.16; 650D-651A. The book of Basil to which Augustine refers is not extant; it is known only from Augustine's mention of it in the above work.
[10] *Homilia in Epistolam ad Ephesios* 2.3; P.G. 62:20B.
[11] *Homilia in Epistolam ad Romanos* 13.1; P.G. 60:508C.
[12] Referred to by Augustine in *C. Jul.* 1:6.22; P.L. 44:655C.

cerning original sin, in public they concealed this teaching as though it were a mystery. They apparently felt that it would foster security and carelessness in men. But by their unfortunate expressions and false praise of the goodness of nature not only was this doctrine obscured, but the seeds of Pelagianism were scattered abroad. The light of the true doctrine would at length have been altogether extinguished had not God, through the Pelagian controversy, aroused sound and faithful teachers. By diligent study of the truth of this question in the fountain of Scripture itself, these men set aside the more questionable sayings of the Fathers, and called for a return to the true form of doctrine, as Paul calls it.

Augustine modestly excuses such quotations from the Fathers. He reminds that the Pelagian controversy had not yet begun, so that the Fathers could speak with great confidence and freedom.

Around that time a certain writing was circulated under the name of Clement of Rome,[13] who had heard Peter and was a companion of Paul. In this document, under the name of Peter, there were many prodigious fables and discussions concerning free will which clearly contradict canonical Scripture. These properly belong to the preceding Locus. However, it can profitably be said here that the most ancient writers of the church neither explained adequately the doctrine of original sin and free will, nor spoke with sufficient exactness and fullness according to the command of the Holy Spirit concerning these articles. The reason was that their dealings were chiefly with pagans who ridiculed, rejected, and persecuted the doctrines of the church as absurdities, when they measured them by the judgment of reason. Justin, Clement, and others therefore thought that the pagans would be less unfriendly if those things which seemed most abhorrent in Scripture were toned down. Thus they accommodated Scripture to the reasoned opinions of the philosophers, thinking that the resulting doctrine of the church would be more plausible to the pagans, so that more of them could be won for the church. But the confusion which followed from this in the doctrine of the church showed itself clearly even in the time of Augustine.

---

[13] This remark does not apply to the letters of Clement to the Corinthians (I and II), but to the Pseudo-Clementine literature (the *Homilies* and the *Recognitions*).

III.   Thirdly, in Augustine's day the Pelagian heresy arose, which did not merely shake certain parts of the doctrine of original sin, but abolished and denied it entirely. In order that the antithesis might be clearer, we shall point out the principal errors of the Pelagians which are condemned.

(1)   They eliminated the true and necessary distinction between original and actual sin, teaching that nothing is sin except what is committed by the action of one's own will.

(2)   They denied the material aspect[14] of original sin, by supposing that infants have no depravity in their souls, nor any sinful defect prior to the action of their own wills. So Pelagius praised the soundness and purity of nature. Augustine thus repeats the words of Pelagius: "None of those good or evil things for which we are either praiseworthy or reprehensible are born with us but done by us; for we are born not fully developed but with the capacity for either kind of conduct. Thus we are procreated without virtue and without vice, and before the action of our own will, that alone is in man which God placed there."[15] Likewise, Augustine records the words of Celestius: "Sin is not born with man, but is afterwards committed by man, for it is obviously not a fault of nature, but of the will."[16]

(3)   They also took away the formal aspect[17] of original sin, i.e., its guilt. For they said that the death of the body is not the punishment for sin. The body of Adam was in the beginning created, they said, so that he would die, not as the penalty for guilt, but from the necessity of nature, which is composed of conflicting qualities and must finally be resolved into its original elements. "To dust shalt thou return because dust thou art" (Gen. 3:19). But they understood Romans 5 to refer only to the second death, which would reign only in those who had sinned by action of their own will.

[14] Literally, *materiale* (matter). In Scholastic usage, this term applies to the concrete content or stuff out of which a thing is formed. On the other hand, *formale* (form) refers to the formative factor itself. Thomas Aquinas considers man's sensual or biological nature as *materiale* (Cf. *S. Th.* II-II: q. 59. a.3). and man's rational nature as *formale* (Cf. *Ibid.* I: q. 85. a.7).

[15] *De Grat. Chr. et de Pecc. Orig.* 2:13.14; P.L. 44:391D.

[16] *Ibid.* 2:6.6; P.L. 44:388C.

[17] Literally, *formale*. See note 14, page 10.

However, lest they seem to deny entirely the grace of Baptism in infants, they said: the unbaptized infants are not in damnation, for they have no sin, no cause for damnation. Neither are they in the kingdom of heaven, because they lack the grace of Baptism. Therefore the Pelagians contrived a certain third place, where infants would indeed not have that supernatural bliss, but would be happily in the state of Adam before the fall.

Augustine says, "Indeed they promise them something outside of the kingdom of God, and yet a certain eternal and blessed life."[18] Again, "They say that infants are to be baptized, not that they may be freed from the bonds of sin and damnation, but that they may be transferred from a good place to a better."[19]

(4)   They taught that the descendants of Adam were stained by sin; not by propagation, but only by example, by imitation, by circumstance. Further, they maintained that Adam by his fall hurt only himself as far as the corruption of nature and penalties are concerned, and that his posterity was in turn harmed only by the bad example.

(5)   They imagined that the regenerate after Baptism could be cleansed so that no traces of sin would remain, barring actual offenses. Whatever movements are naturally present in the mind, in the will, and in the heart of those reborn, are good in themselves and created by God. Man could be perfect and without any sin in this life if he abstained from outward sins.

(6)   Augustine everywhere strongly pressed the argument concerning the efficacy of Baptism. For it was always conferred upon children in the church. It was used from the times of the apostles, and was always given for the remission of sins. Therefore infants must have sins. In the resolving of this argument the Pelagians began to look for different ways of escape. So they spoke like this: Infants are born without sin; thus there is no vice or corruption in their nature which renders them children of wrath. But as soon as they are born they commit certain actual sins of their own by crying, squalling, and other acts of that age. Because of those acts they become subject to the wrath of God, though they are not so by

---

[18] *De Haeresibus ad Quodvultdeum* 88; P.L. 42:48D.
[19] *Ibid.* 88; P.L. 42:48D.

nature. Augustine says that this opinion is refuted by the evidence itself, and adds: "Let everything prove itself by its own evidence. Nowhere have I found the matter stated more clearly than I have stated it here."[20]

There is, however, no doubt, as Solomon tells us, concerning the natural action of believers. Eccles. 9:6 says, "Eat and drink in happiness because your deeds please God." But in unregenerated infants the natural urges displease God, not because of actual sin which requires an action of the will, but because the corrupted nature is subject to the wrath of God. To this opinion Augustine says, "Who recalls for me the sins of my infancy? For in thy sight, no one is free from sin, not even an infant who has lived but one day upon earth. In what ways therefore did I sin in that time? Was it not because I wept with longing for my mother's breasts? . . . Was I not wrong in seeking by crying those things which would be harmful for me, being fiercely indignant at those who bore me, and lashing out insistently to harm them for not obeying me? Thus the innocence of the child is to be found in the weakness of its body, but not in its soul. I have observed a child to be jealous, though it could not yet speak; it was pale with bitterness as it watched another infant nursing. . . . But if I was conceived in iniquity and in sin by my mother nourished in the womb, where, I pray thee my God, where, O Lord, or when was I, thy servant, innocent?"[21] So much for the errors of the Pelagians.

IV. After Augustine's time the doctrine which he had so happily restored began again to be disregarded to such a degree that Damascenus, who three hundred years after Augustine summarized the doctrine as it was then held in the Greek church, did not even use the term "original sin," nor did he anywhere treat the matter expressly.

In the western church this teaching remained because of Augustine's influence but not altogether uncorrupted. Lombard[22] recounts, six hundred years after Augustine, that some had begun to teach in the schools that original sin is only a liability to punishment for the

---

[20] *De Pecc. Mer. et Remiss.* 1:35.65; P.L. 44:147C.
[21] *Conf.* 1:7.11, 12; P.L. 32:665C, 666C.
[22] 2 *Sent.* 30.5; P.L. 192:721C.

sin of the first man, and not guilt. It is a debt, which makes us liable to temporal and eternal punishment for the actual sin of the first man. Thus, they said, sin is in infants, just as children are sometimes by judicial decision of a court in exile for the sin of a wicked parent.

But then Anselm[23] and after him Hugo of St. Victor[24] again promulgated the true doctrine of this Locus. Valla also says, "On account of the disobedience of the first parent, God poured into us the penalty of death, but not his guilt."[25]

Since this doctrine had then been recently corrected by Anselm, Lombard[26] explained it less thoroughly, except that he sowed certain seeds of new doctrine concerning the transmission of original sin and the concupiscence remaining after Baptism. Thereafter among the Scholastics corruptions of this article arose about which we have spoken previously. And in the last chapter certain things are added. From this it is possible to draw up a catalogue of papist errors concerning original sin.

When Alexander[27] had Bonaventure[28] as a pupil, he used to say, "In this respect Adam did not sin." Finally, in our time the Anabaptists have resurrected the old Pelagianism with slightly changed colors, namely, that Christ by his death has taken away original sin from human nature altogether, so that infants are now under the New Covenant, and not conceived or born in sin, but are innocent. Even Zwingli professed the same opinion in a letter to Urbanus Rhegius, [29] for he said that the original evil was not properly guilt or

---

[23] Anselm of Canterbury (1033-1109), an early Scholastic theologian, is considered to be the outstanding theologian between Augustine and Aquinas. His re-affirmation of the traditional doctrine of original sin is found in his well-known work on the atonement, *Cur Deus Homo.*

[24] *De Sacramentis Christianae Fidei* 1:7.25-28; P.L. 176:303A-306B.

[25] *De Libero Arbitrio.*

[26] 2 *Sent.* 30 ff; P.L. 192:720D ff.

[27] Alexander of Hales (c. 1170-1245), teacher of Bonaventure, was the first great theologian of the Franciscan order.

[28] Bonaventure (c. 1221-1274) was a theologian and mystic of the Augustinian-Platonic tradition.

[29] Formerly a humanist and a devoted student of John Eck, Urbanus Rhegius or Rieger (1489-1541) became a Lutheran in 1524. He had known Zwingli in humanist circles and temporarily sided with him in the Eucharistic controversy. Finally he accepted the Lutheran position, and from 1530 until his death he was a strong Lutheran reformer in Lueneburg.

sin, bringing eternal punishment upon children. For sin is properly a breach of the Law of God by one knowing and willing. It is rather a sickness or natural defect such as stammering or a hereditary stone, which cannot be called a crime because it is present in nature. He says therefore that it is called sin in the figurative sense of the word on account of the actual trespass of the first man. Since, however, it is the fount and origin of all sins, that first sin can by itself condemn infants. But through the death of Christ the guilt is already so removed that the children not only of believers but also of the Gentiles, although born with the original defect, are nevertheless free from subjection to the wrath of God even though they are not baptized. And here he distorts the text of Romans 5, which he interprets thus: just as Adam infected and corrupted the whole mass of human nature, so also Christ has restored and purged the whole. Therefore, just as without our consent we acquire the corruption of Adam, so infants receive naturally the benefit of the redemption of Christ without either faith or the Sacrament of regeneration. Otherwise the comparison of Adam and Christ would not agree throughout. He declares that in this way the benefit of Christ is magnified the more, not being restricted to believers only.

And the whole faction of the Sacramentarians[30] concedes a certain material aspect[31] of original sin. Children, however, who are born of believing parents, before they are grafted into Christ by Baptism, are not under the wrath of God. For this was removed through the promise given to believing parents: I will be your God and the God of your seed after you. Baptism, however, is only a sign, because the guilt has already been resolved and taken away.

These are the chief corruptions of this doctrine, to which others can be added if and where they occur.

---

[30] This term is applied to Zwingli, Calvin, and their followers for their figurative interpretation of the real presence of Christ in the Eucharist.

[31] See note 14, page 10.

VI

The Arguments
of the Pelagians

Now that the truth of the issue has been stated and the errors have been pointed out, it will be useful to know what reasons and arguments the opponents have employed, and also whether these have been used for undergirding their errors. This study has a multiple application.

(1) In Titus 1:9 Paul gives the qualifications of a true teacher of the church: "He may be able by sound doctrine both to exhort and to convince the gainsayers." He uses two significant words: ἐλέγχειν, i.e., to uncover and refute the emptiness and falsity of the objections, and ἐπιστομίζειν, which means to refute beyond the possibility of contradiction. These things, however, cannot be set forth unless the arguments of the adversaries are known and the sources of the solutions noted.

(2) The same speculations by which the heretics were once seduced can disturb our faith also. In order therefore that men may be forewarned, it is useful to have the strongest arguments of the adversaries in readiness, lest any mere appearance of truth lead men away from the true doctrine.

(3) The explanation of the true opinion may be more apparent

164

from the antithesis. For when the sources of our solution are shown, many things which pertain to the true fundamentals are clearly seen, which would otherwise not be observed, and faith is strengthened when we can discern the empty and false foundation of the arguments which oppose the truth. Neither can there be that firm assent of the mind which is called πληροφορία [full conviction] unless doubts are removed by the true solutions. For these reasons we ought to note the chief arguments of the Pelagians.

Augustine summarizes them briefly in his treatise against Julian: "These are the heads[1] of your dreadful arguments, by which you terrify the weak. For you say that by asserting the existence of original sin, we declare that the devil is the author of human birth, condemn marriage, deny that all sins are forgiven in Baptism, accuse God of criminal injustice, and make men despair of perfection."[2] Two of these arguments pertain to the dispute concerning concupiscence remaining after Baptism. It seems easier to divide them in the following manner.

I. We could mention all these opinions which the Pelagians took over from philosophy and rational thought in order to do away with original sin: For those qualities which are given by nature itself men should be neither praised nor blamed. By reason of passions we are not good or evil. Accidental traits[3] do not pass from one to another. Sin is an accidental trait. Therefore it does not pass from the parents to the children. An accidental trait is not transferred without a subject. The soul, however, which is properly the subject bearing guilt, is not propagated in generation. Therefore sin is only an accidental trait. An evil act precedes an evil habit. But in infants there was no evil act originally: and hence no evil mode of life. Moreover, all guilt is either an evil act or an evil habit; and because neither

---

[1] Augustine likens the Pelagian arguments of Julian to terrible dragons, the main arguments being the heads of the dragons.

[2] *C. Jul.* 2:1.2; P.L. 44:672D.

[3] "Accidental traits" *accidentia* are those which do not belong to the essence of a person or thing. They can be present or absent according to the individual will or to some random circumstances. E.g., sin does not belong to the essence of man (according to either Augustinian or Orthodox Lutheran teaching). Even original sin is "accidental."

can be present in infants, therefore neither can sin be present in infants as the cause of guilt. Death reigns also in brute animals, which nevertheless cannot be said to have original sin. So it does not follow that since death reigns in infants, they are sinful.

I answer: There is a great difference between brutes and men, as God shows in the creation itself. For of the former he said: Let the earth bring forth living creatures. Into man, however, he himself breathed the breath of life. Man was created in the image of God, thereby becoming immortal by nature. But because man does not only die, but death reigns in him, this is not because he was so created, but because of sin.

Pighius[4] uses this argument, which Pelagius also used: it is certain that man is born from the seed in the propagation of the flesh; but in no manner can there be lawlessness in the seminal elements. Therefore there can be no original sin.

Augustine himself employed many such opinions of the philosophers before the Pelagian controversy arose. Afterwards Pelagius used these opinions against Augustine, as in his book concerning the true religion: "Insofar as sin is voluntary it is an evil. It is by no means sin if it is not voluntary."[5]

He also declares, "To hold someone guilty of sin for not doing what he could not do is the highest perversity and insanity."[6] Again, "Who sins by doing what cannot be avoided?"[7]

However, there is one simple and true answer to all such opinions: What they say concerns only physical or judicial matters. But philosophical or political opinions are not to be indiscriminately mixed with the doctrine divinely revealed in Scripture. . . .

Augustine knew that he had not spoken too clearly or accurately, but he sought some explanation for this. He says in his *Retractationes*[8] that the saying of Paul, "The evil which I would not, that I

---

[4] Albert Pighius (1490-1552) was a Dutch theologian and controversialist. His strong opposition to the Lutheran and Calvinist position on free will led him to de-emphasize the doctrine of original sin.

[5] *De Vera Religione* 14.27; P.L. 34:133D.

[6] *De Duabus Animabus* 12.17; P.L. 42:107B.

[7] *De Libero Arbitrio* 3:18.50; P.L. 32:1295C.

[8] Augustine wrote this work (426-427) to list his works and to correct some of his former statements. In 1:13.5 he does not recant the above-quoted statement from *De Vera Rel.* On the contrary, he continues to maintain it, but he

do" (Rom. 7:19), contradicts his own philosophical opinion concerning the free will. He then adds that original sin is not incorrectly called voluntary, because by the will of the first man it was made, as it were, hereditary. So also concupiscence can in a sense be called voluntary because even though we do what we do not wish, we are not unwilling, but we delight in it.[9] Later in the same work he says, "Little ones are guilty because they are held in the bondage of origin from one who did not do what he was able to do."[10] These interpretations are too farfetched. Nevertheless they show with what sincerity Augustine wished to examine both his own and the sayings of other ancients according to the analogy of faith.[11] Finally, a better answer is simply that such quotations are not properly transferred from philosophy to the doctrine of original sin, which is altogether unknown to reason.

II. The Pelagians accumulated many arguments against original sin from the article of creation, as that of Julian: "If an infant is born with sin, either he sins who bears, or he who is born, or God the Creator, of whom it is written: 'Thy hands have made me' (Job 10:8). But sin cannot be attributed to the Creator, for 'The just God will do no iniquity' (Zeph. 3:5)."[12]

Pighius asks: Since creation was solely the work of God, who was it that, in the very hands of God, at the moment of formation, so corrupted the masterpiece of divine creation that he would render it despised to the Creator himself?

gives an explanation to clarify the sense of his statement. He explains that even the so-called "involutary" sins which are committed without knowledge or forced upon the person are not entirely without the participation of the will of the person. The man who is overcome by concupiscence has still assented to concupiscence. If he acts according to it, he acts according to his own will in spite of the fact that in another sense the concupiscence was against his rational will (man cannot act without will).

[9] *Retractationes* 1:13.5; P.L. 32:604A.

[10] *Ibid.* 1:15.6; P.L. 32:610C.

[11] The "analogy of faith" in Orthodox Lutheran teaching refers to the harmony of Biblical teachings based on the clear passages of the Holy Scriptures. It is a prototype or model of doctrine, containing a minimum of the most certain statements. On the basis of the "analogy of faith" the theologian develops his doctrinal system, explaining the less clear passages by the clearer ones.

[12] This opinion of Julian is quoted by Augustine in *Contra Secundam Juliani Responsionem imperfectum opus* 2:27; P.L. 45:1152C.

Augustine gives the same answer to the objection of Julian with regard to this point: "Only stupid impiety criticizes God because men, who are damnable through their corrupted will, live by his life-giving power, which is given to all. Why do we think that he abhors his works because men born through his creative work are damnable by their corrupt origin?"[13] Celestius says, "Care is to be exercised concerning the doctrine of Baptism lest through it evil be said to be passed on to man by nature before it is committed by man, to the disparagement of the Creator."[14] Pelagius declares: "Before the action of his own will that alone is in man which God has placed there."[15]

Pighius writes that body, soul, and the union of these two are the direct works of God, but concupiscence results from the combination and mingling of the elements of body and soul, which nature tempers with God's cooperation; therefore it is not sin. Such is the doctrine of the union of soul to body that it is unable to be without desires; therefore concupiscence is not sin. I reply: Natural appetites must be distinguished from concupiscence, which is the disorder of all powers. This idea was advanced particularly at the time of Pelagius: "Nature is not evil" (this condemns the error of the Manicheans), "but good." Therefore sin is not original. And because the name of the Manicheans was despised on account of offensive errors, this argument was plausible, and those who opposed Pelagius dared not withdraw from this dictum lest they be encumbered with the hateful dogma of the Manicheans.

When Jerome discussed Romans 7:14 ("I however am carnal"), a Pelagian objected: But is not this the dogma of the Manicheans? Jerome answered, "This you will not impute to me, but to the apostle. From me you will never hear that nature is evil."[16] And Augustine against Julian says that he had not asserted that evil is natural; but that Christ says in John 3:6, "That which is born of the flesh is flesh," and Paul: "We are by nature the children of wrath" (Eph.

---

[13] Cf. *C. Jul.* 6:9.26; P.L. 44:837. This is not a quote but a paraphrase.
[14] Referred to by Augustine, *De Grat. Chr. et de Pecc. Orig.* 2:6.6; P.L. 44:388C.
[15] *Ibid.* 2:13.14; P.L. 44:391D.
[16] *Epistola* 133 (ad Ctesiphontem) 9; P. L. 22:1158B.

2:3).[17] Afterward, when the first fury of the Pelagian controversy had subsided somewhat, the fathers were not afraid to speak thus.

Augustine declares: "What is an evil man if not evil nature, since man is nature?"[18] Ambrose had said previously: "The dissension of flesh and spirit turned itself into nature through the disobedience of the first man";[19] and, "The contagion of procreation is natural."[20]

Augustine says: "Adam was made by nature without sin. When man sinned, however, nature sinned, and nature now became a sinner"; that is, "vitiated by sin, but not built by sins or vices."[21] Again, "Sinful man without doubt begat sinful man. Because he was born from a vitiated nature he has a vitiated nature, that is, a sinful one, because that which is from the earthy is earthy."[22] We call lust a natural evil, not because it is of nature, by God's work innate, but because it passes on from one sinning nature to another."[23] Anselm also clearly says that original sin can be called natural in the sense in which it was defined above.[24] These matters I recall at this time so that we might the more carefully consider the mode of speaking. Augustine often uses this language: "Nature was changed for the worse by a moral fault."[25] "Nature is corrupted by evil."[26] "Nature was weakened and changed through sin."[27] Hence it was customary to say that nature was corrupted, depraved, injured, contaminated, rather than that it is evil. And the reason is that those matters which are works of God remaining in man ought to be distinguished from those which are faulty in themselves.

But let us return to the proposition. Not only in ancient times was this statement debated, but also now the Romanists de-empha-

---

[17] *C. Jul.* 2:8.28; P.L. 44:692D-693A.
[18] *Enchiridion* 4:13; P.L. 40:237C.
[19] *Expositio Evangelii secundum Lucam* 7:141; P.L. 15:1736B.
[20] *Apologia Prophetae David* 11.57; P.L. 14:874C.
[21] *Hypognosticon* (or *Hypomnesticon*) 2:1.1; P.L. 45:1619B. Sin is destructive, not constructive.
[22] *Ibid.* 2:1.1; P.L. 45:1619B.
[23] *Ibid.* 4:1.1; P.L. 45:1639B.
[24] Cf. *Cur Deus Homo.*
[25] *De Grat. Chr. et de Pecc. Orig.* 2:35.40; P.L. 44:405C.
[26] *Ibid.* 2:33.38; P.L. 44:404B.
[27] *De Natura et Gratia* 19.21; P.L. 44:256C.

size original sin. The Archbishop of Cologne, Hermann of Wied,[28] had said in his own reformation: by the Law it was revealed how evil, perverse, and condemned is our whole nature. Gropper[29] criticized this statement. Let it be considered, said he, whether by that unrestrained hyperbole an injury is not imposed upon the goodness of the Creator, which original sin has not wholly extinguished in us. Does not Augustine say, "Our flesh is good, and is not evil, as say the Sethians, Ophites, Patricians; neither the cause of evil, as Florians hold; neither compounded of good and evil, as Manicheus blasphemously says."[30] In what sense these things are said, namely against the wild statements of the Manicheans, the Romanists know; nevertheless they insidiously select such opinions in order to extenuate original sin.

Augustine replies to the arguments from the article of creation: "In a child there is not only human nature, created by the good God. But he also has that corruption which has passed on from one man to all men."[31] "We ought not to consider what good there is in the procreation of nature, but what evil there is in sin, by which our nature has certainly been corrupted. No doubt both nature and the vice of nature are propagated at the same time, one of which is good, the other evil. The former is received from the bounty of the Creator; the latter is contracted from the condemnation of our origin."[32]

Early doctrinal treatises present the case this way: First, in the nature of man there are certain things good in themselves, because they are the works of God, such as ideas, which Paul calls the truth of God, and the affections commanded by the Law of God. Others are in themselves evil. Therefore the distinction must be made be-

---

[28] Hermann of Wied (1477-1552) was bitterly opposed to the Reformation in its early years, but ca. 1539 he became sympathetic to it and attempted a reform movement in his own archbishopric with help from Bucer and Melanchthon. For this he was deposed and excommunicated in 1546, and he spent his remaining years as a Lutheran.
[29] Johann Gropper (1503-1559) was a Roman Catholic theologian educated at Cologne. He is now considered by scholars to be the author of the Ratisbon Book. Following the deposition of Hermann of Wied, Gropper restored Catholicism in the archbishopric of Cologne.
[30] *De Eccl. Dogm.* 43; P.L. 42:1220B. The four groups mentioned in this quotation are heretical Gnostic sects.
[31] *De Nupt. et Concup.* 2:29.49; P.L. 44:465A.
[32] *De Grat. Chr. et de Pecc. Orig.* 2:33.38; P.L. 44:404B.

tween fundamental matters and the depravity which is not fundamental. That is to say, these matters which are good *per se* were
contaminated and became evil through a non-essential trait.

In the doctrine concerning the cause of sin this solution is traditional. God is not the cause of sin although he aids and preserves
the propagation of substance; nevertheless he conserves the mass
such as it is now, just as an artisan might make a cup not out of gold
but out of lead. But the wrath of God is truly and powerfully
aroused toward its destruction.[33]

III. Arguments have also been taken from the institution of marriage, as Julian does. God did not sin when he provided for the
multiplication of the human race through procreation. Neither does
the infant sin who is born, because he does not yet act of his own
will. The only conclusion is that the cause of original sin is the parents who beget. But Scripture says, "Marriage is honorable and the
bed undefiled" (Hebr. 13:14). And Paul calls it sanctification in
1 Thess. 4:3, 4 and 1 Cor. 7:14. Therefore, according to Julian,
original sin is not transmitted from parents to children.

Julian also used to urge this argument with great earnestness:
To condemn marriage is a heresy rejected in ancient time. . . . The
doctrine of original sin, however, manifestly condemns marriage,
because it affirms that corruption is contracted through procreation,
that infants are conceived and born in sin.[34] Augustine replies:
In matrimony there are two things which are good and of divine
ordination and institution, but there is also a desire in marriage without which there is no propagation, and because of that desire infants
are born in sin.[35] But it seems simpler if one says: Marriage is the
order of life instituted by God and thus good and pleasing to God.
Nevertheless marriage does not take away the hereditary evil from
nature, which is certain to remain even in marriage. Original sin is
passed on to posterity by propagation, not by reason of marriage

---

[33] Cf. Rom. 9:22.

[34] Cf. *C. Jul.* 2:1.2; P.L. 44:675C.

[35] Cf. *Ibid.* 3:7.15; P.L. 44:709D. Sexual desire in marriage is not called
sin in the proper sense of the word, but it is a transmitter of sin unto posterity.
In another sense, every human function is in some way stamped by the basic
corruption of human nature.

but by reason of the corrupted nature of man even in marriage. As is the earthy, such are the earthy. "That which is born of the flesh is flesh," says Christ in John 3:6.

IV. At one time the Pelagians, and in our time chiefly the Anabaptists, adduced certain passages of Scripture for the purpose of overthrowing the doctrine of original sin: Children do not know the distinction between good and evil (Deut. 1:39). They know not to discern the left and right (Jonah 4:11). It is said of the childish age, "Before the child shall know how to reject evil and choose the good" (Is. 7:16). Therefore children do not have sin. The reply is clear.[36] The Pelagians are speaking of sin as knowing and willing trespass against the Law. This is actual sin, but the question before us is original sin. Again, it is one thing not to know sin, and another not to have sin. In 1 Tim. 1:13 Paul says, "I did it ignorantly," and nevertheless he confesses himself the greatest sinner. Even the servant who did not know what to do at length received stripes (Luke 12:48).

Augustine says, "This very ignorance demonstrates that nature is corrupt already in the infant." For David in Ps. 25:7 speaks of the sins of youth and ignorance, etc. But this cannot apply to Christ, of whom Isaiah says, "Before the boy shall know how to eschew evil and to choose the good."[37]

In Matthew 19:14 Christ says of infants, "Of such is the kingdom of heaven." Therefore, say these false teachers, they are not the children of wrath. I reply: Christ does not say that infants by nature are heirs of the kingdom of heaven before the action of their own will. For in another place he expressly says: "That which is born of the flesh is flesh," and, "Except a man be born of water and of the Spirit, he cannot enter into the kingdom of God" (John 3:5-6). But of such, he says, who are brought to me, whom I accept, embrace, and bless, of such is the kingdom of heaven, as he plainly says in Mark 10:15, "Whosoever shall not receive the kingdom of God as a little child. . . ." Therefore they do not have it by nature but receive it. However, the kingdom of heaven also comprises the

---

[36] Chemnitz's difficult formulation is paraphrased at this point.
[37] *De Pecc. Mer. et Remiss.* 1:36.67; P.L. 44:149B.

forgiveness of sins. Therefore they have sins, if theirs is the kingdom of heaven.

Psalm 106:37-38 says, "They sacrificed their sons and daughters unto devils and shed innocent blood." Therefore the nature of infants is innocent and without sin. I reply: He calls the blood innocent, because they were not killed like robbers for crimes committed, but were in that age where no act merits civil punishment. Thus this phrase is used in law in a political or civil sense, as in Phil. 3:6, ἄμεμπτος (blameless); Exod. 23:7, ". . . the innocent and righteous slay thou not"; Deut. 19:10, ". . . that innocent blood be not shed"; Jonah 1:14, "Lay not upon us innocent blood." They say this of Jonah who nevertheless was not innocent, because he was disobedient and in flight from the command of God. But they spoke in a political sense because among the sailors he was not deserving of death for any crime. Theologically, however, this phrase is used in another manner, as in Exod. 34:7, "forgiving inquity, and will by no means clear the guilty"; Nahum 1:3, "He will not at all acquit the wicked"; Jer. 30:11, "I will correct thee in measure, lest thou appear to thyself harmless." The infants are therefore innocent in a political sense (as the Psalm says), but theologically they are by nature children of wrath. One can also answer thus: The children of the Jews were grafted into the covenant with God by circumcision. The Psalmist laments the sacrifice of children who are innocent and righteous before God through faith and the remission of sins.

The Pelagians cite Ezek. 18:20: "The son shall not bear the iniquity of the father." Therefore the sins of the parents do not pass on to the offspring, to render us guilty on account of the fall of Adam. The reply is twofold: The prophet is not speaking about hereditary sin; but the Jews complained that even though they remained in the covenant of God, loved the Word, and cherished piety, nevertheless they were finally punished in innocence on account of the sins of the parents. God answers: The son shall not die for the iniquity of his father. And this is simply the teaching of the Decalogue: "Visiting the iniquity of the fathers upon the children unto the third and fourth generation of them that hate me." For the prophet says: If a just man should beget a son who is a thief, one who sheds blood, if an impious man should beget a son who is frightened at the sins of his father, there is only this to say: No one who is himself innocent and without sins is punished on account of the parents' sins. For Ezekiel wishes that in our punishment we should not rail at God and seek the cause of punishment outside of ourselves, but humbly confess with the saints, "We have sinned with our fathers, we have committed iniquity, we have done wickedly" (Ps. 106:6); just as also Daniel does in his prayer (Dan. 9:5).

The second answer is that of Augustine, who says: It is the promise of the Gospel that Christ released the infants grafted into him from the weight of sin contracted from their parents. In Christ therefore the son does not bear the iniquity of the father, because it is forgiven. And Jer. 31:29-30 clearly supports this. Speaking of the New Testament, he says, "In those days they shall say no more, the fathers have eaten a sour grape and the children's teeth are set on edge." But "the days come that I will make a new covenant, for I will forgive their iniquity" (Jer. 31:31, 34).

In John 15:22 Jesus says, "If I had not come and spoken unto them, they had not had sin." Therefore these to whom it is not said have no sin. I reply: it is altogether false that the Jews had no sins before the advent of Christ. In Rom. 2:12 Paul says, "For as many as have sinned without law shall also perish without law." Christ therefore speaks of a certain kind of sin, where every excuse is taken away, that the conscience might convict them. Such sin, he says, they would not have if I had not spoken to them. Augustine explains this as the sin of unbelief, which includes all sins, because it prevents sins from being taken away and forgiven. But the first answer is simpler.

The apostle says in Rom. 5:18: "Therefore as by the offense of one judgment came upon all men to condemnation; even so by the righteousness of one the free gift came upon all men unto justification of life." Therefore by the merit of Christ original sin is altogether taken away from the nature of things. I reply: There is a difference between the merit of Christ and the application of this merit; in other words, because Christ is the propitiation for the sins of the whole world, all are impious without repentance, but they are saved by faith. And in Romans 5:17 the application is explicitly stated: those who receive the abundance of grace and the gift of righteousness shall reign in life through Christ.

Rom. 5:12 reads: "By one man sin entered. . . ." But, says Pelagius, the propagation of it is not through one man. Therefore sin entered into the world, not through inheritance, but by example and imitation. To this argument Augustine gives the following answer: Husband and wife are one flesh, and thus we may say, "through one man." Still, the propagation of offspring is attributed to the man, with the result that women are not recorded in the genealogies. Therefore Paul says that sin entered in through Adam, so that the blessed seed of the woman should be excepted. In other places, too, Scripture speaks the same way about the woman. "In sin did my mother conceive me" (Ps. 51:5).

The Pelagians quote Hos. 6:7: "They like Adam have transgressed the covenant." Therefore the sin of Adam passed upon the world by imitation and example. Augustine answers: "When Scripture speaks of the first author of sin, whom the sinners imitate, then it does not name Adam, but the devil."[38] "The devil sinneth from the beginning" (1 John 3:8). "By the envy of the devil death entered into the world" (Wisdom of Sol. 2:24). So the children of the devil imitate their father (John 8:44): "Ye are of your father the devil," because you do his works; you want to do the desires of your father. When in Rom. 5:12 Paul says that sin entered not through the devil but through one man, he is not speaking of imitation, as he expressly says, ". . . even over them that had not sinned after the similitude of Adam's transgression . . ." (Rom. 5:14). Again, Adam and Christ are compared with each other in Rom. 5. Christ, however, is not only the example of righteousness for imitation. Adam too was harmful not only by his example.

Pighius says on Rom. 5 that death and condemnation are always attributed to the sin of one. Therefore infants do not have sin. I reply: Paul said that sin entered through one man, indeed, not however into Adam alone, but into the world. So he could say: ". . . in whom all have sinned," and "many were made sinners."

Pighius interprets "all have sinned" to mean that they pay the penalty of another's sin; "many were made sinners" to mean that

---
[38] *De Nupt. et Concup.* 2:27.45; P.L. 44:462B.

they are guilty of another's trespass. But in Scripture it is affirmed of Christ alone that he bore the sins of others in innocence. Of no other man is this said. Such an exposition is therefore a perversion of the Pauline text.

The Zwinglians offer in objection the text 1 Cor. 7:14 which calls children "holy." Therefore the children of Christians, before they are reborn in Baptism, are absolved from original sin.

I reply: Paul was born of pious and believing parents. For he says in 2 Tim. 1:3, "I serve God from my forefathers with pure conscience." Nevertheless he affirms: We who were born of circumcised and faithful parents "were by nature children of wrath" (Eph. 2:3). Therefore he calls the children of Christians holy in 1 Cor. 7, not because they are either without original sin or without guilt before they are born and cleansed by the washing of water in the Word, but as he says in the same text, "The unbelieving husband is sanctified by the wife" (1 Cor. 7:14). This he says, not because unbelief can be holy, but because the cohabitation with a believing person is permitted and holy, just as food is sanctified through the Word (1 Tim. 4:5). But in explaining this statement, it ought to be added that the children of Christians are to be called holy, even as in Rom. 11:16 the Jewish nation is called holy, although already blinded. If the offering is holy, the entire substance is holy; if the root is holy, the branches are also. Besides, since they belong to the promise, the children of believers are called holy. For Acts 2:39 says, "The promise is unto you and to your children."

VII

The Remnants of Original Sin
After Baptism

This is an ancient question, keenly disputed at the time of the Pelagian controversy and repeated by Lombard. Even in our time it has aroused violent disputes.

Leo X[1] placed this second among the articles which he condemned in the teaching of Luther, viz., to deny that sin remains in the child after Baptism is to trample on Paul and Christ at the same time.

From that time on this has always been one of the most controversial articles, whether it is right to say that there is sin in infants after Baptism; or whether the concupiscence remaining in adults is sin. This question was disputed at Augsburg, as is apparent from the Apology. Afterwards, in the year 1540, this question was chiefly disputed at Worms.[2] Even in the Council of Trent this

---

[1] The son of Lorenzo de Medici, he was Pope from 1513 until his death in 1521. When the Reformation occurred, he did not understand its real nature and considered it simply a monastic quarrel between the Augustinians and the Dominicans.

[2] The Disputation of Worms was one of the many unsuccessful conferences held to settle the religious differences between Protestants and Catholics. Each side was represented by eleven theologians, with Melanchthon and Eck the spokesmen for the Protestants and Catholics respectively.

article was posited: Injury is done to Baptism if it is said that sin remains in baptized infants and in regenerate adults. In short, there is no one of all the adversaries who did not sharply brandish the sword over this question.

I recount these things so that studies might be promoted which would help us see the true sources of this controversy. Many cry out that this is only a contention about words, for popes call the remaining concupiscence a defect, a weakness, an imperfection of strength, etc. We contend that it is sin. It appears therefore to be a war of words, which should not be of such importance that the Church should be disturbed on its account. Therefore we must diligently consider why the Papists in the beginning of this controversy contended so sharply that the concupiscence remaining after Baptism is not properly sin, although Paul on occasion designates it so. But this matter is not simply a question of terminology, for the Papists are insidiously trying to fortify the main foundations of the whole pontifical rule. They contend that regenerated man is in this life able to satisfy the Law of God by perfect obedience, and that the good works of the regenerate can stand before the judgment of God, withstand the divine wrath, and be worthy of eternal life. Thus they say that the concupiscence remaining is not sin, but only a deformity, not against, but outside of the Law of God. However, in this manner they overthrow the whole doctrine of justification and good works. The conflict is therefore not only over words but concerns the most important issues, which the church must fully understand.

First we must consider why it is necessary that this doctrine be rightly and carefully explained. Otherwise we might think that these controversies have been motivated by contentious minds, without real cause, solely to nourish dissensions. Let us, then, divide this question into several parts.

I. The true status of this question must first be established. Since Baptism imparts the complete, full, and perfect remission of all sins, the Manicheans fancied that sin was so removed from man that after his cleansing it was like a thing existing by itself and having its dwelling in the center of the earth.

Pelagius taught that no remnants of sin remained in those baptized, since otherwise there would not be a full remission of sins.
He also taught that whatever might be in the regenerate beyond
actual reigning sins[3] was holy and good.

However, at this time it is conceded by all without controversy
that concupiscence is and remains in those who are born again of
water and the Spirit, because all Scripture and Christian experience
witness to it. Some of the opponents falsely slander the doctrine of
our churches as if we taught that original sin remained after Baptism and the regeneration of the Spirit in the same manner as it was
before Baptism and regeneration. But this is obvious calumny.
Two true and very significant differences are pointed out in the
Apology between the concupiscence which is in the non-regenerate
and that which remains after Baptism in the reborn. (1) Concupiscence in the unregenerate leaves one subject to the wrath of
God and eternal death, which in Baptism is taken away by the remission of sins. (2) In the unregenerate sin reigns, as its reign is
described in Eph. 2:1-3; 4:17ff.; and Rom. 6:12, 13, and 19. In the
reborn, however, the Spirit begins to heal the nature and to mortify
the deeds of the flesh (Rom. 8:13). The Spirit crucifies the old man
and destroys the body of sin (Rom. 6:6). It lusts against the flesh
(Gal. 5:17), and in place of weaknesses it kindles new aspirations.
What still continues of the old man is termed the "remaining concupiscence" or the "remnants" of original sin. And these are proper
terms, if rightly understood, for concupiscence remains in the reborn after Baptism, but in a way totally different from what is found
in the unregenerate.

The question therefore is not whether it is sin when a regenerate

---

[3] Latin, *peccatum dominans*—sin which rules or has dominion over man
(Cf. Rom. 6:14). Chemnitz will in the next chapter suggest that mortal sins can
be called reigning or dominating (Latin, *regnans seu dominans*) sins. The
Scholastics equate mortal sin with crime, following the words of Augustine: "A
crime is a mortal sin, one that deserves condemnation" (*In Joann. Ev. Tract.*
41:9; P.L. 35:1697C). Aquinas writes, "Mortal and venial sins are opposed as
reparable and irreparable. And I say this with reference to the interior principle,
but not to the Divine Power, who can repair all sins. . . . Venial sin is called a
sin in reference to an imperfect notion of sin, and in relation to mortal sin (to
which the perfect notion of sin is applicable). . . . For venial sin is not against
the Law but outside of the Law" (*S. Th.* I-II: q. 88. a.1).

man gives in and submits to concupiscence so that he acts contrary to the Law of God (for this is certainly beyond all controversy). But this we ask concerning those who do not obey the lusts of sin, who through the Spirit mortify the deeds of the flesh, and who bemoan that impurity: Since it is certain that in regeneration the total disease of original sin is not suddenly removed, are the concupiscence and the defects remaining after Baptism good and holy, or sin, or adiaphora? The question should expressly include both the concupiscence and the defects remaining after Baptism, since each of them belongs to the subject of original sin, as was shown in the definition.

II. The right answer must come from sure and clear testimonies of Scripture. Sufficient for us is the testimony of him who did not receive the Gospel from man, but learned it by revelation from Jesus Christ (Gal. 1:12).

First, then, Paul expressly says of concupiscence that it is not a good thing. "I know that in me (that is, in my flesh,) dwelleth no good thing" (Rom. 7:18). Secondly, he does not talk about the remaining concupiscence in the same way that he speaks on indifferent matters: "Circumcision is nothing, and uncircumcision is nothing" (1 Cor. 7:19). Again, "For neither if we eat, are we the better; neither, if we eat not, are we the worse" (1 Cor. 8:8). On the other hand he complains in Rom. 7:24, "O wretched man that I am! Who shall deliver me from the body of this death?" In the third place, he sometimes calls concupiscence "sin" in express terms. For example, he writes in Rom. 6: ". . . that the body of sin might be destroyed, that henceforth we should not serve sin" (v. 6); and further, "Let not sin reign" (v. 12); "for sin shall not have dominion over you" (v. 14). Of himself Paul says, "I am carnal, sold under sin" (Rom. 7:14), and he makes reference to "the law of sin, which is in my members" (Rom. 7:23).

Various sophistical objections have been raised, by which the papists would escape from clear testimonies. Eck at Worms dared to argue that the Church Fathers interpreted Paul to be speaking here of a Jew not reborn. But Augustine in the Retractations[4] ex-

---

[4] *Retract.* 1:23.1; P.L. 32:620C-621B.

pressly confesses that he had wrongly expounded these passages in this manner before the Pelagian controversies arose. And in *Against Julian*[5] he cites among the ancients especially Ambrose, who taught that Paul was here speaking of himself already reborn. Even the text itself is plain against all objections. For he is speaking of the inner man when he says, "I delight in the law of God," and "With the mind I myself serve the law of God" (Rom. 7:22, 25).

These things cannot be ascribed to the unregenerate man unless we wish to be clearly Pelagian. And the witness is clear; because the eighth chapter of Romans is joined with the seventh by a particle which gives the reason in this manner: "There is therefore now no condemnation to them which are in Christ Jesus" (Rom. 8:1). Paul therefore is speaking of himself as reborn. This is equally apparent in Rom. 6:14: "Sin shall not have dominion over you: for you are not under the law, but under grace." And in Rom. 7 Paul states that though sin is dwelling in him, he does not allow sin to dominate him, and to accomplish its purpose. For he says, "That which I do, I allow not; what I hate, that do I" (7:15); and "The evil which I would not, that I do" (7:19); "To will is present with me" (7:18); "I delight in the law of God" (7:22). And in 8:4, "We walk not after the flesh, but after the spirit." Paul therefore, who had labored more than twenty years in mortifying lust and destroying the body of death, whose inner man had been continually renewed from day to day for more than twenty years, who says in 1 Cor. 4:4, "I know nothing by myself," confesses with earnest complaint that the concupiscence dwelling in him is sin.

These things are very secure against all slander. But hitherto the Romanists have objected that though Paul indeed calls the concupiscence left in the reborn "sin," he does so, not in the proper sense, but by a figure of speech, just as he says that "Christ was made to be sin for us" (2 Cor. 5:21). And yet Scripture declares, "He knew no sin, neither was guile found in his mouth" (Is. 53:9).

Therefore these Pauline texts should here be more diligently considered, so that after the clouds of sophistry are dispersed the true teaching might be more clearly apparent. For Paul does not only

[5] *C. Jul.* 2:4.8; P.L. 44:678C.

apply the name "sin" to the concupiscence remaining in the reborn, but he explains himself in various ways about what he means by the name "sin." He describes it (1) *negatively:* "The good that I would I do not" (Rom. 7:19); "How to perform that which is good I find not" (Rom. 7:18). "The mind that is set on the flesh . . . is not subject to the law of God, neither indeed can be" (Rom. 8:7). (2) *Positively:* ". . . the evil which I would not, that I do" (Rom. 7:19). "I see another law in my members, warring against the law of my mind [i.e., against the Holy Spirit], and bringing me into captivity to the law of sin . . ." (Rom. 7:23). (3) He says that it is not good but evil: ". . . when I would do good, evil is present with me" (Rom. 7:21). (4) He says that he struggles with that law: "Thou shalt not covet" (Rom. 7:7). (5) He says, "The carnal mind is enmity against God" (Rom. 8:7). (6) He commands to mortify (Rom. 8:13), to crucify, to destroy lest we die (Rom. 6:6). (7) On account of that sin he calls it the body of sin, from which we have need of liberation.

If this is not clear, then I do not know what could be produced from Scripture that is clear. For in the above quotations Paul has spoken very plainly: Concupiscence dwelling in the reborn is sin, but not prevailing so that the desires of the flesh are accomplished. For that which I do, I allow not, but with the mind I serve the Law of God, etc. Nor is it such a sin that it brings damnation, for there is "no condemnation in those who are in Christ Jesus" (Rom. 8:1). But it is and is called "sin," because it is evil and opposes the Law of God. And Paul knows that that evil is by itself and in its nature worthy of eternal death, unless it is forgiven and the obedience of Christ reigns.

It is obvious that the Papists employ the same reasons whenever they contend that concupiscence should not be called sin. These reasons are: (1) that concupiscence is not an evil that wars against the Law of God; and (2) that it is venial in its nature and thus not worthy of eternal death. This antithesis must be carefully observed.

Here belong other testimonies of Scripture also, which affirm that sins remain. "For this (namely, forgiveness of sins) shall every one that is godly pray unto thee in a time when thou mayest be found" (Ps. 32:6). "Who can say, I have made my heart clean,

I am pure from any sin"? (Prov. 20:9). "If I justify myself, mine own mouth shall condemn me; if I say, I am perfect, it shall also prove me perverse" (Job 9:20).

Augustine, in a letter to Jerome, embraced many such testimonies in one significant statement: "Charity in some is greater, in others less, and in still others wanting altogether. It is in no one so plenteous that it could not be increased while a man lives. However, as long as it can be increased, that which is less than it ought to be is of evil. Because of this evil there is not a just man upon earth that doeth good and sinneth not, and therefore no man living shall be justified in the sight of God. On account of this vice, if we say that we have no sin, the truth is not in us. And whatever our deeds, we are compelled to pray, Forgive us our sins, though in Baptism all words, deeds, and thoughts are forgiven."[6] I have quoted this opinion because it shows why this doctrine should be retained. It is thus demonstrated and proved from sure testimonies of Scripture what the right teaching in this matter is.

III. The chief arguments of the adversaries should be reviewed, for their explanation gives us a helpful statement of the doctrine. They are threefold:

(1) They set in opposition certain testimonies of Scripture, chiefly those which speak of the efficacy of Baptism, such as Acts 2:38: "Be baptized every one of you . . . for the remission of sins." Now such remission is not erroneous or superficial, but true, full, and perfect, as the prophet says, "The Lord also hath put away thy sin" (2 Sam. 12:13). For we are baptized into the death of Christ, who is ". . . the Lamb of God which takes away the sin of the world" (John 1:29). And as Micah says, "Thou wilt cast all their sins into the depths of the sea" (Micah 7:19). "As far as the east is from the west, so far hath he removed our transgressions from us" (Ps. 103:12).

This argument was chiefly used by the Pelagians. For so Augustine states their objections: "If the concupiscence remaining after Baptism is sin, it follows that Baptism does not give remission of

---

[6] *Epistola* 167:4.15; P.L. 33:739C.

all sins or take away transgressions, but shaves them like hair on
your head, so that the roots of all sins remain in the evil flesh, and
the sins cut off grow again."[7] But to hold this is a gross abuse of
Baptism, and a blasphemy against the death of the Lamb of God,
which takes away the sins of the world.

It should be noted that the Council of Trent was not afraid to
borrow from Pelagius the same accusation that he used against
Augustine: that sins are not forgiven in Baptism, but only shaved,
if the remaining concupiscence is called sin.[8]

But before we proceed to the true solution, it will not be unprofitable to observe that this argument troubled Augustine greatly. For
he tried in every way to soften the shame or disgrace of this slander,
that in Baptism true, full, and perfect forgiveness of all sins was
not granted. It seemed to him, however, that he could find no way
out unless he said that the concupiscence which remains after Baptism is not properly sin. For if he said that anything of sin remained, then all were not truly and perfectly forgiven in Baptism.

From this Pelagius drew the inference that no one can transmit
to another what he himself does not possess. But the baptized cannot transmit original sin, because it is completely forgiven. Therefore children born of baptized parents do not have original sin.
Augustine is constrained to reply: "It happens in a wondrous manner, not easily understood or explained in a sermon, that when a
parent is freed from sin and damnation, he begets children subject
to sin and damnation; nevertheless it does happen, because Scripture affirms it: 'And we (the circumcised) were by nature the children of wrath.' "[9] He adds two similes, moreover, in which he somewhat explains himself. The first is: The seeds of grain are cleansed
from hulls, beards, stems, and chaff by the labor and skill of the
farmer, and the bare seeds are stored away. But if they are after-

---

[7] *C. Duas Epp. Pel.* 1:13.26; P.L. 44:562D.

[8] The Trent article (Session 5, Part 5) reads as follows: "If anyone denies,
that, by the grace of our Lord Jesus Christ, which is conferred in Baptism, the
guilt of original sin is remitted; or even asserts that the whole of that which
has the true and proper nature of sin is not taken away; but says that it is only
shaved [Latin, *radi*], or not imputed; let him be anathema." Certainly, neither
Augustine nor the Lutherans taught that sins are only "shaved" in Baptism.
This is simply "calumny" on the part of the Trent article.

[9] *C. Jul.* 6:5.11; P.L. 44:828D.

wards sown, they do not produce bare and winnowed seeds, but seeds united with their hulls and beards. For it is not their nature to be bare seeds, but they are made such by artificial means. The multiplication of the seed is, however, according to nature.[10] The second simile is: The circumcised Jew does not have a foreskin. But he passes on the foreskin, which he does not possess, to the children, because he begets such, as he is by nature. The foreskin is not wanting by nature, yet by circumcision it is taken away.[11]

By these similes Augustine tries to explain himself; but he does not find the true basis of the solution. The baptized man begets children with original sin, because his renewal is made by the Spirit, while the old condition remains in the flesh. "The body is dead because of sin; but the Spirit is life because of righteousness" (Rom. 8:3). Reproduction, however, is not by the Spirit but by the flesh. Therefore it is called carnal generation. Thus the old nature of sin dwelling in the flesh is propagated. For this reason Augustine, when he could not extricate himself from the previous argument, unfortunately chose to say that the lust remaining is not properly sin. These unhappy words contributed to the eventual corruption of this doctrine, as we shall see.[12]

The true and simple answer is this: Baptism is called the washing of regeneration and renewal (Titus 3:4, 5). That is, it confers two gifts: forgiveness of sins and the beginning of renewal, breaking down the old nature of the flesh (2 Cor. 4:16). The forgiveness of sins, however, is one thing; the mortifying, cleansing, destruction, or despoiling of sin is another. Forgiveness takes away the guilt of all sins, so that there is no condemnation for them that are in Christ Jesus. And this remission is full and perfect. The renewal,

---

[10] *Ibid.* 6:6.15; P.L. 44:831D.

[11] *Ibid.* 6:7.20; P.L. 44:834B.

[12] Chemnitz is too severe in his judgment of Augustine, who is much closer to his viewpoint than he presumes. It is true that Augustine says that concupiscence in the regenerate is not properly sin (Cf. *De Nupt. et Conc.* 1:23.25; P.L. 44:428B, C). On the other hand, in *Against Julian* Augustine clearly calls the remaining concupiscence "evil"; though he emphasizes that the guilt-character of it is taken away in Baptism (Cf. *C. Jul.* 6:17.51-52; P.L. 44:853ff.). If Augustine's words contributed to the corruption of the doctrine of original sin, they did so by the fact that later writers could hold to one side of the above dialectic while ignoring the other side.

however, cleansing the old ferment, plundering and destroying the
body of sin, only begins; neither is it full and perfect in this life
so that nothing of the old or of sin remains. Since "the new man is
renewed from day to day" (2 Cor. 4:16), the fallacy of the Papist
argument can easily be observed: In Baptism there is complete
forgiveness of all sins; therefore nothing of sin remains in the baptized. What they are trying to prove is that in Baptism a full and
perfect renewal is made, which leaves no remnant of sins in the
flesh of the reborn. But against this opinion all Scripture cries out.
Augustine also saw this, as many of his statements show, upon which
Lombard commented; and when he could not in another way free
himself from this argument, he said that it was not properly sin.[13]
"Ye are clean . . ." (John 13:10). "Ye are washed, ye are sanctified"
(1 Cor. 6:11). Therefore the concupiscence remaining in the baptized is not sin. So Gropper argues. I answer: Christ affirms that
the disciples are clean because of the Word; but then he says that
it is necessary to cleanse the feet (John 13:10). And Paul expressly
says of those previously washed and sanctified, "Let us cleanse
ourselves . . . , perfecting holiness . . ." (2 Cor. 7:1). They are
therefore clean, washed, and sanctified by imputation and by the
beginning of a transformation within them; but since this is not
completed, both are true: you are clean—cleanse yourselves; you
are sanctified—perfect your sanctification.

Paul declares that by the washing of water Christ established for
himself a glorious church, "not having spot, or wrinkle, or any such
thing; but that it should be holy and without blemish" (Eph. 5:27).
Therefore, they say, the original lust remaining after Baptism is
not a blemish before the Law of God. I reply that the Pelagians once
also used this argument. But Augustine answers rightly: Paul does
not say that because Christ perfectly cleansed the church in Bap-

---

[13] Chemnitz has here represented only one side of Augustine's dialectical
position. The other side may be seen in his *Tractates on the Gospel of John,*
where he emphasizes that Christians should wash their emotions (which are the
"feet" for bringing them into sensible contact with society) and pray daily
for the forgiveness of sins (Cf. *In Joann. Tract.* 56:4; P.L. 35:1788D-1789A.)
And a little later in the same work he writes, "But although believers are clean
in comparison to other men, because they live righteously, yet they need to
wash their feet, because they are certainly not without sin" (*Ibid.* 56:5;
P.L. 35:1789B).

tism by the forgiveness of sins, he likewise by renewal at once caused it to be without blemish. But the text says that he cleanses the church (namely, by the remission of sins), that he might show it to be glorious, without blemish. However, that demonstration is not made in this life; but the Son of God covers its uncleanness. The Spirit then mortifies the sin, and the inner man is renewed from day to day, to the end that, when the Lord shall be all in all, the church shall appear without spot or wrinkle. He speaks therefore concerning the benefit of Christ in its fulness, which begins in this life and will be perfect and full in the life to come.

Our opponents say on the basis of 1 John 3:8 that the son of God has fully and perfectly destroyed the works of Satan. Therefore after Baptism nothing is left in the reborn of the works of the devil. But as far as the merit of Christ is concerned, Scripture says: "The Prince of this world is judged" (John 16:11); "He led captivity captive" (Eph. 4:8); "He spoiled principalities" (Col. 2:15). But concerning the effective work of Christ in us, by which he applies his merit to us, John does not say that the Son of God has already fully and perfectly destroyed the works of the devil in us. But he says, "For this the Son of God appeared, that he might destroy the works of the devil."

They also cite the statement of Paul: "All things work together for good to them that love God" (Rom. 8:28). On this basis, they contend, the remaining concupiscence is good, so that, as once virtue failed because of complacency, thus now it should be made perfect in weakness. However, by the same reasoning even the devil should be called good, whose angel smote Paul so that strength might be made perfect in weakness (2 Cor. 12:7, 9). However, we are not now asking how God works things out to the advantage of those who love him, but what things are in themselves and according to their nature. The following principle is relevant here: When the formal aspect of a thing is removed, the thing itself is destroyed.[14] Concerning this principle we recall that at Worms in 1540, before the public colloquy began, our men deliberated privately on the application of this principle to the doctrine of sin.

---

[14] In Aristotelian teaching, form makes a thing what it is; without form a thing cannot be.

Some attempted to answer dialectically, i.e., that the formal aspect of sin is two-fold: qualitative and relational. They contended that the relational aspect[15] was taken away, and the mortification of the qualitative aspect[16] only began in this life.

Others attempted the simpler answer, that there is a twofold guilt of sin: actual and potential. Actual guilt results in damnation because of the deed, as in unremitted sin. Potential guilt is that guilt of original concupiscence, whose nature is against the Law of God, so that it would make one subject to eternal damnation unless remission were made, and it were covered by Christ's righteousness.

Osiander[17] at this point came up with another solution, namely, that in Baptism the guilt is not taken away from concupiscence, so as to render it worthy of eternal life; but it is taken away from the person baptized, to whom it is not imputed unto condemnation, although by itself it is a matter meriting the wrath of God.

This answer seems at first glance to be too subtle. But rightly considered it clarifies this entire dispute, i.e., how sin is still present after Baptism when original sin was forgiven in Baptism. And it becomes clearer if we observe what Augustine answered Julian on exactly the same subject. Augustine had said, "Concupiscence, even though its guilt is forgiven in Baptism, can still remain."[18] Julian twisted this statement and added that therefore after Baptism the original concupiscence absolved from guilt is no longer an evil thing, but worthy of eternal life.[19] To this slander Augustine answered, "We do not say that concupiscence, which remains in the regenerate, is sanctified and made believing through Baptism. . . . But we do say that its guilt, not a guilt by which it is itself guilty (for it is not a person), but the guilt by which it origi-

---

[15] By the relational aspect of sin is meant the guilt or condemnation before God, which was taken away and replaced by the relation of forgiveness.

[16] By the qualitative aspect of sin is meant the sinful nature of man, which is in the process of transformation but not completely transformed.

[17] Andreas Osiander (1498-1552) was one of the friends and fellow workers of Martin Luther and was champion of the Reformation in Nuernberg. Later he separated from the Lutherans because of his peculiar doctrine of justification (justification by the indwelling righteousness of God rather than by imputation of Christ's merits).

[18] C. Jul. 6:17.51; P.L. 44:852C.

[19] Ibid. 6:17.51; P.L. 44:853A.

nally made man guilty, has been forgiven and made void; whereas the lust itself is evil, so that the regenerate longs to be healed from this pestilence."[20]

(2) Certain opinions of Augustine were raised against us, which we have tried to put in their proper context. Thus he says: "Concupiscence itself is not sin in the regenerate when consent is not given to it for illicit deeds, . . . but only in a manner of speaking is it called sin, because it may produce sin. According to the same manner of speaking we call Latin speech the 'Latin tongue,' although it is not a tongue, but is done by it. Similarly concupiscence is sometimes called sin because it generates sin when it prevails, just as cold is called sluggish because it makes men sluggish."[21]

Augustine observes further: "They say that Baptism grants indulgence for all sins, wipes out and takes away transgressions. Only the lust remains. But although this is called sin, it is so called not because it is sin, but because it is caused by sin. In this same way, a writing is said to be someone's 'hand' because the hand has written it. But they are sins because they are unlawfully done, said, and thought, according to the lust of the flesh or according to ignorance."[22]

A little further on they say: "Because the guilt [of concupiscence] is contracted through generation, it is remitted by regeneration. Thus it is not sin any more, but it is called so, either because it is caused by sin, or because it has been stirred by delight for sin, although overcome by the love of righteousness it is not consented to."[23] The adversaries therefore conclude that it is the consensus of all antiquity that the concupiscence which remains in the reborn after Baptism is not properly sin.

Let us reply briefly. Our faith is built upon the foundation of the prophets and apostles, and all the statements of the fathers must conform to the analogy of faith, which in this question is supremely clear, as has been shown above. Yet, a few words must be added to show with what fairness the papists employ the testimonies of

[20] *Ibid.* 6:17.51; P. L. 44:853A.
[21] *De Nupt. et Conc.* 1:23.25; P.L. 44:428B, C.
[22] *C. Duas Epp. Pel.* 1:13.27; P.L. 44:563A.
[23] *Ibid.* 1:13.27; P.L. 44:563B.

antiquity. What was said above should be repeated, so that the statements of Augustine may appear in context. It should also be honestly considered in what sense Augustine denies that the remaining concupiscence is sin. For also in Scripture sin was regarded from two viewpoints. On the one hand it is lawlessness which wars against the Spirit and renders guilty, unless it is forgiven. Thus in Rom. 6:12 and 7 and 8 concupiscence is called sin. On the other hand, it defiles the conscience and condemns to death. So James 1:15 applies: "When concupiscence hath conceived, it bringeth forth sin; and sin, when it is finished, bringeth forth death." Augustine therefore explains fully in what sense he denies that concupiscence is sin. For he says to Boniface, "Those things are sin, which are done, said, or thought contrary to the Law, because of concupiscence or ignorance."[24] And to Valerius he declares, "For not to have sin means not to be judged guilty of sin."[25] And elsewhere he says, "The baptized lacks all sin, not all evil,"[26] which is more plainly said thus: "He lacks not all evils, but the guilt of all evils."[27] In this sense Augustine rightly denies that concupiscence is sin. For the distinction between mortal and venial sin must necessarily be retained. It is one thing when the desires of the flesh are accomplished, and another when the deeds of the flesh are mortified by the Spirit. And Paul clearly establishes that distinction in Rom. 7 and 8, as has been shown above.

When the papists, however, contend that original concupiscence in the baptized is not sin, they do not ask whether the sin reigns. But they hold like the men of Cologne,[28] that it is not a sin against the command of God, nor a matter in conflict with the Law of God.

---

[24] *Ibid.* 1:13.27; P.L. 44:563A. Boniface, pope from 418 until his death in 422, was the one to whom the above work was written.

[25] *De Nupt. et Conc.* 1:26.29; P.L. 44:430C. Valerius, to whom the above work was written, was an African count and a strong defender of orthodox Christianity.

[26] *C. Jul.* 6:13.40; P.L. 44:844C.

[27] *Ibid.* 6:16.49; P.L. 44:851A.

[28] The University of Cologne was a strong center of Scholasticism, and its theologians were active in opposing the Reformation. Johann Gropper was considered the author of *Enchiridion Coloniense* in 1536 (Cf. Gerhard III:348.). Albert Pighius edited his polemical work against Luther (*De Libero Arbitrio*, 1542) at Cologne.

On the contrary, it is something good, or at least indifferent, which clearly contradicts Paul.

Finally, it should be added that Augustine in later writings corrected himself when his more unfortunate statements were thrown at him by Julian. For Julian argues thus: "Augustine teaches that the concupiscence remaining is not properly sin. Therefore it should not only not be criticized, but should even be praised."[29] Here Augustine answers: "Just as blindness of the heart . . . is not only sin, in which a man does not believe in God, as well as punishment for sin, in which a proud heart is punished with a deserved punishment; it is also a cause of sin when evil is committed in the error of that blind heart. Thus concupiscence is not only a sin because it is disobedience against the rule of the mind (the punishment of sin is there because it is rendered as the wages of disobedience). It is also a cause of sin by the failure of him who consents to it, or by the contagion of birth."[30] You see the retraction. Earlier he had said that it was only the penalty or the cause of sin. Now he adds a third, that it is sin; and he adds that it is a cause, because it opposes the mind in which the good Spirit "lusts" against the flesh.

The papists, however, objected to this quotation. Eck said at first that Augustine was speaking of concupiscence in the unregenerate. But since this was clearly false, he later scurried away from this position, lest he should "get his foot stuck" at the place where Augustine was contending with his opponents.

The theologians of Cologne quote Augustine to the effect that concupiscence involves disobedience against the rule of the mind,[31] but they add: He does not say that such disobedience in the baptized is sin, when the mind rules in them. But this is a manifest untruth. For Augustine explicitly states that concupiscence is sin because disobedience is present in it.

Augustine has many similar statements: the "law" of sin . . . is forgiven in Baptism, not abolished.[32] "For it is also sin, when in a man either the higher parts basely serve the inferior, or the inferior

---

[29] *C. Jul.* 5:3.8; P.L. 44:786C.
[30] *Ibid.* 5:3.8; P.L. 44:787C, D.
[31] Cf. Rom. 7:25.
[32] *C. Jul.* 2:4.8; P.L. 44:678C.

parts basely oppose the higher, even though they are not permitted to prevail."³³ Again, he says that it is evil.

Augustine is cited in the Apology: "*Sin* is remitted in Baptism, not that it no longer exists, but that it is not imputed."³⁴ Eck objects that this is a falsification, for Augustine said, "*Concupiscence* is remitted, not that it no longer exists, but that it is no longer imputed for sin." But it is certain that this opinion is found elsewhere in Augustine, who says, "That sin might not reign." The apostle does not say that it would not exist, but that it should not reign. "For as long as you live it is inevitable that sin is in your members; but let its dominion be taken from it, let not its demands be obeyed."³⁵ And writing against Julian he assembles the opinions of those who were before his time. Ambrose calls the concupiscence remaining in the reborn "iniquity."³⁶ Hilary calls it "corruption."³⁷ The Romanists therefore try in vain to whitewash their errors with the witness of antiquity.

(3) They object that this doctrine is not profitable for edification, because it renders men complacent and negligent. For when they hear that, although they do not live according to the flesh, nevertheless the original concupiscence dwelling in them is sin before God, they think at once: "It is all the same whether I obey lust or resist. For I am nonetheless a sinner before God, whether I fulfill the lust of the flesh, or oppose it. In vain do I labor therefore in mortifying the deeds of my flesh."

My answer is twofold: (1) It is nothing new when, in the teaching of the church, many accept with the left hand what is given with the right. Paul, an excellent craftsman, no doubt chose his words

---

³³ This quotation is not found in *Contra Julianum* 6:8, the place cited by Chemnitz.

³⁴ *Apology* II (*Triglotta* 115, 36). The quotation is from Augustine's *De Nupt. et Conc.* 2:25.28; P.L. 44:430A. Literally, Eck is right (as Chemnitz seems to admit) in his objection that the Apology misquotes Augustine. In the Augustine text it is concupiscence, and not sin, that is spoken of (*"dimitti concupiscentiam carnis in Baptismo, non ut non sit sed ut in peccatum non imputetur."*) In defence of the *Apology*, however, it should be said (as Chemnitz indeed does) that the misquotation in the *Apology* is still a genuinely Augustinian viewpoint.

³⁵ *In Joannis Evangelium Tractatus* 41:12; P.L. 35:1698D.

³⁶ *C. Jul.* 2:6.15; P.L. 44:684C.

³⁷ *Ibid.* 2:8.26; P.L. 44:691D.

with great care in delivering the doctrine of heaven. Nevertheless his doctrine of justification was publicly burdened with abuse, as if he had said: Let us do evil so that good may result. And in 1 Peter 2:16 there is the complaint that many misuse the Christian doctrine of liberty as a cloak of malice. And yet, on account of such abuse and sinister understanding by hearers, the apostles did not alter the nature of their doctrine nor suppress anything which belonged to the truth of their teaching. For Paul says in Acts 20:20, 27: ". . . I kept back nothing that was profitable unto you, . . . for I have not shunned to declare to you all the counsel of God."

(2) It is not true that the following doctrine is taught in our churches, viz., that it is immaterial whether one obeys lust or resists it; or that a murderer can stand before God, who relaxes the reins of his wrath and does not allow the sun to go down upon his rising anger. For we teach diligently that true and necessary distinction between *prevailing sin* and the sin which does not prevail. According to Gal. 5:21, we teach that those who do such things shall not possess the kingdom of God. At the same time we teach as Paul does in Rom. 8:1: "There is therefore now no condemnation to them which are in Christ Jesus."

It is extremely important when this doctrine is taught to upbraid that error frequently and seriously. For when the world hears that sin remains in the saints, and that before God they are still sinners even when they are conscious of nothing, it immediately adds its perverse interpretation, so as to confirm and increase its false security and license to sin.

It should not be said lightly that sin remains in the saints also after Baptism; but it must be explained what kind of sin it is, and why it is so called. But most important of all, the true and pious use of this doctrine should be made clear. For Peter rightly says (2 Pet. 3:16) that the Pauline Epistles and the rest of Scripture are twisted by many to their own destruction. This happens because they are untaught and unstable, that *is*, they are neither instructed in the true fundamentals of the Word of God nor taught rightly and thoroughly in the sound doctrine; but they seize upon one word or another superficially. Neither are they strengthened by serious and pious exercises in sound doctrine. With these two reasons Peter explains how the doctrine of heaven is by many distorted to their own liking. And therefore "rightly dividing" is especially to be retained in teaching the doctrine concerning the concupiscence left in the reborn.

It is, however, possible to show the right use of this doctrine, but its abuse by carnal men must be upbraided. And it must be further shown what perversions follow in the principal articles if this doctrine is not faithfully expounded. Note the case of the Romanists who contend that the remaining concupiscence is not sin. Thirdly, the reasons must be stated, why this doctrine should be retained, and how it should be applied. We linger only with the chief matters.

(1)   The first is that we should rightly understand the article of forgiveness of sins. For it is not a certain "quality" which is infused once for all, either in Baptism or when we are converted from mortal sin. But just as we always carry about the body of sin in this life, just so the remission of sins is ours (with us), because the Son of God daily lets his shadow cover the flesh of his members, in which no good thing dwells, in order that sin should not be imputed.

(2)   On this depends also the article of justification. For in this life the believers are pleasing to God after reconciliation; they are accepted into life eternal, not so that nothing more dwells in them which is worthy of the wrath of God and eternal death; but by humble confession they acknowledge that in their flesh no good dwells, and that it is therefore the body of death. But they give thanks to God through our Lord Jesus Christ, on whose account there is in the believers nothing of damnation.

(3)   From this God's love for man is known. In the flesh dwells no good thing, but it is the body of sin; and nevertheless our bodies are temples of the Holy Spirit. For God pours out His Spirit upon the flesh (Joel 2:28). The Father and the Son come and make their abode with us (John 14:23). And since God is a consuming fire, we can hereby judge in some manner what this means, that Christ is gone "to appear in the presence of God for us" (Heb. 9:24); so that they are blessed whose sins are covered (Ps. 32:1).

(4)   Why good works cannot stand in the judgment of God, and why therefore believers are in need of the grace of God and for-

giveness of sin, even when they are preserved by the Spirit from sins against their own conscience, is impossible to understand unless this doctrine is considered in serious meditation. For on account of the indwelling sin the good works of all believers are imperfect and unclean in this life. And without this doctrine they cannot understand our Lord's words: "When ye shall have done all those things . . . , say, we are unprofitable servants" (Luke 17:10); or Paul's: "I know nothing by myself, yet am I not hereby justified" (1 Cor. 4:4). For these are the very sinews of Pharisaism, to think that as long as we have not lapsed against conscience we have no need of remission of sins.

(5) This doctrine also helps us to grieve over the inherent filth of our sin, to be more diligent in purging out the old leaven, in crucifying the old man, and in despoiling the body of sin. For if a man feels that the concupiscence remaining in him is not sin, why should he crucify and mortify a thing which is good, or at least indifferent? Why should he exclaim with Paul: "O wretched man that I am!" Because venial or pardonable sin drives us to acknowledge that nothing good dwells in our flesh, to grieve over this vileness, to fight back, and to pray that our filthiness be covered by the Mediator. You see then how great is the need for this doctrine. For those who say that it is not sin, but an indifferent matter, do not acknowledge their vileness, do not grieve over it, do not pray to be covered.

(6) It is well also that we learn to look at our wretchedness more closely. For not only those are wretched who are the servants of sin (John 8:34) and "are taken captive by him (the devil) at his will" (2 Tim. 2:26). But Paul, though he was snatched from the power of darkness and freed from sin, complains that he is miserable because the law of sin in his members rebels against the law of the mind and holds him captive. Let us not think that we need the aid of the Holy Spirit only when we are called to repent of mortal sins. But let us earnestly pray that we may always be governed and aided by the Holy Spirit on account of the sin that remains in us. For it is so great an evil that even Paul complains that he is held captive.

Now I think we can see the true use of this doctrine in the serious exercise of repentance, faith, prayer, and the new obedience. And in this use consists the true recognition of the doctrine.

ACTUAL SIN

Original sin is darkness of the mind, aversion to the will of God, and stubbornness of the heart against the Law of God. These evils are not called actions, but out of them arise the actual sins, both inner and outer. In the mind come persistent doubts and blasphemies. In the will arise false security, neglect and mistrust of God, admiration of self, and the placing of our life and wishes before the command of God. Then come great confusions and a flood of vile affections. Let us not imagine that original sin is an inactive thing. For though indeed a few men are held in check by honest discipline, nevertheless there are great doubts in the minds of men, and many inner drives pulling them away from God and running contrary to his Law. It is as Jeremiah says: The heart of man is wicked, brazen, and inscrutable (Jer. 17:9).[1]

Thus with the original depravity there are always actual sins, which in the unregenerate are all mortal. And the total person is damned with his fruits, as John says: "He that believeth not the Son . . . , the wrath of God abideth on him" (John 3:36). Although there are the great virtues of Aristides, Fabius, Pomponius Atticus, and others, we know that the original depravity nevertheless remained in them, and that their hearts were full of doubts and corrupt desires. The knowledge of Christ was lacking and there was no true worship of God.

Let us never forget that many excellent men of outstanding virtue were nevertheless defiled by extraordinary vices, demonstrating that they were in the power of the devil. How great was the depravity in the morals of Hercules, Themistocles, Pausanias, Alexander, and many others, who in the beginning were very restrained. These examples warn us that we may not disparage the knowledge of Christ, as many do by transferring the heathen to heaven. Let us rather fear the wrath of God the more, because we see them rejected and defiled in various and fearful ways, even though there

---

[1] This is not a quotation but Chemnitz's paraphrase of the verse.

were many excellent qualities in them. Let us not despise the Son of God; let us not imagine that men have been saved without the Son of God; let us not trample upon the blood of the Son of God. These matters we have prefaced concerning the unregenerate, in whom all actual sins are mortal, even as is original sin.

VIII

The Gravity of Actual Sin

When we speak of the reconciled, we distinguish between venial and mortal sins; and original sin itself is called "venial" sin. "Actual" sins are the many internal things which war against the Law of God, against which nevertheless the reborn fight, also the many sins of ignorance and omission.

Neither do we extenuate these evils as the Sentence Writers, who falsely say that venial sin is something beyond the Law of God, not against the Law of God. This error must be rejected. For those things which are called venial are great evils in conflict with the Law of God. They would be mortal by their nature, that is, on account of them a man would be damned with eternal wrath, unless they were forgiven, for the sake of the Son of God, to those who are reconciled. It is, however, necessary to distinguish between the sins which remain in the reborn in this life and those sins on whose account grace, the Holy Spirit, and faith are lost. An actual sin in one who falls after reconciliation, is therefore mortal when it is contrary to the Law of God and against conscience, whether it involves an inward or an outward action. Such action makes one subject to eternal wrath. To imagine that the elect do not expel the Holy Spirit when they run counter to their conscience, is a crass error which must be rebuked. Let us not ask whether or not we are elected while we are trying to judge concerning sin; but let us look

198

to the Word of God, given to us to show us his will. Let us tremble, knowing the judgment of God proclaimed by word and example; and let us not confirm the complacency and blindness in the foolish.

Adam and Eve were elect; nevertheless they lost the Holy Spirit in the fall, being turned away from God and made subject to eternal wrath. Thus Paul says that through the sin of one, condemnation came upon all men (Rom. 5:12).

In Deut. 9 we are told that God was greatly angered against Aaron, so that he would destroy him. But Moses prayed for him. Let not the tragic words of the Holy Spirit escape us when he says that God was greatly angered, and let us not imagine God as a stone or a Stoic. For although God is angry in one way and man in another,[2] let us nevertheless observe that he was angry even with Aaron, and that Aaron was then not in grace but subject to eternal punishment. It was a fearful lapse of Aaron when out of fear he gave in to the frenzied men who instituted the Egyptian worship. Admonished by this example, let us not encourage false security, but let us recognize that the elect and the reborn can fall miserably. Let the fallen know the wrath of God and be converted, and let not the depth of our own fall deter us from returning to God. For where sin abounds, grace abounds the more (Rom. 5:20). And this story of Aaron gives witness to those who repent, that great and atrocious sins are forgiven, as we learn from the lapses of David, Solomon, and Manasseh.

John says plainly, ". . . let no man deceive you; he who doeth righteousness is righteous . . . and he that committeth sin is of the devil . . ." (1 John 3:7-8). And Paul declares: ". . . because of these things cometh the wrath of God upon the disobedient" (Eph. 5:6).

It is evident, therefore, that the elect and regenerate can lose grace, and that a distinction must be made between the sins which remain in all the reborn who do not expel the Holy Spirit and other lapses whereby grace is lost.

---

[2] Chemnitz emphasizes the personal character of God's wrath while clearly distinguishing between divine wrath and human anger. On this distinction Augustine writes the following: "God shows his wrath, not indeed as a disturbance of mind, which is what the wrath of men is called, but as a righteous and consistent decree of punishment" (*Epistola* 190:3.10; P.L.32:860B).

Paul has also drawn the distinction in Rom. 8: "If ye live after the flesh, ye shall die: but if ye through the Spirit do mortify the deeds of the body, ye shall live." It is admitted that in the believers there are the deeds of the flesh, that is, many evil inclinations, doubts, complacency, indifference, false confidences, depraved affections. But against these, he says, one must fight in the Spirit, that is, with spiritual effort, prayer, fear, faith, looking to God with spiritual endurance and chastity. And the reborn remain in grace even though these evil desires are in them, if they only resist and by faith acknowledge forgiveness for Christ's sake. But if they do not resist, he says, they will die.

However, in order that we may know who the non-resisting are, the apostle has established a standard: the non-resistant are those who sin against conscience, who indulge knowingly and willingly, or yield to those evil drives and fires in their outward acts. Therefore men should be carefully instructed concerning this distinction, so that they may beware of lapses against conscience, and that the fallen might again be converted to God.

But the teachings should be denounced which proclaim abroad that all sins are equal and that the elect always retain the Holy Spirit even when they are guilty of atrocious backslidings. Now, although I do not wish to spawn quarrels over words, it is nevertheless necessary to remind students that what they customarily call mortal sin can be called reigning or dominant sin. For when Paul says in Rom. 6, "Let not sin therefore reign in your mortal body" (v. 12), he already passes on this same distinction of which we have spoken. We confess that there is sin in the reborn, but not reigning or dominating as long as they hold on to faith and a good conscience, that is, as long as they do not yield to sin, but resist.[3] But if sin gains control, it leads to eternal perdition, and the term "reigning" in itself reveals its atrocity and power.

Sin reigns when guilt is not remitted. It kindles the wrath of God and drives man from God. And the man abandoned by God is driven by his own weakness and by the devil, so that he runs from

---

[3] This place and many others show how serious and stern are the ethical teachings of the orthodox Lutherans. These teachings should be carefully observed by those who are too willing to criticize them for laxity in this area.

evil to evil and heaps up crimes and punishments. He is like Saul who, when he had been endowed with the Holy Spirit and adorned with most beautiful virtues and illustrious victories, succumbed to the first flames of jealousy. At first it was easy to repress, just as Aaron repressed the jealousy against his brother. But then, as Saul indulged, sin began to dominate him, that is, guilt remained, and the wrath of God was kindled. The Holy Spirit was cast out and vexed, and the mind abandoned by God became weaker and more enslaved to lust. The devil increased his fury. There followed the murders of the priests, and open disaster, until finally, when the army was lost, Saul was killed and went to his eternal punishment. This most tragic picture should be viewed often, so that we might think upon the magnitude of God's wrath against sin.

All histories are full of tragic examples, the reading and hearing of which impress on us how awful is the dominion of sin.

The Anabaptist king[4] promotes sedition under the pretext of religion, falsely boasts of divine inspiration, indulges in lusts, kills wives, is finally captured, and is torn by a burning sword. This is what happens when sin has dominion.

The word "sin" appears to be very old. In Ps. 119:133 it is said, "Establish my footsteps . . . ; let not any iniquity have dominion over me," These words we should use in daily prayer and consider at the same time what a horrible thing sin is when it gains control. Direct my steps, lest sin dominate me, lest I become a vessel of wrath like Cain, Saul, Judas, Ahab, Nero . . . and other scoundrels of the human race.

I think, however, that the term "dominion" is taken from Moses. For in Gen. 4:7 it is stated: "If you will be good, you shall be accepted, but if evil, your sin is quiet until it be revealed."[5] Your desire

---

[4] John of Leyden or Jan Bockelson (1510-1535) was the leading disciple of the Dutch Anabaptist prophet, John Matthys. At the death of Matthys (1533), he proclaimed himself king of the Anabaptist community at Muenster, which was at that time being besieged by forces led by the formerly ruling Catholic bishop of the city. He claimed to be King David redivivus who would reestablish the Davidic kingdom at Muenster among the Anabaptists. He established the practise of polygamy and had sixteen wives of his own. When the town was recaptured by the bishop's forces (1535), John of Leyden was tortured to death.

[5] This is not a quotation but rather Chemnitz's paraphrase.

is made subject to you, and you shall rule over it. This sermon on the Law should be diligently considered, for it contains the doctrine of three outstanding articles. First, it yields the distinction between "inner righteousness" and that of sacrifices. Sacrifices are pleasing, if you are good. If the mind is not devout, sacrifices are not pleasing to God. Secondly, the judgment to come is taught and the complacency of the world is described, when he says: Sin lies dormant, that is, it is not recognized, nor does it strike terrors, until the mind is smitten with a sense of the wrath of God and punishment. Thus Nero, Caligula, and an infinite multitude of men indulged very securely in their folly until the penalties came.

This is, however, a universal sermon, because it teaches that there remains a universal judgment. For when the crimes of the wicked are not punished in this life, it is necessary that there remain another life and another judgment in which all things will be punished. Thus in this first sermon the doctrine of the judgment to come is presented. Thirdly, there is instruction concerning the beginning of obedience: let your desire be subject to you, and you shall dominate it.

Since Moses spoke of the judgment of God, one can ask: What shall I do then when wicked desire is kindled within me? Here he answers and sets forth the first law; he teaches that we should resist corrupt desires. But it is not enough to know the law. It behooves us also to know whether that diligence in restraining desires pleases God, to know how to repress the devil in so great weakness, and to know how the natural weakness can be overcome. These things are learned by considering the promise: The seed of the woman shall crush the head of the serpent. Thus there is no doubt that the patriarchs brought in the promise in this teaching of the Law, instructed their sons regarding the origin of their stubborn affections, and taught them that a reconciliation was promised through the Seed to come, that on his account God would help our weakness and the devil would be restrained.

So also John has most eruditely interpreted the promise that the Son of God came to destroy the works of the devil, that is, to free us from sin, to help us obey God, and to defend us against the devil, that at length he might wholly abolish sin and death and restore righteousness and life eternal. Thus the patriarchs not only taught the Law so that desires might be restrained. They also set forth a doctrine showing how, in spite of such great weakness, men might render obedience and please God, both of which are signified by the word "reigning." For without the help of the Mediator we are not able to reign,[6] i.e., to be freed of guilt and to overcome the devil and our own weakness. . . .

---

[6] Cf. the words of Augustine: "They alone reign with Christ who are so present in his kingdom that they themselves are his kingdom" (*De Civ. Dei* 20:9.1; P.L. 41:673B, C).

IX

Actual Sin in Relation
to Original Sin

This topic is short and can be briefly stated. For from those things which have already been said about sin in general and original sin, the doctrine of actual sin can more easily be established, just as from the genus the species can be understood and from the cause the effect. In addition, reason already to some degree sees and understands those sins which consist of acts, whether inward or outward. We shall therefore briefly note matters which primarily concern actual sin and which have not been considered earlier.

I. Concerning the division of sin into types, it was said above that the actual are to be distinguished from the original, and that this division did not come into the church by mere speculations, but upon a sure foundation in the Word of God. For Scripture in many places differentiates expressly between the evil tree and the evil fruits (Matt. 7:17-18; Luke 6:43; Matt. 12:34-35).

Christ applies this figure thus: How can you speak good things, when you are evil? An evil man out of the evil treasure of his heart brings forth evil. For out of the abundance of the heart does the mouth speak.[1] And from within, out of the heart of man, proceed evil thoughts, foolish things, pride, adulteries, etc. Christ clearly distinguishes, therefore, between the storehouse, that is, the intrinsic or original cause, or the origin itself, and the actions proceeding therefrom. For thoughts are internal, and yet Christ says that they proceed out of the heart from within. And, indeed, he criticizes the Pharisees because they teach only concerning actual sin. "Either make the tree good and the fruits good, or make the tree bad and its fruit bad. You cleanse what appears before the public, but within you are full of uncleanness; you are like white sepulchres."[2] Thus, in Deut. 29:18 the distinction is posited between the root and the seed. Paul also distinguishes between sin dwelling within and sin in action. Original and actual sin are then properly and profitably distinguished according to Scripture.

II. The name "actual sin" should be given consideration. Augustine speaks of sins "added" and "one's own." In the *Enchiridion* he says, "Christ took away not only the one original sin, but at the same time all the other sins which have been added."[3] Again, "Each man has committed many sins on his own, in addition to that one which he has inherited in common with all men."[4] In the *Hypognosticon* there appears the name "actual sin," but the learned dispute whether this book is by Augustine.[5]

The term "actual sin" has now, however, been accepted by the common consent of teachers for these reasons: (1) Sins, whether internal or external, which proceed from the root of a corrupt nature, are more suitably named by the term "actual sin," than if with Augustine they are called "one's own" or "added." (2) The term comes closest to the Scriptural phrase which speaks of evil actions: ". . . . to commit sin . . ." (James 2:9); "Love worketh no

---

[1] This is Chemnitz's paraphrase of Mark 7:18-23.
[2] Paraphrase of Matt. 23:25.
[3] *Enchiridion* 1:14.50; P.L. 40:256A.
[4] *Ibid.* 1:14.50; P.L. 40:256B.
[5] Actually, the term which appears in the *Hypognosticon* (5:1.1; P.L. 45:1649D) is *peccata propria* ("one's own sins"). However, the term "actual sins" does appear in the genuine Augustinian work, *De Pec. Mer. et Remis.* 1:10.11; P.L. 44:116B.

evil to his neighbor" (Rom. 13:10); ". . . ye that work iniquity" (Matt. 7:23); "sin, taking occasion by the commandment, wrought in me all manner of concupiscence" (Rom. 7:8); "it is no more I that do it, but sin that dwelleth in me" (Rom. 7:17); ". . . upon every soul of man that doeth evil . . ." (Rom. 2:9); "The motions of sins . . . did work in our members to bring forth fruit unto death" (Rom. 7:5). "Whosoever committeth sin is the servant of sin" (John 8:34). "Every sin that a man doeth is without the body" (I Cor. 6:18). "The lusts of your father you will do" (John 8:44). ". . . fulfilling the desires of the flesh and of the mind" (Eph. 2:3). These passages are most suitably explained under the term "actual sin."

Moreover, those which are usually called actual sins, have in Scripture appellations such as "works of the flesh" (Gal. 5:14); "works of darkness" (Eph. 3:11); "the old man with his deeds" (Col. 3:9); "dead works" (Heb. 6:1; 9:14). These terms point to the "efficient cause"[6] of actual sin.

Paul writes to those who "were once enemies, with a mind in evil works" (Col. 1:21); Peter speaks of "unlawful deeds" (2 Peter 2:8); and Jude of "ungodly deeds" (v. 15). These point to the "formal cause."

Elsewhere the apostle speaks of "unfruitful works" (Eph. 5:11); "fruits, whose end is death" (Rom. 6.21); and those whose end shall be according to their works (Rom. 2:6). These belong to the "final cause."

This comparison of terms offers instructive illustration for the matters involved in the doctrine of actual sin.

III.   A definition of actual sin can now be given on the basis of this material. Augustine defines it thus: "It is every deed, word, or desire against the Law of God."[7]

Philip Melanchthon's definition is this: Actual sin is every action in conflict with the Law of God, whether in the mind, such as doubts concerning God; whether in the will and heart, such as the fires of evil lusts; or whether in the external members, such as out-

---

[6] For the Aristotelian distinctions of efficient, formal, and final causes, see Note 7, p. 5, MS IV.

[7] *Contra Faustum Manichaeum* 22:27; P.L. 42:418C.

ward acts contrary to the Law of God. And elsewhere he says: Actual sin means the fruits of the corrupt nature, inner or outer, that is, desires, thoughts, deeds, words against the Law of God.[8] Thus it includes both the person and the deed.[9] These definitions are gathered from sure testimonies of Scripture. For in Matt. 5 Christ shows in a long discourse that the Law declared not only the actual to be sins, but also the original; and that the actual sins are not only outward actions but also the lusts within which oppose the Law of God. And Paul gives one common name to both the inward and outward acts of wickedness when he numbers among the works of the flesh not only fornication and drunkenness, but also heresies, idolatry, and wrath (Gal. 5:19-21).

The Scripture, however, lists the inward actual sins in almost the same order as they are recited in the definition.

There are the sins of the mind: "Out of the heart proceed evil thoughts . . ." (Matt. 15:19), that is, they are fruits of a corrupt heart. Rom. 14:1 speaks of "doubtful disputations"; James 1:6, of him "that wavereth." It is observed, however, that thoughts sometimes belong to original sin, when they are mere suggestions; sometimes to actual sin, namely when they signify deliberation or design. Such is 1 Cor. 13:5: "Charity . . . thinketh no evil" (for speaking from the standpoint of original sin, even charity is not free from evil thoughts).[10] In John 11:53 "they took counsel together" to kill Jesus. Likewise, actual doubts are mentioned in this connection e.g., in Rom. 14:1).

---

[8] These two definitions appear to be summaries of Melanchthon's doctrine of sin as found in his *Loci*. Cf. *Loci Praecipui* (1559) 5. 27, 29, 33.

[9] It is interesting to compare the position of Peter Lombard with these definitions of Melanchthon. Lombard writes that sin, as Augustine says, is everything said, done, or desired against the Law of God; it is the will to retain or attain what is forbidden by justice. Lombard is here defining, not venial, but actual mortal sins (Cf. 2 *Sent.* 35:1; P.L. 192:734.). Concerning original sin, Lombard writes that it is not an act or movement of the soul; if it were, it would be actual sin. Original sin is, rather, the tinder, the concupiscence, or the proneness to concupiscence which is called the "law in the members" (Rom. 7:23). He also calls original sin a weakness of nature or the tyrant in our members or the law of the flesh. (Cf. 2 *Sent.* 30.7; P.L. 192:722.).

[10] This is not to say that acts of Christian charity call forth evil thoughts. It means rather that the Christian, who is living a life of charity, still can have some evil thoughts and desires coming out of the depths of his personality against his own will and against his acceptance.

There are also sins of the will. Eph. 2:3 speaks of "the will of the flesh and of the thoughts."[11]

Then there are the sins of the heart. Concupiscence is original sin. But according to Scripture it becomes actual sin if we live in "evil concupiscence" (Col. 3:5), or obey the evil desires (Rom. 6:12). And the internal affections are expressly named in many texts of Scripture. But Scripture locates the external actions opposing the Law of God in the members (Rom. 6:13, 19); in the feet, mouth, lips, and tongue (Rom. 3:13, 14, 15); in the eyes (1 John 2:16); in the ears (2 Tim. 4:3); and in the hands (Is. 1:15; 59:3).

Scripture likewise divides good external works into words and deeds. Rom. 15:18 speaks of "making the Gentiles obedient by word and deed"; and Col. 3:17, of all that men "do in word or deed." Thus the external actual sins are spoken of as "deeds" (2 Pet. 2:8); as words, or "corrupt communication" (Eph. 4:29). "Restrain the lips, that they speak no guile" (1 Peter 3:10).

Finally, it must be observed that the definition of actual sin covers not only actions which in themselves and by their very nature are corrupt; "for whatsoever is not of faith is sin" (Rom. 14:23). That means that all works done by those who are not members of Christ by faith and reconciled to God come under the definition of actual sin. For God requires that works, in order to be good by themselves and by their nature, should be done according to the Law. It is therefore lawlessness when men do not conform to the norm of the Law. To the believers, however, is imputed the perfect fulfilling of the Law by Christ. This is the simple and true definition. The Scholastics contend that actual sin is to be defined only as an evil act of the will. For the impulses themselves, whether external or internal, are a good creation of God, according to Acts 17:28: ". . . in him we live, and move, and have our being." They become sins only through an evil act of the will, which governs the actions.[12]

---

[11] According to the Vulgate.

[12] Cf. Peter Lombard, 2 *Sent.* 39.1; P.L. 192:746B: "The power itself (i.e., the will), which is inborn in man as are the powers of memory and understanding, is never a sin. However, an evil action of that power is a sin." Also 39.3; P.L. 192:746D: "Man who is doing evil is subject to sin because the will naturally wills the good."

But Scripture simply names those actions, as we have shown.[13]

There is also dispute over the sin of omission: in what manner is it to be included under the definition of actual sin? And indeed the Scholastics argue subtly that the sin of omission is always joined to some act which is either the cause or the occasion of the omission. This may be inward, as when the mind reflects that alms should be given, and other thoughts persuade it differently; or when the soul, occupied with other thoughts, does not meditate on the Word of God. Or it may be external, as when unnecessary labors hinder our service, that is, when one does something which keeps him from doing what he ought. These things help us understand what a sin of omission is. It can be said even more simply. Just as defects and inclinations are included in the definition of original sin; so also the sin of omission comes under the definition of actual sin.

IV. It should be observed what the true difference is between original and actual sin. For many quarrelsome sophistries are employed to obscure important matters and to give support to errors. The diligent reader can also see why this is discussed in Article 3 of the Refutation[14] of Luther and in Article 2 of the Apology. For the Scholastics taught that original sin is a dormant evil, an inactive quality. Therefore, unless actual sins result, the concupiscence remaining is not sin, because it does nothing against the Law of God. And this they drew from the disputation concerning the difference between original and actual sin. For since the actual is distinguished from the original, and since the actual includes the actions and impulses, what else can the original be than a quiescent tinder, without impulse or action? Thus original sin is diminished, and its definition rendered almost completely meaningless.

Eck[15] also spoke scornfully of the description of original sin in the Augsburg Confession, charging that it confused the distinction between original and actual sins, as it is presented in the Apology. Whenever this question is treated too subtly, the discussion is ren-

[13] I.e., Scripture considers the actions themselves sinful and simply names them as belonging to the realm of sin.
[14] Cf. *Grund und Ursach* 3; W.A. 7:345ff.
[15] *Confutatio Pontificia* 1:2.1.

dered more difficult, so that it only conceals and confuses matters. For in adults original and actual sins are so intertwined that it is not easy to show a contentious man the exact point at which they are distinguished. And the papists purposely press such disputations, teaching that the regenerate man can be without actual sin, and that his original sin is an extinguished ember. He can therefore be without sin, and the good works of the pious can be so perfect that they satisfy the judgment of God. Therefore something more ought to be said regarding this distinction.

But let it be said simply and clearly, so that the essential doctrine of sin is not confounded by argumentative and long-winded distinctions. The common difference has come down through tradition, that original sin is, as it were, the cause, and actual sin the effect. Ambrose also says: It is original concupiscence which makes both child and adult inclined to lust.

Lombard cites Augustine as saying that "Concupiscence is original sin, while desires, which are the expression of concupiscence, are actual sins."[16]

Scripture uses only one word, but the translator correctly renders it sometimes concupiscence, sometimes desires, though the distinction is at times difficult. For in adults original and actual ought to be distinguished so that the definition of original sin is retained and is not made out to be a dormant evil or an inactive quality.

It seems simpler and clearer to accept the distinction which lies in the definition itself. Let us accept that distinction made in the article on original sin in the Ratisbon Book,[17] because it is accepted and approved by our people. For since original sin is defined as the lack of original righteousness, a depraved habit or corrupt inclination of the human powers toward evil, the distinction can be correctly stated in the following way: Whatever there is in man beyond that lack and the corrupt inclination of his nature, which

---

[16] 2 *Sent.* 30.7; P.L. 192:722B.

[17] The Ratisbon (Regensburg) Book was prepared as a basis for the Ratisbon colloquy of 1541. It was presented to the theologians at Ratisbon as the work of some already dead Dutch theologians. However, we now know it to be essentially the work of Johann Gropper. It was prepared by him during the Worms colloquy (Nov. 1540-Jan. 1541) with secret advice from Martin Bucer and Wolfgang Capito (Protestants) and Gerhard Veltwyck (Catholic).

breaks forth into any action in conflict with the Law of God, whether it be by omission or by commission, this is called actual sin. And this difference can be more clearly understood from the "stages of sins," of which the Fathers spoke: (1) the tinder, or the inherent depravity, which embraces also the defects; (2) the suggestions of thoughts and emotions, that is, when the original depravity is stirred by some inclination; (3) the delight therein; (4) the consent; (5) the act itself.

Of these stages the first two belong to original, the remaining three to actual sin.

This difference can be understood; and if it is defined in this manner, it beautifully illustrates the doctrine of mortal and venial sin. Augustine in *Against Julian* says of original sin that ". . . by rebelling it strives to drag us into guilt."[18] Later in the same work he says that it is the cause of actual sin in the fall of him who consents.[19] In his *City of God* he states: "If that disobedient concupiscence, which still dwells in our death-bound members, is stirred against our will, as if by its own law, surely its stirring in the body of one not consenting is as blameless as its stirring in the body of one asleep."[20] James puts it this way: "Every man is tempted, when he is drawn away of his own lust, and enticed. Then when lust hath conceived, it bringeth forth sin . . ." (James 1:14-15), namely, actual sin. Therefore concupiscence, whether it is stirred by inclinations or aroused by the fires of lusts, belongs to original sin. It is active concupiscence, however, when delight and consent are added (Col. 3:5). These matters are clear.

Now someone might claim that this distinction is too clumsy, and might sophistically urge that all impulses and acts against the Law of God belong to actual sin by definition. Then it is time to invoke the two ancient rules which state the essential doctrine of original sin without any double talk: (1) Original sin is not an inactive thing (*res otiosa*). (2) In original sin there are always present at the same time actual sins. Thus Luther said in his *Resolutiones*[21] that the tinder

---

[18] *C. Jul.* 2:9.32; P.L. 44:696C.

[19] *Ibid.* 5:3.8; P.L. 44:787C.

[20] *De Civ. Dei* 1:25; P.L. 41:39A.

[21] *Resolutiones Lutherianae super Propositionibus suis Lipsiae Disputatis* (1519), conc. 2; W. A. 2:414.

or natural state *(fomes)* is actual sin, i.e., the lack of what should be present, and the presence of weakness and desires which should be absent. For since the law of the members wars against the law of the mind and holds it in captivity, the natural tinder *(fomes)* can never be without actual sin; indeed, a thing so alive and constantly active is sin. This natural tinder is therefore a most lively and restless origin of actual sins. . . .

In conclusion I will give several classifications of actual sin which are used by Scholastic theologians and are in agreement with the Scriptures. It is useful to consider these divisions in order to know the many ways in which we offend God, and the many kinds of trespasses we have. These divisions cannot do justice to the multiplicity of sins. However, they can give some good advice.

(1)   Some sins are inward, some outward. Thus Augustine and Jerome discriminate between sins of the heart, thoughts, mouth, works, and members.

(2)   Some are venial sins, others mortal, and some are sins against the Holy Spirit.

(3)   Some sins are directly against God; some are against the neighbor and consequently also against God. . . .

(4)   1 Cor. 6:18 presents the following division: sin outside of the body and sin in the body itself.

(5)   Some sins are committed because of weakness or ignorance (Gal. 6:1). Others are committed in bold shamelessness, in purposeful maliciousness, or by hardened habit. Such a division is stated in Num. 15:22; Ps. 19:13, 14; Acts 3:17; 1 Tim. 1:13; Heb. 10:20; 2 Pet. 3:5.

(6)   There is sin of commission and sin of omission (James 4:17; Matt. 7:19 and 25:30; Luke 13:7). . . . We have to observe that there are some sins of omission which belong to original sin, arising from weakness or deficiency. There are others again which belong to actual sin and have corresponding guilt, viz., sins of purposeful omission having some interior, volitional cause in the mind, will, and heart. The mind deliberates and because of some desire or passion inclines to omit a duty.

(7)   There are sins which are ours alone and sins which are

only indirectly ours (which are "alien" sins—1 Tim. 5:22; Eph. 5:7, 11). Involvement with such alien sins occurs when we consent to those who commit them.

(8) Some sins are hidden, some are manifest. 1 Tim. 5:24 mentions open sins which lead to divine judgment.

(9) There are sins which God overlooks because of his patience, as Paul mentions in Acts 17:30. There are again some very crass trespasses, which fill up the measure of iniquity (Matt. 23:32; Gen. 15:16; Amos 1:3, 2:1). Scholastics call them crying sins, because Scripture says that such sins are crying unto God and require God's vindictive judgment even though men are silent (Gen. 4:10; 10:20; Ex. 3:7, 22, 25; James 5:4).

(10) Some sins consist mainly in turning away from God and from obedience to his Word. Others consist in turning to objects which are prohibited by law. . . .

(11) Some sins are at the same time causes of other sins or punishments for sin (Rom. 1). There are four modes of them: (1) as efficient, accidental cause:[22] because sin casts out faith, grace, and the Holy Spirit; (2) as disposing cause, because an evil action leaves a disposition for similar action; (3) as material cause,[23] as immoderate appetite is material cause of luxury; and drunkenness of immodesty; (4) as final cause, if for instance somebody kills for the sake of revenge.

(12) Some sins are capital, being the principal root and origin of others,[24] which grow as members from the head. Augustine[25]

---

[22] The life of Emperor Nero presents a striking example of efficient, accidental cause. A number of historians judge that Nero, as a result of killing his mother, lost all moral sense, and from that point on committed all sorts of wicked deeds. There was nothing in the act of killing his mother that made it absolutely necessary that all the evil deeds would follow, yet they did in fact follow. Thus, the act of matricide was the efficient, accidental cause of all the evil deeds which followed.

[23] On material and final causes see Note 7, p. 5, MS IV.

[24] Aquinas comments: "The word capital is derived from *caput* (a head). Now the head, properly speaking, is that part of an animal's body which is the principle and director of the whole animal. Hence, figuratively speaking, every directing principle is called a head, and even men who direct and govern others are called heads. . . . In this way a capital sin is one from which other sins arise . . ." (*S. Th.* I-II: q. 84. a. 3).

[25] *Ennarationes in Psalmos* 79.13; P.L. 37:1026A.

mentions two: desire and fear. Others mentioned are self-love, fear, desire of useful good, greed for delightful good,[26] pride. Gregory[27] notes seven: pride, envy, wrath, depression ($\dot{a}\kappa\eta\delta\dot{\iota}a$),[28] avarice, immoderate appetite, unchastity. It is possible from Scripture to enumerate also unbelief and disobedience. . . .

(13) Not all sins are equal. But one sin is more grievous than the other, as can be seen from John 19:11; 1 Tim. 5:8; 2 Pet. 2:20, 21. . . . There are several ways by which one sin is more serious than the other. I will enumerate them for better understanding of the subject.

(1) Depending on the person who commits the sin, as Luke 12:47. There is mentioned a servant who knows the will of God (Matt. 10:15; 5:13). The powerful man deserves more powerful punishment.

(2) According to the person who is offended, either God or man, faithful or unfaithful (Zech. 2:8; 1 Tim. 5:4, 8). Sins against special persons are emphasized, as against parents, members of the family, friends, rulers, little children, and poor people.

(3) According to the value of the things to which damage is done. E.g., to falsify God's Word, and to blaspheme Christian worship are very serious offenses. . . .

(4) Sin which is done with purposeful maliciousness is much more grave than that which is done through infirmity or because of disturbed emotions.

(5) Sin is aggravated because of continuation, multiplication, repetition, or because sins are excused or defended.

Here we have considered many different kinds of sin. Diligent study of them is profitable to prevent Christians from false security, and to make them understand that the maliciousness of their life is a most terrible thing since they have to fight against so many beasts hiding in their own flesh. Every true Christian has to act, with Paul

---

[26] Desire of useful good and greed for delightful good become the sources of sins when they become immoderate, trespassing the limits set by divine law.

[27] *Moralia in Librum b. Job* 31: 45.88; P.L. 76:621A.

[28] Aquinas, following Damascenus, describes $\dot{a}\kappa\eta\delta\dot{\iota}a$ as " 'an oppressive sorrow' which so weighs upon man's mind that he wants to do nothing . . ." (S. *Th.* II-II: q. 35, a. 1).

(1 Cor. 9:27), to discipline his own body and to deliver it into service, not to be reprobate, because outside of God's grace nothing good can exist in man, and nothing is harmless in him. Therefore we have to pray daily to the heavenly Father in the name of our Savior Jesus Christ to be present with us in the grace of the Holy Spirit and to give us bounteously that we might truly acknowledge our sins, seriously deplore them, and pray for forgiveness in the name of our Savior Jesus Christ, and in this way gain eternal blessedness. Amen.

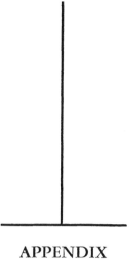

APPENDIX

Biographies

Johann Gerhard

Doctor Johann Gerhard, "the eternal light of the church and the priceless adornment of the University of Jena,"[1] was born October 17, 1582, at Quedlinburg, an ancient town in upper Saxony. His father, Bartholomew Gerhard, a highly esteemed man, was treasurer of the senate of Quedlinburg. He died in the year 1598. From Johann's earliest childhood his mother, Margareta Berndesia, had a very profound influence upon her son. She was deeply religious and experienced God's guiding hand in her daily life. A characteristic thing happened while she was pregnant. By accident she received a very severe blow in her lower abdomen from her quick-tempered husband, who wanted to chastise a disobedient servant. All the doctors prophesied either a miscarriage or a crippled child. When the child was born healthy, this was considered a gracious act of Providence.

In his childhood Johann suffered from several serious illnesses. At the age of fifteen he fell into a severe mental depression. He withdrew from people, avoided all conversation, and prayed and cried through many sleepless nights. Through the help and counseling of

[1] Preface of the Dean of the Faculty June 4, 1656, printed in Gerhard's *Loci*, Hertel's edition, 1657—.

the great Johann Arndt (1555-1621), at that time pastor in Quedlinburg, Johann achieved a spiritual and emotional recovery. In
the year 1589 Quedlinburg was smitten by a pestilence which killed
over three thousand of its citizens. Johann Gerhard became sick,
and his friends had little hope that he would recover. His recovery
came in an almost miraculous way. Again Margareta and her son,
as well as the doctor, saw the gracious hand of God.

In 1599 Johann traveled to Wittenberg and started studying
philosophy and medicine. He was a successful student. However,
he felt that his proper field was theology. He began his theological
studies at Wittenberg, continued at Marburg, and from there went
to Jena (1605), mainly because of filial attachment to his mother.

Already at the age of twenty-four years his unusual mental and
spiritual abilities were noticed by the authorities. So Duke Johann
Casimir appointed him superintendent in Heldburg. Meanwhile he
became a doctor of theology. In the year 1615 he was appointed
to a higher post, general superintendent (bishop) in Coburg, the
appointment being made by Johann Georg I, Archduke (Kurfürst)
of Saxony.

As his proper field Johann Gerhard considered academic teaching. "Outside of the academic world there is no life." He received
a post in 1616 at Jena. Besides the fact that he was an intensive
lecturer and a prolific writer, he was a real father and friend of
the students who constantly sought his moral and academic help.
Sometimes they received substantial material assistance as well.
Gerhard made large contributions to the theological faculty of
Jena to raise its academic standards. Thus it became, even according to the characterization of the Roman Catholics, the greatest
Protestant faculty in Europe. In the midst of his exhausting labors
he experienced the horrors of the Thirty Years' War.

Johann Gerhard is characterized by his contemporaries as a man
of deep piety, high moral character, and warm Christian charity.
"The generosity of Gerhard and his compassion were great and befitting a true disciple of Christ. When somebody was sick he was
there in person. He gave consolation. He provided food and medicine to heal sickness and to restore vigor. He helped rehabilitate
the sick people by his care and by his very person. When they were

naked he sent them clothes. When they were thirsty he gave them alms. And he did not permit anyone to go away in despair."[2]

"If one member in the body of Christ suffers, but the other does not suffer with him, certainly he is a dead member, not having the spirit of life."[3] This is what Gerhard taught and lived.

He could be hilarious and humorous, but nothing mean or offensive would enter his mind. The greater his authority grew the more humble and meek he became. His character was so noble that whoever nursed bad feelings against him felt guilty and later always regretted it.[4]

Gerhard had two most precious gifts of grace: a faithful, kind pastor's heart and a keen, profound scholar's mind. He was a cherished public preacher and personal counselor, with a unique ability to comfort people in distress, to heal their hearts, and to return them to active life. He did not discriminate between the rich and the poor, and he was equally respected by princes and dukes and the poor and humble.

The amount and the intensity of his work were incredible. He maltreated his not too healthy body with overwork. Moreover, he was grieved by the death of his wife and four of his ten children and other near and dear friends and relatives. He suffered the perils of war and the plundering of his property. Overwork and disasters ruined his health. He died August 17, 1637.

Death was one of the great subjects of his meditations. We have to keep death before our eyes to make life really meaningful and responsible. We have to wait the coming of our Lord, and throughout our whole life we have to prepare to meet him.

In a letter to Solomon Glassius, Gerhard expressed a clear presentiment of death six months before he died. In his last days, after receiving Holy Communion, he sent some money to arrange a meal for his poor people that they might share in the joy he had from Communion. His last words before his quiet expiration were, "Come, O come, Lord. Amen."

The literary activity of Johann Gerhard was rich and manifold.

---

[2] *Vita Ioannis Gerhardi,* Erdmann Rudolph Fischer, Lipsiae, 1723, p. 152.
[3] *Schola Pietatis* III, p. 787.
[4] Fischer, p. 181.

There are exegetical works, purely linguistic or historical investigations, voluminous systematic treatises, many practical articles, and warm devotional books.

One of the finest works in all devotional literature, written under the influence of Johann Arndt, is his *Sacred Meditations* (1606).[5]

Another significant book of religious meditations is his *Schola Pietatis* (1622-23). Philip Spener prized this book very highly as a "pattern of sound words," able to impart the true form of godliness to the reader.[6]

A warm glow of emotional piety is noticeable even in the great dogmatic masterpiece of Johann Gerhard, *Loci Theologici* (1610-22). This work has a much stronger and clearer systematic organization than the systems before his. It presents a monolithic, theocentric, dogmatic body. A characteristic of the whole work is that it is centered around Bible texts even more than we find in his great predecessor, Chemnitz. In all his use of philosophy Gerhard avoids metaphysical and epistemological problems. In spite of his extensive studies of Aristotle, he is much less "Aristotelian" than Martin Chemnitz. He is always concerned to relate his theology to the Christian life. If in Luther we hear the voice of the prophet and in Chemnitz the voice of the scholar, then Gerhard's is the voice of the evangelical pastor, the shepherd of souls and the man of wisdom.

EDMUND SMITS

---

[5] *Meditationes Sacrae ad Veram Pietatem Excitandam et Interioris Hominis Profectum Promovendum* (Sacred Meditations to Create the True Godliness and to Promote the Progress of the Interior Man).

[6] Fischer, p. 454.

Martin Chemnitz

It was in the second half of the sixteenth century that Martin Chemnitz was to play a decisive role in the formative years of the second generation of the Reformation. Born November 9, 1522, he was the son of a cloth-maker in the town of Treuenbritzen in the district of Brandenburg.

The path of his preparation for the role he was to play was filled with frequent interruptions. At an early age he was recognized as a child of exceptional intellectual gifts. His teacher, realizing that the local school in Treuenbritzen was inadequate, encouraged his parents to send him elsewhere. At the age of fourteen (1536) he was sent to the *Trivial Schule* in Wittenberg, but was called home after only half a year.

In 1538 it was necessary for him to discontinue his schooling to learn the trade of a cloth-maker. Unable to find satisfaction in his work, however, he yearned to continue his studies. A distant relative in Magdeburg, impressed by a letter which Martin had written to him in Latin, made it possible for him to study classical languages and literature at the university there from 1539 to 1542. His financial situation forced him to alternate his studies with teaching. Thus, he taught a year, and then studied for another year at the University of Frankfurt on the Oder; once again he sought employment as a teacher; and then in 1545 matriculated at the University of Wittenberg. Although he had occasion to hear Luther, it was not yet in theology that he concentrated his attention, but rather in mathematics. In this he was encouraged by Melanchthon. From mathematics his interest shifted to astrology.

The outbreak of the Smalcald War caused another interruption of his university studies. In May, 1547, at the invitation of the poet Sabinus, a son-in-law of Melanchthon, he arrived in Königsberg, where he occupied various posts as a steward for some Polish nobles and later as administrator in the school of Kneiphof. In September, 1548, he was promoted to *magister,* supported financially by Albrecht, Duke of Prussia. Meanwhile he continued to practice astrology and prepared an almanac which was to attract the attention of Albrecht. Evidence of an awakening interest in theology is indicated by the fact that he accompanied Sabinus on a trip to Wittenberg in 1549 and later wrote Melanchthon for suggestions about pursuing theological studies. Melanchthon replied that the most important method in the study of theology is the proper distinction between Law and Gospel.

Because of the outbreak of a plague in Königsberg, Chemnitz withdrew with Sabinus to the village of Salfeld. This enforced period of isolation furnished the occasion to study the sentences of Lombard and the sermons of Luther. When he returned to Königsberg he resolved to leave Prussia but was persuaded by Duke Albrecht to remain. The duke was interested in his achievements in astrology and offered him the post of castle librarian. He accepted the position on April 5, 1550. Although his interest in astrology diminished as he became convinced of the uncertain foundations of the discipline, nevertheless he continued as librarian, making use of its facilities for pursuing his now-central theological interests. In his autobiographical remarks he observes that he studied the Bible in the original languages and in connection with important commentaries and translations; he studied the writings of the church fathers; finally he turned his attention to the principal religious controversies of the time.

The happiness of these days, which Chemnitz refers to as "die allerbesten Herrentage," was brought to an end by the arrival of Andreas Osiander in Königsberg. Since the duke was a good friend of Osiander, Chemnitz was not able to express his criticisms of Osiander freely. He resolved to leave Königsberg. In April, 1553, he arrived in Wittenberg to continue his study of theology under the guidance of Melanchthon. As the long period of interrupted study came to a close, it appeared as though Chemnitz was about to begin the career of a university professor. At Melanchthon's own suggestion, he began lecturing on the *Loci Communes*[1] of his teacher. So successful was this venture that it was soon necessary to secure a larger classroom.

Chemnitz might have remained as a member of the Wittenberg faculty, but elected instead the role of a churchman. He accepted a call to Brunswick as preacher at the St. Aegidienkirche and coadjutor to the superintendent of the Brunswick church, Jacob Mörlin. He took over the office in December, 1554, and continued in it until 1567, when he accepted the call to be the superintendent. He remained in office until the pressure of deteriorating health caused him to resign in September, 1584. He died April 8, 1586.

Not from an academic chair but from the office of a Brunswick churchman did the influence of Chemnitz begin to be felt throughout Germany. Examples of his churchman's work are preserved in a major collection of sermons, *Postilla oder Auslegung der Evangelien.*[2] In the work of P. J. Rehtmeyer[3] there is a collection of his letters which reflects some of the practical problems of church leadership which he faced. For the improvement of the pastors he wrote *Die fürnehmsten Hauptstücke der Christlichen Lehre wie darin die Pastores examiniert und unterwiesen werden.*[4]

Together with his work as a churchman, Chemnitz continued to grow in stature as a theologian. Part of his responsibility in Brunswick was to hold weekly theological lectures in Latin. For this pur-

---

[1] He used the 1543 edition of this work.

[2] Frankfort am Mayn, 1593.

[3] *Der Beruhmten Stadt Braunschweig Kirchenhistorie*, Teil III (Braunschweig, 1710). This work, containing a partial autobiography of Chemnitz, a complete history of his life, and a collection of relevant documents and writings, remains the most important single source for the study of his life.

[4] Wolffenbüttel, 1569.

pose he continued the lectures on Melanchthon's *Loci* that he had begun in Wittenberg.[5] He continued to study and use the biblical languages; his exegetical concerns bore fruit in a harmony of the Gospels, *Harmonia Evangelica*.[6] It is not without reason that Chemnitz became known as one of the most learned theologians of his time and that the weight of his arguments and opinions began to be felt beyond Brunswick.

In the first place, he emerged as an important defender of the Reformation against the revived energy of Roman Catholicism manifested in the Counter-Reformation. His participation on this front was touched off by a controversy which developed over a catechism written by Johannes Monheim, rector of a school in Düsseldorf. This catechism, written from a Reformation point of view, was severely attacked by the Jesuits of Cologne. As the dispute became more than a local contest, Chemnitz wrote a small work in defense of Monheim, entitled, *Theologiae Jesuitarum Praecipua Capita*.[7] The Jesuit answer-bearer was Diego Payva d' Andrada, a Portuguese theologian and participant at the Council of Trent. At the suggestion of the Jesuits at Trent he rejoined with a work entitled *Libri orthodoxarum expositionum de controversis religionis capitibus*.[8] Recognizing the importance of the decrees of the Council of Trent to the Counter-Reformation, and fully aware of Andrada's association with Trent, Chemnitz beamed his reply at the decrees of Trent, using the work of Andrada as a key to their interpretation. The result is a major work which appeared in four parts between 1565 and 1573 entitled, *Examen decretorum concilii Tridentini*.[9] The many editions of this work, the last appearing in 1861, attest to

---

[5] This work was collected and published posthumously by Polycarp Lyser (Frankfurt a.M., 1591).

[6] Francofurti, 1593. This work is incomplete. It was continued by Polycarp Lyser and finished by Johann Gerhard.

[7] Lipsiae, 1562. Included in later editions of Chemnitz's *Loci*, op. cit., 1690.

[8] Further bibliographic information on this work is not available to this writer.

[9] Frankfurt. A complete German translation by Nigrin was published in Frankfurt, 1576. An abridged translation by Bendizen, Leipzig, 1884. A reprint of the 1861 edition appeared in Leipzig, 1915. Andrada published a reply, *Defensio Tridentinae fidei Catholicae*, which did not enjoy the same prominence as the *Examen*.

its influential role as a classic Protestant criticism of the Council of Trent.

More than a defender against anti-Reformation forces, Chemnitz became, in the second place, an architect of concord in the center of the controversies which threatened to dissolve the Lutheran wing of the Reformation from the inside. A few examples from his writings and activities will demonstrate this. In January, 1557, he attended a conference with Mörlin on the adiaphora controversy. In 1561 he contributed an article to the emerging dispute on the mode of the real presence of Christ in the Lord's Supper entitled, *Anatome propositionum A. Hardenbergii de Coena Domini.*[10] In 1565, in connection with the controversy over good works, he wrote, "Concerning the controversy, whether the proposition ought to be retained in the church: that good works are necessary for the regenerate."[11] His concern with the question raised by Flacius, whether or not original sin is of the substance of man, appears in "Regarding the proposition: whether sins are the substance or soul of man."[12] In 1567 he spent some months with Mörlin in Prussia to reorganize the church there in the wake of the Osiandrian controversy. The problem of the relationship of the two natures of Christ is discussed in his most important single theological monograph, *Libellum de duabus naturis in Christo.*[13] He criticized sharply the Wittenberg Catechism of 1571 for being crypto-Calvinistic.

The position which Chemnitz took in these controversies may be described as that of a mediating theologian. Although himself an appreciative student of Melanchthon, he did not hesitate to accept the criticisms of the strict Lutherans on Melanchthon's doctrine of the will and the Lord's Supper. He was anxious to avoid error and wished to fight error by formulating pure doctrine. The impor-

---

[10] Islebii, N. D. The preface is dated 1561.

[11] "De controversia, utrum in Ecclesia retinenda sit propositio: Quod bona opera renatorum sint necessaria." The German edition was published in Eisleben, 1568. The Latin version was included at the end of the Locus on good works in the *Loci, op. cit.,* Pars Tertia, pp. 27ff.

[12] De propositione: An peccata sint ipsa substantia hominis, aut ipsius anima." Included at the end of the Locus on sin in the *Loci, Ibid.,* Pars Prima, pp. 241ff.

[13] Jenae, 1570.

tance of Chemnitz's voice in these difficulties is attested by the many invitations he had to other offices—superintendent in Austria in 1569, coadjutor in Prussia in 1570, *Professor primarius* at Heidelberg in 1579. He rejected these invitations in order to remain in Brunswick, although he did on occasion take leaves of absence to perform work outside Brunswick. As Chemnitz grew in prominence as churchman and theologian, he appeared to Jacob Andreae to be the natural choice to help write a *Formula of Concord* which by its exposition of pure doctrine was intended to bring unity to those churches which stood in the tradition of the Augsburg Confession. From 1573 until his retirement in 1584 Chemnitz was actively involved in the preparation, formulation, and defense of this document.

Concerning Chemnitz and the period of Orthodox theology which followed, there has been a variety of estimates ranging from praise to blame: praise for conserving the Reformation heritage, blame for losing it. Contemporary historical scholarship has examined anew the principal Reformation figures of Luther, Melanchthon, Zwingli, and Calvin; but little attention has been paid to the generation of theologians which followed. As scholarship moves on now to a reappraisal of the second generation, it would seem that a proper evaluation of Chemnitz and those who followed him presupposes new research into their times and their writings. To assess the work of Chemnitz requires insight into the work of a churchman and theologian who was so highly regarded by his peers that it was said of him at the time: "Si Martinus (Chemnitz) non fuisset, Martinus (Luther) vix stetisset." (But for Martin (Chemnitz), Martin (Luther) would scarcely have endured.)[14] However he is finally judged, he must be seen as an important link in the development of Protestantism in general and Lutheranism in particular.

ARTHUR L. OLSON

---

[14] Quoted by Johannes Kunze in the article on Chemnitz in the *Realencyklopädie für protestantische Theologie und Kirche*, herausgegeben von D. Albert Hauck, Vol. III (Leipzig, 1897) p. 803. The English translation is my own. For the above I am indebted also to the article on Chemnitz by Dr. Schenkel in the first edition of the *Realencyklopädie*, Vol. II (Stuttgart und Hamburg, 1854) as well as P. J. Rehtmeyer's *Der berühmten Stadt Braunschweig Kirchenhistorie, op. cit.* and Reinhard Mumm's *Die Polemik des Martin Chem-*

---

nitz gegen das Konzil von Trient (Naumburg, 1905). Other important secondary sources on the life of Chemnitz are C. G. H. Lentz's *Dr. Martin Chemnitz, Stadtssuperintendent in Braunschweig* (Gotha, 1866), and Hermann Hachfeld's work, *Martin Chemnitz nach seinem Leben und Wirken insbesondere nach seinem Verhältnisse zum Tridentinum* (Leipzig, 1867). The only recent monograph on his theology is that by Gottfried Noth, *Grundzüge der Theologie des Martin Chemnitz* (Erlangen, 1930). By no means all of Chemnitz's writings have been cited above. A complete biography of the primary sources appears both in Rehtmeyer and in Noth.

Index

Academic, necessity of the, 220
Actual sin (see also Original Sin and Sin)
    arising out of original sin, 196
    in believer, 200
    causes of, 206
    classification of, 207f, according to Scriptures, 212ff
    conviction of because of deeds, 133
    definition of, 206f, in Scholastics, 208
    distinct from original sin, 139, 159, 172, 204f, 209ff
    and guilt, 134
    and the Law, 134, against Law of God, 198
    mortal in unregenerate, 196, when it becomes mortal, 198
    Rom. 5:12, 144
    reasons for acceptance of term, 205f
Albrecht, Duke of Prussia, 224
Alexander of Hales, 133fn, original sin, 162 & fn
Alexandria, School of, original sin, 157
Ambrose, actual and original sin, 210
    concupiscence remaining after baptism, 192
    death of body and soul, 47
    grace and works, 104
    influence on Augustine, 124
Anabaptists, original sin, 162, 172
Andreae, Jacob, 228
Angels, servants of God, 28
Anselm of Canterbury, location of sin, 152
    original sin, 162 & fn
Anselm of Laon, 133fn
Apology (to Augsburg Confession)
    distinctions of concupiscence in regenerate and unregenerate, 179
    free will and external conduct, 79
    original and actual sin, 209
    remission of sin in baptism, 192 & fn
Aquinas, Thomas, "capital" a term applied to sin, 214fn
    definition of *good*, 79fn
    definition of *inherence*, 44fn

distinctions of sin, 179fn
free will, 89fn
theology, xix
Aristotle, cause of sin, 155
    causes of sin, 156fn, distinction of four causes, 137 & fn
    contingency and necessity, 92
    influence on Gerhard, 222
    φύσει, 145fn
Arndt, Johann, 220, 222
Augsburg Confession, conversion, 105
    free will and external conduct, 79f
    original and actual sin, 209
Augustine, actual sin, 205 & fn, defined, 206, distinctions of, 213f,
        related to original sin, 211
    bondage of will, 98f
    Confessions of, 113, 124
    conversion, 106, 112, 123
    concupiscence, 188f (also Original sin and Baptism)
    death of body and soul, 47
    desires of man inspired by Spirit, 108fn
    Enthusiasts, 121
    experience, 126
    free will, 72, 74f, 77ff, 84, 93f, 114
    fulfillment of Law, 89f
    grace, distinctions of, 102, and good works, 103ff, 111f,
        degrees of, 105ff & 105 fn, 113ff
    good works, 91
    image of God, as mind, 49, in woman, 53fn
    mind must be opened by God, 100
    nature and evil, 169
    original sin, 167, remnant of, 183, and Baptism, 183ff,
        as bodily desire, 153, lack of treatment in Fathers, 158, in infants, 161,
        infants released from, 174, and creation, 170, and procreation, 171f.
    Paradise, 55 & fn, 57
    Pelagians, 121
    philosophy, 166
    procreation of soul, 150
    Romans 5:12, 143, 175
    sin, location of in man, 152
    summary of Pelagian arguments on original sin, 165ff
    will, 122f, 125f

Baptism (see Sacraments)
Basil the Great, original sin, 157
    Paradise, 55f & fns
Bellarmine, Robert, distinction between image and likeness, 33 & fn
    Paradise, 56f
Berndesia, Margareta, 219f
Bernhard, free will and grace, 114f
    image of God, 49f, 50fn
Beza, 50fn
Body, creation of, 30
    death of, 47
    image of God, 49

immortality of, 50
   relationship to soul, 59
Bonaventura, 162 & fn
Boniface, 190fn
Brandenburg, 223
Brunswick, 225, 228
Bucanus, image of God, 50 & fn

Calov, image of God, 39fn
Capito, Wolfgang, 210fn
Casimir, Duke Johann, 220
Cassianus, 111fn, 133fn
Celestius, free will, 78 & fn
   original sin, 168
Chemnitz, Martin, x, xii
   categories of tradition, xvii, xviii fn
   divine wrath and human anger, 199fn
   life of, 223ff
   Melanchthon's influence, 224, 226
   relationship of Church to Scripture, xv
   relationship to Osiander, 225
Christ, apprehended by faith and reason, xv
   Baptism of, 28
   benefits of in relation to sin, 132
   blessings of, 117
   enlightens mind and converts will, 100
   grace of, 116
   intercession of, 194
   kingdom of heaven explained, 172
   Mediator, 117, 133, need of, 203
   restoration of image of God earned by, 64f
   revealer of Gospel, 180
   work of Son of God, 202
Chrysostom, John, conversion, 105
   free will, 73
   original sin, 157
   Paradise, 55
Church, denunciation of sin, 131
   doctrine of sin in, 131
   established and cleansed through Baptism, 186
   interpreter of Scripture, xiv
   strengthened by Holy Spirit, 132
Cicero, cause of sin, 155
   influence on Augustine, 113, 124
   virtue and habit, 155
Clement of Rome, original sin and free will, 158
Coburg, 220
Cologne, men of, 190fn, 191
Concupiscence (see Original Sin)
Contingency, definition of, 92fn
Conversion (see also Free Will)
   accomplished through grace, 112, 120f
   earlier stages of, 123
   flesh not beginning of, 113

not instantaneous, 122
origin of according to Fathers, 105f
prevenient grace, beginning of, 122
Cosmos, teaches knowledge of God, 38f
Council of Mileve, 94 & fn
Creation, of body and origin of soul, 30
corporeal things, 39
distinctions of, 60
Eve, 39
God's rest from work of, 59
man, 27, 29, 38f, as good, 170f
new man, 38
original sin in Pelagians, 167f
world, 29
Creationism, refutation of, 59
Ctesiphon, 78, 104

d'Andrada, Diego Payva, 226
Damascene, John (or Damascenus), original sin, 161
Paradise, 55f & fns
Death, of body and soul, 47
as punishment for sin, 47f
Doctrine, of free will, 95, and original sin, 135fn
importance of, ix, x
Orthodox, regulative principle of, xviii
and Scripture, 143
of sin and relation to vices, 136
Dominican School, 133fn
Düsseldorf, 226

Eck, John, 163fn, 177fn, 180
comments on doctrine of original sin in Augsburg Confession, 209
concupiscence, 191f, 192fn
Eden (see Paradise)
Election (see Predestination)
Emser, 97 & fn
Enthusiasm, 110, 119
Erasmus, free will and Luther, 119
nature of man, 145f & fns
works and faith, 91
Eugubinus, immortality in creation, 46

Faith, analogy of, 167, defined, 167fn
apprehends Christ, xv
as assent and trust, 110
beginning of, in prevenient grace, 122
correlated to Gospel, 110
created by God, 111
experience, feeling not preceding, 126
gift of God, 107, 109, 114
good works, 111, no works pleasing to God without faith, 91
out of hearing of Word, 126
relation to reason and revelation, xv
relation to Holy Spirit, 108f

sin of unbelief, 174
two senses of, 108
Fall, consequences for mind, 82
    free will, prior and subsequent to, 120
    loss of image, 61f, of Holy Spirit, 62
    man before, 39f, 63, 72
    man following, 39f, 63, 72
    remnants of image after, 63
Faustus of Maxilio, 106fn
Fides historica, definition of, 112
Flavius, Josephus, location of Eden, 56 & fn
Flesh, and conversion, 113
    helplessness of, 118
    mind of, and Law, 78
    righteousness of, 83f
    work of, 95
Franciscan School, 133fn
Frankfurt, University of, 223f
Free will (see also Will)
    attitudes of Church, 77
    categories excluded from discussion of, 72
    classified Scriptural testimonies, 77
    conversion, 103, 120
    distinction of phases of, 120
    distinctions of, in external conduct, 73
    doctrine of, not taught to encourage vices, 117
    in civil affairs, 86f, need of Divine help, 87
    in mind and will, 76, 81f, and/or heart, 77
    in spiritual action and external conduct, 81
    in unregenerate, 82f, 92, 96
    meanings of, 77
    "nominal definition" of, 76
    not able to carry on spiritual activities, 102
    not perfect in this life, 74
    object of, 78f
    only to do evil, 74
    original sin, 135fn
    principal point in doctrine of, 95
    proper stating of problem of, 72
    reasons for doctrine of, 117
    and regeneration, 73, 120
    after renewal will has liberty, 121
Freedom (see also Free Will)
    doctrine of liberty, 193
    in new creature, 122
    of choice and contingency, 86
    of choice in unregenerate, 92
    meaning of, in Scripture, 73

Gennadius of Constantinople, 106fn
Georg I, Johann, 220
Gerhard, Batholomew, 219
Gerhard, Johann, life of, 219ff
    immortality of God and man, 50fn

influence of Aristotle, 222
predestination, 27fn
theology, center of, xix
Glassius, Solomon, 221
God (see also Creation)
counsel of, concerning man, 28f
Creator of good, 59, 170
directing way of man, 86f
divine attributes of xxf fn
foreknowledge of, and necessity of man's willing, 70f
foresight of sin and death, 28
immortality of, 50fn
is Spirit, 49
knowledge of, related to cosmos, 38f
love of, 194
majesty of, xix
not cause of sin, but preserver of substance, 171
will of, necessitates man's action, 71
working in us to will, 115
Good (*Bonum*), definitions of, 79fn
Gospel (see also Scripture, Word)
Christ as revealer of, 180
correlated to faith, 110
ministry of Holy Spirit, 109f
proper distinction from Law necessary, 224
Grace, according to Scriptural and practical psychology, 105fn
Augustine's distinctions of, 102
and conversion, 112, 120f
cooperating, 115f
gift and work of Holy Spirit, 106
given threefold to man, 54
given to mind and will, 98, 114
of God restores image of God, 66
and good works, 103
not merited by external conduct, 91
operating, 115
persevering, 116f
preparatory, 113f
prevenient, 105f, 110, 112f, beginning of faith and conversion, 122,
beginning in Word, 125
subsequent, 107, 116
Gregory the Great, creation of man, 27
seven sins, 214
Gropper, 170 & fn, 210fn
Grynaeus, 50fn

Harnack, Adolph, evaluation of Hugo St. Victor, 56fn
Heart, acted upon by God, 100
and mind in New Testament, 76
must be regenerated and renewed, 101
in Old Testament, 76
Heidelberg, 228
Heldburg, 220

Herman of Wied, 170 & fn, 186
Hilary, concupiscence remaining after baptism, 192
conversion, 105
Hollaz, image of God, 39fn
Holy Spirit, begins work of salvation, 118
creates new man, 38
efficacious through Word, 107, through Gospel, 125
gifts of, 109, 117
given to those who seek, 111
illumines the soul, 36
lost in fall, 62
losing by elect, 198f
moves will in conversion through Word, 124
not discerned by emotions, 111
opposed by men, 118
received by faith, 110
relationship to faith, 108ff
relationship to will, 125
restoration of image, 37, 62f
reveals sin, 132, 136
strengthens Church, 132
and theology, xix
work of, 142f
Hugo of St. Victor, location of Eden, 56 & fn
original sin, 162

Ignatius, the Christian life, x fn
inspiration of Scriptures, xiii fn
Image of God, before and after the fall, 39f
as mind, 49
as righteousness and holiness, 62f
as the unifying principle of the Trinity, 28
beginning and realization of, 66
distinguished as material and formal, 39fn
elements of, 38
how related to the soul, 33, 36f, 43ff, 49f
in the Fathers, 34
in Hebrew Scripture, 35
in Pauline thought, 34ff
in woman, 52f
includes immortality, 46f
lost, 31, in fall, 61f
Luther on, 34f
man in, 30, man's reason, 38
meaning of, 32ff, 66
not a supernatural gift, 43 & fn
original righteousness and original image, 41, 140
propagation of, 42, 58
relationship to essence of man, 43f, to likeness, 33, to renewed man, 35f
remnant of, 31, 41, after fall, 63, 82
restored, 37f, by Holy Spirit, 62f, 66, through Christ, 64f
senses of, primary and secondary, 52f
various definitions of, 61f
work of the Trinity, 66

Immortality of God, 50fn, and image of God, 46f
 man created with, 47
Innocent I, 93 & fn
Interims, meaning of, 107fn
Irenaeus, free will, 72fn, 73
 inspiration of Scriptures, xiii fn
Isidor of Seville, 133fn

Jena, 220
Jerome, conversion, 105 & fn
 distinctions of sin, 212
 free will, 72, 78
 grace and works, 104 & fn
 nature and sin, 168
Jesuits, 226
John of Leyden, 201fn
Jovinian, degrees of sin, 91 & fn
Judgment, future and universal, 202
 and wicked desire, 202
Julian, cause of sin, 154, 157, 167 & fn, 171
 concupiscence and Baptism, 188
 good works, 91 & fn
Justification (Justified)
 forgiveness of sins, 194
 righteousness, 132
Justin Martyr, doctrine of Church confused, 158
 free will, 83 & fn
 inspiration of Scriptures, xiii fn

Kneiphof, 224
Königsberg, 224

Lactantius, creation of man, 30
Law, and actual sin, 134
 complete obedience to, 88f, impossible for unregenerate, 89f
 confusion of external conduct and complete obedience, 90
 Decalogue governs external acts, 81
 demands of, 95
 distinction between external observances and internal works
  or spiritual activities, 79, 104
 fulfilling of by imputation, 208
 and grace, 107, 116
 in heart of Gentiles, 41, of men, 61
 material cause of sin, 137
 of mind and members, 195, of mind of flesh, 78
 object of free will to unregenerate, 84
 properly distinguished from Gospel, 224
 restraining desires, 203
 reveals God's wrath, 135
 righteousness of, 83f
 and sacrifice, 202
 satisfied by regenerate man according to Papists, 178
Leo X, 177fn
 doctrine of original sin, 177

Likeness (see also Image)
    and soul, 33
Lombard, Peter, actual and original sin defined, 207fn, 210
    free will, 75, 78
    grace, distinctions of, 102, and mortal sin, 92
    location of sin in man, 151
    original sin, 162, and Baptism, 186
    Paradise, 55f & fns
    Sentences of, 133 & fn, studied by Chemnitz, 224
    works, 92
Luther, Martin, actual sin related to original sin, 211f
    attitude toward Lombard, 133fn
    free will, 89, 119
    image of God, 34f
    importance of doctrine, ix, x
    interpretations of original sin, 147
    Lutheran Orthodoxy appraises, xviii
    opinion of Melanchthon's *Loci*, xi
    original sin in Genesis, 146f
    orthodoxy in the conduct of life, x
    reason, xv, and faith, xv
    relation to the ancient Church, x, xi
    Romans 5:12, 143
    Scripture as divine source of truth, xiii
    traducianism, 151
    work of, xi
Lutheran Orthodoxy, analogy of faith, 167fn
    attitude toward theology, xix, toward Peter Lombard, 133fn
    Christian life, x
    distinction between emotion and mind and will, 76fn
    meaning of, x, xi
    relationship to Luther, xviii, xix
    sin as accidental trait, 165fn
    understanding lost and retained in fall, 82fn
    view of Scripture, xiv
Lyser, Polycarp, 226fn

Magdeburg, 223
Malvenda, 108
Man, before and after fall, 39f, 63, 72
    corrupted by sin, 170, fatally, 98
    creation of, 27, 29, 38f, as good, 170f
    creation of body and origin of soul, 30
    differentiated from animals, 82, 166
    dominion of, 52f, 61f
    free will in unregenerate, 82f, 92, 96
    immortality, 47, 50fn
    in image of God, 28, 30, 49, 166
    inner man is renewed daily, 186
    liberty in new creature, 122
    lost sinner, xix
    "natural" in Pauline thought, 97
    origin of, 30
    perfection of, 40fn, created in, 42

predestination of, 27
propagation of whole man, 59
relation to woman, 53
uniqueness of, ix
unregenerate man sins in all he does, 90, in bondage, 99,
    and good works, 112
without power to do good, 106, 117
Manicheans, 124, 149, 156f, 168, 170, 178
Manicheus, 156fn, 170
Marburg, 220
Melanchthon, actual sin defined, 206f & fns
    Father of Lutheran Orthodoxy, xi
    influence on Chemnitz, 224, 226
    Luther's opinion of *Loci*, xi
    at Worms, 177fn
Merit, fitting, 92
    of Christ different from application of His merit, 174
    Scholastic distinctions of, 90fn
Mind, affected by fall, 82
    definition of, 153
    differentiates man from animals, 82
    enlightenment of, 100
    and free will, 76f, 81f, in unregenerate, 96
    and heart in New Testament, 76
    identical to heart in Old Testament, 76
    and image of God, 49, 82
    power of, after fall, 82
Monheim, Johannes, 226
Mörlin, Jacob, 225, 227

Necessity, definition of, 92fn
New Creature (see Regeneration)

Origen, creation of souls, 156
    original sin, 157
    Paradise, 55 & fn
Original, as perfection, 41, righteousness and original image, 41, 140,
    and likeness, 140
    description of, 153
    meaning of, 140
    original sin as lack of, 62, 140
Original sin (see also Actual sin and Sin)
    ancient rules of, 211
    applications of to man, 146, not his essence, 44
    arguments of Pelagians on, 164ff
    and Baptism, 174, 176, 178ff, 183ff
    characteristics of, 140, 196, a positive evil quality, 59
    comparison of in Old and New Testaments, 146
    concupiscence, 179ff, 211, and natural appetites, 168
    depravity and imputation, 141
    distinct from actual sin, 139, 159, 172, 204f, 209ff
    doctrine of, basis for, 143, need for, 194f
    effects of, 153fn, upon the whole man, 152
    efficient cause of, 149, 156, as will of Adam, 150

erroneous views of, 135, in Manicheans, 156f, in Pelagians, 159ff
  form and matter of, 153fn, 159fn
  as formal cause, 137
  and free will, 135fn
  holds us guilty, 134
  in definition of sin, 134
  in infants, 146, 176
  in Romans 5:12, 144f
  in Scriptural passages, 143ff, proofs of, 145, 152
  in Western Church, 162
  as lack of original righteousness, 62, 140
  taught by Fathers as a mystery, 158
  through fall, 62, of Adam, 141
  transmission of, 171, in marriage, 171f
Osiander, controversy, 227
  relations with Chemnitz, 224f
  removal of guilt in Baptism, 188 & fn

Paradise, man's dwelling, 54f
  nature of, 54f
Pelagianism, a deviation, 119f
Pelagians, Baptism, 160, and remission of sins, 183f
  concerning Augustine on original sin, 166
  controversy caused sound teachers to arise, 158,
      involved free will entirely, 117
  conversion, 106
  free will, 75, 81fn, 93 & fn, 94, 125f
  good works, 91, and grace, 103f
  guilt, 166
  immortality in creation, 46
  original sin, 159f, 172ff, arguments concerning, 164f, and creation, 167f
  procreation of soul, 150
  sin, cause of, 149, description of, 165 & fn
  use of Scripture, 108
Pelagius, free will, 74, 78, 79fn
  fulfillment of Law, 90
  Holy Spirit, 107
  original sin, 168, and Baptism, 178f, 184f
  Romans 5:12, 175
Pererius, Benedict, 32fn
  relation of image to likeness, 33f
Perfection, man created in, 42
  meaning of, 40fn
  original righteousness, 41
Photinians, immortality in creation, 46 & fn
Pighius, creation and sin, 167f
  original sin, 166 & fn, 175f
Predestination, distinguished from foresight, 28fn
  election before creation, 27fn, of Adam and Eve, 199, and
      possibility of falling, 199
Propagation, blessing not lost in fall, 58
  image of God, 42, 58
  involves whole man, 59
  of the soul, 58, 60, manner of, 59

Prosper of Aquitania (Prosper Aquitanus), 111fn, 133fn

Quedlinburg, birthplace of Johann Gerhard, 219f
Quenstedt, Holy Spirit and theology, xix fn, xx
    image of God, 39fn

Ratisbon Book, 210fn
Reason, apprehends Christ, xv
    frailty of, xvii
    image of God, 38
    Martin Luther on, xv
    necessity of, xv
    relationship to the good, xv, to faith and revelation, xv, to revelation, 156
Regeneration (Renewal, Restoration)
    Baptism, 185
    by Christ, 64f, grace of God, 66, Holy Spirit, 62f, 66
    concupiscence, 194
    continuous need for grace, 116
    free will, 73, 120f
    growth in, 123
    image of God, 35ff
    Law of God, 116
    of mind and will, 98
    and sin in Pelagians, 160
    strength, 116
Revelation (see also Scripture), relationship to faith and reason, xv,
        to reason, 156
    and Scripture, xiv
Rhegius, Urbanus, original sin, 162f & fn
Righteousness, defined by the wise, 132
    of flesh, 83f
    and justification, 132
    of those outside of Christ, 84
Romanticism, 76fn
Rousseau, 76fn
Rupertus, Paradise, 56 & fn
    work of Trinity, 29fn

Sabinus, 224
Sacramentarians, application of term, 163fn
Sacraments
    Baptism and concupiscence, 179, and original sin, 178ff, and original sin
        according to Zwingli, 176, and Pelagians, 160, and remission of sins,
        183ff, and removal of guilt of original sin, 174, of sins, 185, defined,
        185, efficacy of, 160, gifts of, 185
    Lord's Supper, controversy over real presence, 227
Sacrifice, distinct from "inner righteousness," 202
Salfeld, 224
Sanctification, description of, 140
Scholastics (Papists, Romanists)
    actual sin, defined, 208ff, classifications of, 212ff
    concupiscence, 182, 189, 194
    contingency and necessity distinguished, 92

distinctions of *merit*, 90fn, of *causes*, 137fn, between *materiale* and
    formale, 159fn, of sin, 179fn
faith and works, 91f
free will, 88ff, 94, 102f
fulfillment of law, 89, 178
image of God, 50
mind, 153
mortal sin and faith, 92
original sin as bodily pleasure, 153, as doctrine corrupted, 162,
    as doctrine deemphasized, 169f, and rebirth, 181
preparatory grace, 113
procreation of soul, 150f
remission of sin in Baptism, 186
sin, location of in man, 151f
Scripture (see also Gospel, Word)
    and actual sins, 207f
    authority of, xiii
    distinguished from philosophy, 166
    divine revelation, xiv
    divine source of truth, xiii
    doctrine, 143
    image of God in, 33ff
    Lutheran Orthodoxy view of, xiv
    meaning of freedom, 73
    mystery of, xiv
    Pelagian use of, 108, against original sin, 172f
    propagation of soul, 60
    "spiritual interpretation" of, xx
    testimony of, on bondage of will, 96, on free will, 77
    use of as testimony, 142
    verbal inspiration of, xii, xiii, in Fathers, xiii, in
        Reformed Confessions, xiii, xiv
Seneca, cause of sin, 155
Sentence writers, venial sins, 198
Sin(s) (see also Original sin and Actual sin)
    accidental trait, 165 & fn
    of Adam according to Pelagians, 160
    causes of: efficient, material, formal, final, 137, 154f
    causes of other sins, 213
    death as punishment of, 47
    definition of, 134, need for, 133, as disobedience, 134,
        as concupiscence, 188ff
    distinguished, as from vice, 135f, prevailing and non-prevailing, 193
    doctrine of, in Church, 131, revealed by Holy Spirit in Word, 136
    forgiveness of, rightly understood, 194
    generated by concupiscence, 189f
    guilt of, as actual and potential, 188
    in believer must be resisted and forgiven, 200
    inevitable in man, 192
    knowledge of, inherent in all, 136
    law of, in our members, 118
    location of, 151f, in the will, 98
    mortal and venial, 92, 198, 212, and concupiscence, 190, 195
    mortal dominating, 200f

omission, 209, and commission, 212
relational and qualitative aspects of, 188 & fn
remission of, and Baptism, 183ff, 192
remnant of, after Baptism, 188
revealed by Holy Spirit, 132
signifies a certain guilt and condemnation, 134
stages of, 211
of unbelief including all others, 174
of unregenerate, all mortal, 92, contingent and necessary, 93,
    in all he does, 90
wrath of God, 131, 134
Smalcald War, 224
Soto, Dominic, free will, 78 & fn
    immortality, 46fn
Soul, concepts of, 30fn
    conscience as natural characterization of, 42
    creation of, 156
    death of, 47
    illumined by Holy Spirit and Word, 36f
    image of God, 33, 36f, 44
    origin of, 30
    original sin, 152
    procreation of, 150f
    propagation of, 58ff
    relation to body, 59
Spener, Philip, 222
Spiera, Ambrosia, works, 92 & fn
Supernatural Gift, conscience not a, 42
    image of God as, 43fn

Tarquinius, Sextus, 71
Tertullian, creation of man, 27
    reason and the good, xv
Theology, center of, xix
    definition of, xix
    and Holy Spirit, xix fn
    revealed wisdom of God, xx fn
    spiritual medicine, xxi
Theophilus, inspired Scriptures, xiii fn
Tradition, categories of, in Martin Chemnitz, xvii, xviii fn
    and the Reformation, xvii
Traducianism, held by Luther, 151
Trajus of Saragosa, 133fn
Tremellius, Johannes Immanuel, 47fn
Trent, Council of
    Baptism and remission of sins, 184 & fn
Treuenbritzen, 223
Trinity, mystery of, 28
    work of, 29, and image of God, 66

Valerius, 190fn
Valla, Lorenzo, 70ff
    free will, 78
    original sin, 162

Veltwyck, Gerhard, 210fn
Victor, Marius, Paradise, 56 & fn
Vitales, 114

Will (see also Free Will)
    assents, 123
    bondage of, testified by Scripture, 96
    captivity to sin, 94
    cause of good works, 125
    conversion of, 100
    depravity of, 88
    dwelling place of sin, 98
    moved by God through Word, 123
    necessity of man's willing, 70f
    power and weakness of, 93
    in regenerate man, 108
    relationship to action, 71, to Holy Spirit, 125, to free will, 76
    renewal of, 98
    in unregenerate man, 98
William of Champeaux, 133fn
Wisdom, limitations of, 131
    righteousness defined by men of, 132
Wittenberg, University of, 220, 224ff, Catechism, 227
Woman, image of God in, 52f
    relation to man, 53
Word (see also Gospel, Scripture)
    creation of new man, 38
    God moves will through, 123
    and Holy Spirit, 107
    illumines soul, 37
    ministry of, 107
Works, good works, spiritual fruits
    cause of, in will, 125
    controversy on, 227
    divided into word and deed, 208
    doctrine of original sin, 194
    and faith, 111
    and free will, 73, 81
    and grace, 103
    imperfect in this life, 195
    in lives of all men, 91
    of man must be governed by God, 85
    man without power to begin good works, 106
    unregenerate man, 112
    without faith, not pleasing to God, 91
Wrath (of God)
    against sin, 201
    distinct from human anger, 199fn
    revealed by God's Law, 135
    and sin, 131, 134

Zanchius, 50fn
Zwingli, original sin, 162f & fn
Zwinglians, sin in children and Baptism, 176